LEAVE IT AS IT IS

* * * A JOURNEY THROUGH * * *
THEODORE ROOSEVELT'S AMERICAN WILDERNES

DAVID GESSNER

Simon & Schuster

NEW YORK   LONDON   TORONTO   SYDNEY   NEW DELHI

Simon & Schuster
1230 Avenue of the Americas
New York, NY 10020

First Simon & Schuster hardcover edition June 2020

SIMON & SCHUSTER and colophon are registered trademarks of Simon & Schuster, Inc.

For information about special discounts for bulk purchases, please contact Simon & Schuster Special Sales at 1-866-506-1949 or business@simonandschuster.com.

The Simon & Schuster Speakers Bureau can bring authors to your live event. For more information or to book an event, contact the Simon & Schuster Speakers Bureau at 1-866-248-3049 or visit our website at www.simonspeakers.com.

Interior design by Paul Dippolito
Maps by Alexis Seabrook

Manufactured in the United States of America

1   3   5   7   9   10   8   6   4   2

Library of Congress Cataloging-in-Publication Data
Names: Gessner, David, 1961– author. | Simon and Schuster, Inc.
Title: Leave it as it is : a journey through Theodore Roosevelt's American wilderness / by David Gessner.
Other titles: Journey through Theodore Roosevelt's American wilderness
Description: First Simon & Schuster Hardcover Edition. | New York : Simon & Schuster, 2020. | Includes index.
Identifiers: LCCN 2019051718 (print) | LCCN 2019051719 (ebook) | ISBN 9781982105044 (Hardcover) | ISBN 9781982105051 (Paperback) | ISBN 9781982105068 (eBook)
Subjects: LCSH: Environmentalism--United States--History. | National parks and reserves--United States--History. | Nature conservation--United States--History. | Forest conservation--United States--History. | Conservation of natural resources--United States--History. | Gessner, David, 1961---Travel. | Roosevelt, Theodore, 1858-1919--Travel--California--Yosemite Valley.
Classification: LCC GE195 .G385 2020 (print) | LCC GE195 (ebook) | DDC 333.78/3160973--dc23
LC record available at https://lccn.loc.gov/2019051718
LC ebook record available at https://lccn.loc.gov/2019051719

ISBN 978-1-9821-0504-4
ISBN 978-1-9821-0506-8 (ebook)

For Edmund Morris and Walter Jackson Bate,
great biographers whose lives continue to inspire

CONTENTS

Theodore on the Edge

He stands on the edge of the world, the great shimmering orange-red-and-bruise-colored chasm opening below him. Ravens lift off and ride the wind. He is bristling with energy at this moment. Which is to say it is like most of his waking moments.

Curious, always curious, he is a lover equally of the world and books about it. On the ride up here through the small juniper forest, always the show-off, he pointed out and named all the birds he saw to his companions. From his horse he studied the chickadees and towhees and pinyon jays and nuthatches—their calls higher pitched than those back east—and stopped to listen to the sound of a woodpecker cracking open a piñon nut. He knows these birds, knows their names, and he knows this canyon, too, though until today only through the words of others.

The president came to this place with expectations, like almost everyone else. The earliest explorers might not have known what to make of the canyon, and the first white settlers might have been surprised, and even angered, by what they saw as a colossal hole blocking their way west. But for more than a century now almost everyone who arrives here at the South Rim, who ascends out of the desert into the cool pine-scented air, does so knowing that something astounding awaits. Theodore Roosevelt is no different in this regard: even before he encountered the place, he had seen drawings and photos, and read plenty of descriptions. In fact he wrote most of the speech he will deliver an hour from now—when he will talk to the crowd of eight hundred gathering near the canyon's edge—without having ever laid eyes on the Grand Canyon itself. He did so, as he does many things, in a hurry, writing it this morning in his sleeping car as his train hurtled through New Mexico and into Arizona.

For the last month his life has been a paradox of speed and stillness, as he travels on his private train to some of the most beautiful and awe-inspiring places in North America, and then, after a few speeches, rushes off to the next place. It is 1903, and he is on a campaign tour for reelection, the first of its kind for a sitting president, during which he will travel more than a hundred miles a day, by train and car, and give close to two hundred speeches. An occasional insomniac and chronic coffee drinker (always with plenty of sugar please), he bristles with plans and schemes, ideas popping into his head at all hours, his famous enthusiasm bordering on, and perhaps sometimes slipping over into, mania. "We humans are an elsewhere," the poet Reg Saner will one day write. Teddy is more elsewhere than most.

Except when he isn't. Because for someone so ambitious, so eager to get on with the next task, he is shockingly good at slowing down time, at what we might call, in a phrase he would no doubt find disagreeable, being in the now. Whether he is staring down a charging grizzly or diving into the bracing winter water of Washington, D.C.'s Rock Creek Park or listening to the music of wind tinkling the cottonwood leaves, he seems to have the gift of *becoming absorbed*. This comes through most famously in his bouts of roughhousing with his children on the White House lawn. Even while burdened by the presidency, he has an enviable ability to slough off his heavy loads and simply enjoy himself.

Nothing quite takes him out of himself, nothing quiets his restless, fact-filled, febrile mind, like nature. He has already snuck off while camping at Yellowstone, walking eighteen miles alone to study a herd of elk. And in less than two weeks his fourteen-thousand-mile road trip will climax when he leaves his Secret Servicemen behind and embarks on a legendary excursion with the great prophet and protector of the natural world John Muir. That excursion in Yosemite will be long remembered as perhaps the most famous camping trip since Jesus spent his forty days in the desert. Think of it. The president of the United States sleeping outside under the stars with the country's most famous lover of nature. Details from the night are sparse but we do know that the president was critical of the prophet's bird knowledge and that the prophet questioned the morality of the president's bloodlust as a hunter. But I wonder what else happened as they stared into the fire and talked? Perhaps a form of osmosis affected Roosevelt. Perhaps the idea that wilderness was vital, not just for any human purpose, but for itself, began to grow.

That the seed of this knowledge, of this love, was already there is obvious. All you have to do is go back and read the man's sentences. Not the jingoistic, chest-beating, America-first rants or the bloody descriptions of killing things. But the words in between. The clean sentences that describe the stillness on the prairie or a morning full of birdcall, or a simple description of packing it in for the night in the North Dakota Badlands: "At the edge of the dark cedar wood I cleared a spot for my bed, and drew a few dead sticks for the fire. Then I lay down and watched drowsily until the afternoon shadows filled the wild and beautiful gorge in which I was camped. This happened early, for the valley was very narrow and the hills on either hand were steep and high." This is where the secret, quieter Roosevelt lies.

Theodore Roosevelt *got it*, something that few people, and no other president, ever understood and felt to the same degree. The raw fact that there are worlds beyond the human world. Muir might have helped him evolve, but Roosevelt already knew. He might have been an imperialist, a bellicose, limited man, anchored down by the prejudices of his times, but in this he was different. To say he was ahead of his time would be wrong, since many thinkers of the past, especially many Native peoples, had had similar insights before. But whatever his flaws, in this way at least he was definitely outside of his time, and his culture. Not in his embrace of hunting or hiking or birding, all of which were fashionable (and becoming more so in part because of him). But in the beginnings of something deeper. The sense that there is a world out there that cares little about the grid man lays over it. The biocentric sense that we are just one animal in a world of many, and the corresponding thrill, and freedom, that humans can feel when they step out of themselves and understand this.

Perhaps this is giving Roosevelt too much credit. After all, he often responded to the beautiful things he saw in nature by killing them. And his fascination with the world was balanced out by his fascination with Theodore Roosevelt. So let me reiterate an earlier, more modest claim. The man had the gift of going outward.

Which brings us back to the edge of the canyon. Let us imagine that he has already dismounted his horse and asked the others to give him a moment alone. As he moves to the spot where the world falls away, he will experience the vertiginous sensation we all do, leaning backward for fear of toppling a mile downward. He nods and understands. A place of danger. A place where you can't help but step back. And it is true. We pay lip service to feeling small in the natural world, to being part of it. But here the idea is not lip service. It is unavoidable.

He has already peeked over the edge a few times, but now he gives it his full attention. Perhaps he, like you or me, was worried that the canyon would not meet his expectations, would not be quite so grand. But what he sees does not disappoint. He stares far down to the canyon floor, at a scribbled green line of vegetation along the river, tracing it toward its roots. Morning comes late here, and though he has missed the molten show of sunrise, he delights in the way the light plays off the notches in the walls, bringing out purples and reds and oranges he has never seen before, even back in the Badlands. A gust of wind blows in from the east, and a small group of ravens ride it, tracing the edges of the canyon's cleaves and curves. He follows their flight with bespectacled eyes.

I have been speculating as I write this—*supposing*—and I will suppose one final time. There is a mystery from this day, May 6, 1903, that has not been solved. It has been assumed that the president wrote most of his soon-to-be-delivered speech before he arrived. But some researchers suggest he revised it after he saw the canyon. I don't know whether that is true or not. But I do know what the experience of seeing wild places does to me. It brings me to a wordless place. But then that wordlessness succumbs to words. In fact it has been my experience that places prompt sentences, as if the place itself were asking you to celebrate and protect it. So, yes, based on absolutely no evidence at all, except the fact that we know Roosevelt went on a horseback ride and saw the canyon before he gave his speech, I will suggest that at least some of the words he later spoke came from the canyon.

Whatever the case, an hour or so later he is standing on a hotel balcony above a crowd of eight hundred, declaiming, in his distinct, clipped, and surprisingly high voice about the need to save the place he has just seen for the first time. It is a perfect match of subject and stage. More than a few Rough Riders, members of Roosevelt's regiment in Cuba, are in the crowd. They play their parts well, hooting and hollering for the man who famously led them up San Juan Hill during the Spanish-American War. Roosevelt charged up the hill in a berserker's frenzy, later calling it the best day of his life. But many close to him had died on that best day, and he now mentions one of them in his introductory remarks, a man named Bucky O'Neill, who owned a cabin on the canyon's edge not a hundred yards from where the president speaks. O'Neill, like Roosevelt, had faced the Spanish bullets that day, and bragged that no Mauser bullet could kill him, right before one did.

It is thanks to an industrious newspaperman from the *Coconino Sun* that we have a transcript of what the president said that day. The words blew off with the wind, but they are still with us.

"I am glad to be in Arizona to-day," Roosevelt begins. "From Arizona many gallant men came into the regiment which I had the honor to command. Arizona sent men who won glory on hard-fought fields, and men to whom came a glorious and honorable death fighting for the flag of their country. As long as I live it will be to me an inspiration to have served with Bucky O'Neill."

Luck had been with Roosevelt, as it had not been with O'Neill and thousands of others, including the eighty-eight Rough Riders who died in Cuba. But Roosevelt gained more than the hill that day. The political capital earned as a war hero allowed him to lead much more unpopular charges, and he is about to lead one now. And if you are going to launch into what is essentially an environmental manifesto, it is not such a bad thing to have the local cowboys on your side. Some have been drinking, and they are not about to turn on their colonel or let anyone else do so. As they have already proven, they will follow him anywhere.

Roosevelt acknowledges the Rough Riders again—to more hooting—and says some nice things about the governor of Arizona. And then he gets down to it. The essence.

"In the Grand Canyon, Arizona has a natural wonder which, so far as I know, is in kind absolutely unparalleled throughout the rest of the world," he tells the crowd. "I want to ask you to do one thing in connection with it in your own interest and in the interest of the country—to keep this great wonder of nature as it now is. I was delighted to learn of the wisdom of the Santa Fe railroad people in deciding not to build their hotel on the brink of the canyon. I hope that you will not have a building of any kind, not a summer cottage, a hotel, or anything else, to mar the wonderful grandeur, the sublimity, the great loneliness and beauty of the canyon."

He is a newcomer here while most of these people have known the canyon for years or, in some cases, their whole lives. But he is the one telling them how they should treat it. He has never lacked for confidence. Or moral certainty. He speaks as he always speaks, emphatically. He is also a gesticulator of the first rank, and his hand hammers home the points. Writers of the time describe how sharply he clips his words, as if biting them off with his famous flashing teeth.

"Leave it as it is," he tells the crowd. "You can not improve on it. The ages have been at work on it, and man can only mar it. What you can do is to keep it for your children, your children's children, and for all who come after you, as one of the great sights which every American if he can travel at all should see."

Leave it as it is. While the crowd is delighted that the president of the United States is here, not everyone is pleased with this message. The enemies of the message then are the same enemies of the message now. Locals thinking in the short term. Entrepreneurs trying to make a buck off the big hole. Ranchers and miners. Extractors. *Leave it as it is? But this chasm is our meal ticket, our big chance, our bread and butter.* In some way Roosevelt's speech is the opening shot in a war still going strong over a century later.

No one in the audience can know the reverence with which the speech will one day be regarded, or the fact that environmentalists, an as of yet un-invented word, will come to regard it as being as important as Churchill's "Blood, Toil, Tears, and Sweat" and Lincoln's Gettysburg Address. The five words that the speech is most remembered for will become synonymous with the Grand Canyon and will be repeated so often that they become irritating to locals.

"We have gotten past the stage, my fellow-citizens, when we are to be pardoned if we treat any part of our country as something to be skinned for two or three years for the use of the present generation, whether it is the forest, the water, the scenery. Whatever it is, handle it so that your children's children will get the benefit of it."

Over the next century the environmental appeal to our children's children will become a cliché. But at the moment it is fresh. It is an appeal to that vague place, the future, and to its as yet nonexistent population, our grandchildren and great-grandchildren. It is genius: to connect us by our own blood to the land and the future. But it is an appeal that requires an act of imagination to succeed, a tenuous and brittle appeal easily broken by the urges and needs of *now*.

Those in the crowd cannot yet know that by the time he leaves office the president will have been responsible for saving 230 million acres of land for his country. And no one knows that he will find a clever way, through the use of a not-yet-created presidential act, to protect not just other treasured landscapes but the canyon itself. Or that, as he predicted, the grandchildren of angry locals will delight in what was saved.

From the distance of 117 years, it might look like some fights, including this one for the canyon, have been won. Secured and safe. But they never really are. Though no one could have known it then, in those early days, each battle can be lost, at any point in the future, even if it has been won multiple times before. Old threats return in new ways, requiring new words, and new acts to protect them.

But for the moment the battle, like so many similar battles across the country, has a champion. Someone to defend and articulate ideas that most people don't know they have yet. Someone who doesn't mind that the ideas are often unpopular and who can handle having scorn heaped on him for thinking and expressing something new. Someone to describe what can be gained and what can be lost.

What has happened today on the canyon's edge is just an early skirmish in what will be a never-ending war. But what has also happened is this: the fight has found its leader. And a rallying cry.

Leave it as it is.

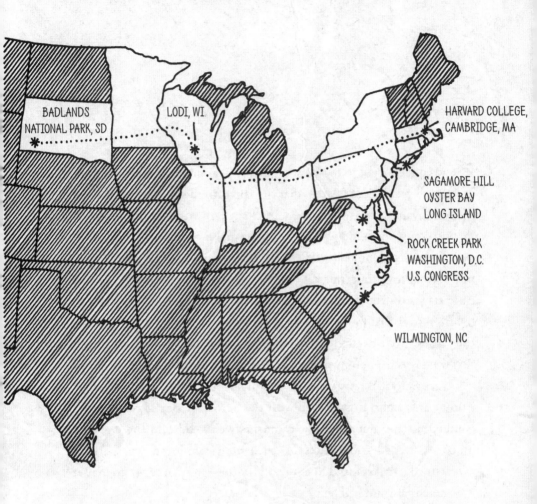

BADLANDS
NATIONAL PARK, SD

LODI, WI.

HARVARD COLLEGE,
CAMBRIDGE, MA

SAGAMORE HILL
OYSTER BAY
LONG ISLAND

ROCK CREEK PARK
WASHINGTON, D.C.
U.S. CONGRESS

WILMINGTON, NC

* * * CHAPTER ONE * * *

Into the Badlands

I t was once we got to the West—just the beginnings of the West, true, but the real West I insist—that the trip turned strange. From down in the valley, amid the hoodoo rocks where we were camping, the buffalo up on the ridge appeared to be making love to our car.

Of course, technically, they were American bison, and they were not making love to it, not yet at least, but rather seemed to be in the early stages of wooing. There were three, maybe four—it was hard to tell from over a half mile away—and they were rubbing up against the car's sides. My traveling companion, my nephew Noah, pointed out that what was happening made some sense, given the fact that the boxy vehicle, a Scion xB, was curiously bison-shaped, humped back and all. And he was right: it fit in well with the herd. The next day, when we climbed up and out from our campsite, we would find the rearview mirrors flattened and streaks of dried mud running down the car's sides, streaks that refused to come off for the rest of our trip no matter how much rain and hail fell.

We had been on the road for ten days, having worked our way up the East Coast from North Carolina to Washington, D.C., then heading to Boston before making the turn westward. At last we had crossed the Mississippi and encountered large animals in what were at least semi-wild places, which meant that for both of us the trip had really begun. For my twenty-one-year-old nephew it was only the second time that he had crossed America's great dividing river, and the first when his destination was the ocean on the other coast.

Noah is a quiet kid, so quiet that sometimes I didn't know if he was appreciating what we were seeing or experiencing, but after our trip was over he would send me a letter that let me know he had seen and felt it all.

"The drive through the middle of the US is a tough pill to swallow to get to the West," he would write. "It is miles and miles of plains, farms and the occasional creek or river. Then after driving in fairly flat, grassy plains forever you reach the outskirts of Badlands and you just see the earth drop off. After hours of driving with boring views the badlands hits you with an insane array of colors, landscape out of a fairy tale and bison as common as people."

The trip was my graduation present to him, an attempt to offer up some of what I had experienced when I headed west right after college. It was also a present to myself, an attempt to reconnect with an old hero of mine, one who had inspired me in the past, and, I hoped, wasn't done inspiring. Like that hero, I was an Easterner who believed deep down that some of the best years of his life had been in the West, and that the region, like the buffalo on my car, had left its indelible mark.

"I am myself at heart as much a westerner as an easterner," Theodore Roosevelt would say, though his grand total of time spent actually living in the West added up to just over a year. My own total came in at close to a decade, and those years changed me. One thing that had changed was my vision of nature. Born in Massachusetts, I saw the natural world as something small and private. The West had blown the doors off that old vision, teaching me about size and scope. Now I lived and taught in the East during the school year, but every summer I eagerly headed back to the place where this vision first formed. My hope was that Noah would develop a taste for the same landscapes.

"It was here the romance of my life began," Roosevelt wrote. He was talking about the badlands of North Dakota, not their southern cousins where Noah and I were camping, but in my life, and in Roosevelt's life, and in the lives of so many others, past and present, the sentiment applies to the West in general. A change in geography would lead to a change of character in the young Roosevelt, or at least an expansion of that character. And an expansion in values, especially in the value of all that is wild.

It is in the West that the central creation myth of Theodore Roosevelt began. At the age of twenty-five, Roosevelt left the East behind, and moved to the cattle ranch he had purchased near Medora, North Dakota. It was a not uncommon practice among his wealthy peers, to buy a ranch as an investment, but for him it became much more. Twenty years later, when he was president, he wrote:

"Do you know what chapter of my life . . . in all my life . . . looking back on all of it . . . I would choose to remember, were the alternative forced upon me to recall any portion of it, and have erased from my memory all other experiences? I would take the memory of my life of the ranch with its experiences close to nature and among men who lived nearest her."

*   *   *

Laugh if you want at the idea of Roosevelt, wealthy scion of an Eastern family, playing at being a Westerner. And to some degree laughter is merited: the future president and new cowboy would pose for publicity shots in his buckskin outfit with his silver engraved gun and a Tiffany knife tucked into his belt. But don't laugh too long. The buffalo we saw up on the ridge that were coming on to my car, and the individual buffalo that I would observe the next morning, grazing outside my tent—sniffing and snorting and kicking up dirt—those same animals owed their lives to the former effete Easterner who found himself in the West.

I don't mean that metaphorically. If Roosevelt hadn't headed west as a young man, it is unlikely Noah and I would have had a chance to see these massive animals anywhere except a zoo. The connection between his life and the buffalo strolling around our camp was a very real and direct one. There were several individuals who made the preservation of the buffalo possible, but he was one of those most responsible for the fact that we have buffalo herds in the United States in the twenty-first century. Not just in the habitat he saved or because of his efforts to protect the Yellowstone population. He also helped to save the species by promoting the breeding of remnant populations in the Bronx Zoo and elsewhere, populations that would later be interbred with the last wild animals in the West.

That was what was so exciting to me about Roosevelt and that was why I had returned to him. My reasons for coming to the life of Theodore Roosevelt were personal. I *wanted* something from him. The great writer and lexicographer Samuel Johnson valued biography above other genres because what we find there can be "put to use" in our own lives. My former professor, Walter Jackson Bate, who wrote lives of Samuel Johnson and John Keats, taught me to value the same. We have selfish uses for biography: we hungrily read the lives of others in hopes that we can find something that changes or enhances our own.

Though I was a writer who had dabbled in biography before, I had no interest in writing a proper life of Roosevelt. There were plenty of good ones already. They told the well-known story: the sickly child who made himself into the muscular, hardy young man who would later celebrate the strenuous life. The fledgling politician, still dandified and Eastern, and, in the vocabulary of the time, effeminate, with a high-pitched voice, who heads west, to the Badlands no less, where he transforms himself into a Westerner, a cowboy, a rancher, and returns a new man. The rising politician whose early popularity reaches its peak in a charge with his Rough Riders up San Juan Hill, a charge captured by a media (who he turns out to be masterful at manipulating) that makes him a national hero. And then the accidental president, after an assassin's bullet kills William McKinley in 1901, making Roosevelt the country's youngest leader ever at forty-two. Finally, the Roosevelt of legend: wielding power from the bully pulpit, fighting the trusts, carrying his big stick, and saving millions of acres of American land. The constant captivator of the country's attention, of whom his daughter Alice famously said: "My father always wanted to be the corpse at every funeral, the bride at every wedding, and the baby at every christening." But also the man who, at the peak of his popularity, announced he was quitting, and left the public stage too soon, only to come roaring back as a Bull Moose, before falling short, and heading into his last act: the worn-out traveler to the Amazon, exhausted but leaving behind one of the shining political epochs in American history.

As fascinating as his full biography was, it was not the story that interested me. The story I wanted to reacquaint myself with, the one I had some *use* for, was the story of Roosevelt and the land, his love of it, his words about it, his ferocious fight to preserve it. This, with our public lands threatened as never before, was what had brought me back to the life of the twenty-sixth president. More specifically, after years of writing about nature I wanted to begin to fight for it. And in that effort I couldn't think of a better role model than Theodore Roosevelt.

Over the previous few years I had been relearning an old lesson: no matter how often public lands are "saved," they are never really safe. With environmental safeguards being rolled back on land once thought protected, I had come to feel I could no longer sit on the sidelines. I began to ask myself a simple question. *What would Teddy do?*

He would fight like hell to preserve the land, I knew that, but what else? I jotted down a quick list of answers to that question in my journal:

- Get into the wild
- Study birds
- Drink lots of coffee
- Get into (spirited) battles
- Speak his mind
- Read/Learn about threatened places
- Write about those places
- Get in fighting trim
- Offend some people

I began to envision a project. I wanted to see if Roosevelt's life could stand as a challenge. For someone who called himself a conservationist, I had done precious little conserving. I wanted to find my voice, not just as a writer, but as a fighter, an advocate, and I wanted to help others do the same. It occurred to me that spending more time with Teddy, who in the end had saved millions of acres of American land through parks, national monuments, national forests and preserves, might have a rousing effect. Even better, I would spend that time outside in places that mattered to him.

We had been on the road for almost two weeks, but our arrival in Badlands National Park, a 244,000-acre geologic wonderland in western South Dakota, felt like a beginning, and, as I stared at the buffalo lurking around my car, a basic lesson came to me. That how we regard the land and its creatures has consequences. That our actions in the present ripple into the future, and that maybe, sometimes, our ideas can affect the world. Of course as soon as I write that sentence, a cynical voice inside me points out that we do not all have handy bully pulpits. And that often I feel about as in control of events as a dried leaf riding a flooded river. But remember: Roosevelt fought for buffalo in the early twentieth century and here was one grazing near our tents in the twenty-first.

The usual Roosevelt paradox applies here. He came west to hunt and to ranch, and it was men of his ilk, not long before his arrival in the West, who threatened the herds of bison in the first place, who diminished to the point of near extinction a seemingly un-diminishable number of animals, the great sea of beasts on the endless prairie. It is telling that under "Buffalo" in the index of Douglas Brinkley's massive biography of Roosevelt, *The Wilderness Warrior*, the many entries for "Conservation of" are matched in number only by those for "Hunting of."

This was part of what had turned me away from Roosevelt for a while. I loved him when I was young, and read multiple biographies when I first moved west, but over the years he had transformed into a caricature in my mind. I tired of the image of the great white hunter, eyes gleaming with manifest destiny while ignoring or hastening the fate of Indigenous people, charging about and yelling "Bully!" Though I was aware of all the land he had saved, and his well-earned reputation as perhaps our country's greatest conservationist, he was, in some ways, the very embodiment of the sort of manic, driven, America-first personality that had gotten the world into the mess we were in. Worse, sometimes he seemed plain silly.

And yet: buffalo.

How many human beings can offer such a solid and bulky rebuttal when questioned about their worth?

And there they were right in front of us. His burly legacy. Surrounding my car as the sun died, their hulking black shapes silhouetted up on the ridge.

And I thought: To have *saved* something. What must that be like?

*   *   *

The idea of launching our cross-country journey was born on October 27, 2017. That day happened to be Theodore Roosevelt's 159th birthday. It was also the day that the secretary of the interior of the United States held a press conference and recommended a drastic reduction of two national monuments that had been created by previous presidents. The two targets were Grand-Staircase Escalante and Bears Ears in southern Utah. The interior secretary also recommended opening these public lands to private interests.

The irony in the air, already thick, was made thicker by the fact that the secretary, Ryan Zinke, made his announcement standing below a portrait of Roosevelt. In fact, the secretary, who fancied himself an outdoorsman, claimed to be "an ardent admirer and disciple" of Roosevelt, but what he proposed was an effort to weaken and possibly overturn the 1906 Antiquities Act, the very tool the twenty-sixth president had used to save millions of acres of American land.

Bears Ears, the country's newest monument at less than a year old, was especially hard hit. No one was surprised that this was what this particular administration wanted, or that their weeks of "studying" Bears Ears had resulted in a recommendation to reduce the acreage. But the degree of suggested diminishment would prove extraordinary, the monument reduced to almost a tenth of what it had been.

With so much news bombarding us at such a fast pace it is easy to become numb.

But I took this story personally. Not just because I had already been studying Roosevelt's life, but because the national monument that was in the crosshairs was one where I'd often hiked and paddled and camped over the years. Bears Ears is a spectacular landscape that includes the hundred-mile sandstone spine of Comb Ridge, the high meadowland of the twin peaks that give the monument its name, and canyons that drop down out of that meadow to the San Juan River. It contains a varied assortment of natural bridges, redrock spires, and buttes, surrounded by creeks, mountains, and mesas, all in one of the most remote corners of the Lower 48. In 2016 I, along with many other writers, had contributed to a book that would aid the effort to save the Bears Ears Wilderness, part of the appeal to then President Obama to designate this land as a national monument. *Red Rock Testimony* was distributed to all members of Congress, and when Obama declared Bears Ears a national monument before leaving office I experienced a sense not just of elation but of empowerment.

Even as I felt that way, I also understood that this was just my small, personal response. Something larger was going on. Bear Ears for me had offered some of my most formative experiences in the wilderness, but for others it was much more. It was a place inhabited long before Europeans came to the continent, and if I considered it "sacred," for others it actually was.

That was the important thing to remember about Bears Ears, the thing that got lost in the coverage. The important thing was that there was one difference between Bears Ears National Monument and all the other national monuments that came before it: it was the first national monument to fully grow out of the thinking, support, and political power of Native American tribes. What made the threat and reductions even more painful was that they followed a great moment of hope.

While we've heard America's national parks called "our best idea," the part of that idea that was never so great was the exclusion—and sometimes expulsion—of Native peoples. Bears Ears was a *better* idea.

Something akin to a Native American attitude toward the land, and its sacredness, had always been floating around in the minds of those who fought to preserve this country's public lands. This was true even if their behavior when it came to actual Native Americans didn't reflect this. But until Bears Ears, actual Indigenous thinking played little part in the creation of our national monuments. Our policy toward public land had mostly ignored those who had lived longest on that land and for whom that land was sacred. The proclamation of Bears Ears as a national monument was the first step in recognizing the wrongness of this and of putting forth a new vision.

Which was why the news of October 27 hit so hard. That earlier victory, and that stunning place, a place that got at the essence of the ideal of public lands and why it mattered to have places that no one but the country's citizens owned, were now threatened.

On a personal level, slumping seemed an appropriate response. That and feeling overwhelmed. Once again something in the news, something seemingly remote and far beyond my life and powers, had swept me off like that leaf in the flood.

But this time, instead of slumping, I took action. Two months after Zinke's press conference I flew west to Bears Ears. It was a kind of scouting mission for the larger trip to come, and those ten days were filled to the brim. I talked to the activists who had argued with Zinke, hiked into ancient Anasazi dwellings that were tucked into cliff sides, as integral to their surroundings as the nests of cliff swallows, drove south for a side trip to the Grand Canyon, and hiked through the snow to the base of the western Bears Ear with an old Navajo friend. For all that, the highlight might have been the very first stop of my trip, at the Ute Indian Museum in Montrose, Colorado. I had traveled there to speak with the museum's education director, Regina Lopez-Whiteskunk.

Regina had been the head councilwoman of the Ute Mountain Ute tribe during the initial battle for the designation of Bears Ears as a national monument. She was a small woman, who sometimes got lost behind the podiums she had recently found herself so often speaking from, but she had a big personality. Her wide smile and quiet charm had made her a go-to spokesperson for Bears Ears. Regina gave me a brief history of the creation of the newest national monument, from idea to reality and, perhaps, back to idea. It was a story that was already getting lost as the likes of Donald Trump, Zinke, and Utah senator Orrin Hatch were being elevated to central characters in the drama.

The story began when a Navajo group, Dine Bikeyah ("People's Sacred Lands"), initiated the project of culturally mapping the Bears Ears area, a large region of public land almost empty of people but full of cultural and religious significance for Native peoples. Opponents of the Bears Ears designation sometimes portray it as a rash and sudden decision by Obama, but in fact the monument's roots grew from the Dine Bikeyah's assiduous collection of data and identification of sensitive cultural historical areas in the region.

Once the initial work was done, the Navajo organization invited other tribes to join in the creation of a proposal for a national monument. The five tribes that would eventually make up the Bears Ears Inter-Tribal Coalition—Navajo, Hopi, Ute, Zuni, and Ute Mountain Ute—were not exactly on the best of terms. The Utes were in active litigation with the Navajo over water issues and the Navajo and Hopi were at odds and in active litigation over land issues.

"Those first meetings were so intense," Regina told me. "And we had some really long meetings. We had to heal ourselves first. We agreed that when we met, all other issues, all other politics, would stay outside. In the end we set our disagreements aside and focused on the conservation of the land, continued access to the land, and trying to keep the mining and the roads out."

The coalition proceeded slowly. Dozens of elders were interviewed about Bears Ears and the significance that particular places had for their clans and tribes.

"While we were putting the proposal together, we worked really hard not to spend time recounting the historical trauma of the Indigenous people. We didn't want to say, *We want our land back*. Ours was an effort to heal. We worked hard to stay away from terms like 'racism.' We tried to focus on the light, not the darkness."

I told her about a friend back in North Carolina, who, when I brought up Bears Ears, had said: "I don't object to them saving the land. I love wilderness. But they shouldn't have saved it under the Antiquities Act. It's a misuse. That is not what the act was created for."

Regina laughed.

"I'd like to talk to your friend," she said. "I feel like I have the Antiquities Act memorized. We went over it so carefully, every word and aspect."

She knew the history of the act, too. Knew that "An Act for the Preservation of American Antiquities" had slipped fairly quietly through both houses of Congress back in 1906. Knew that what the members of Congress seemed to fail to notice, or at least failed to alter, was just how little Congress would have to do with the future designation of these monuments. From its inception the Antiquities Act was solely a tool of the president, and the president at the time was not one to leave effective tools unused. She also knew that for conservationists Roosevelt's creative interpretation of the act had been a cause for joy; for those who opposed it, a cause for consternation, and sometimes rage.

When I sat down with her, Regina had been fighting hard for Bears Ears for four years—though she didn't like the war metaphors, all the "fights" and "battles" so common among environmentalists. By the end of our talk Regina's healing approach toward Bears Ears had me questioning my own more aggressive approach to environmentalism. In a time of raised voices did I really need to add another raised voice? Furthermore, I wondered about the wisdom of my barging in and telling *her* story.

When I brought up this concern directly, Regina was typically generous.

"We need *your* story, we need *my* story, we need *all our* stories right now," she said.

* * *

I came back from my scouting trip animated and energized. My proposed cross-country trip, the seed of which had been planted when Zinke announced the reductions on TR's birthday, began to feel like a reality. I was going to do it. Equally animating was the idea of confluence. Could Roosevelt's old-school park ideals about leaving it as it is be united with the new ideas that Regina was proposing? I didn't know, but my gut said yes. In a time of division why not try to unite?

Four months later, on May 21, I left my home in Wilmington, North Carolina, picked up Noah in Durham, and drove north. For the first ten days of our trip Noah and I slept in hotels, dorms, and the homes of friends and relatives. In Washington, D.C., I hiked and swam in Rock Creek Park, where Roosevelt had gone for bracing swims with members of his cabinet, even in winter. I'd always felt so disconnected from Washington, but recently an old college classmate, Jamie Raskin, had been elected as a representative from Maryland. Walking down the corridors of the congressional office building, I felt as if some real and personal connection to national politics was possible, though when I saw Jamie he confirmed my sense of the state of the nation, shaking his head slowly and saying: "It's even worse than you think."

Noah, who had gone to school in Asheville, in the mountains of North Carolina, had been an avid Bernie Sanders supporter. He was unimpressed with D.C. and the droves of young workers outside of the congressional offices. It occurred to me that I would have thought the same thing upon my graduation. "Tools," I would have called them. "I wouldn't want to live here," Noah said to me. "Everyone is wearing ties."

Nor was my nephew crazy about our next stop, Sagamore Hill, Roosevelt's home on Long Island, a dark, cedar-shingled cave full of mounted animal heads and zebra rugs. "Too much death and darkness in there," he said. But he did enjoy the wicker rocking chairs on the house's expansive front deck, and we sat there for a while in the shade above the great sloping hill of a front lawn while swallows, chasing insects, shot through the unmown grass and daisies. "What true American does not enjoy a rocking chair?" Roosevelt once interjected exuberantly in the midst of what was otherwise a staid and buttoned-down sentence.

We continued north to New England and spent five days in a cramped dorm room in Cambridge so I could study Roosevelt's papers in Houghton Library. Less than a hundred yards from where we stayed was a sign:

Here lived Theodore Roosevelt During Four Formative and Fruitful Years as a Member of Harvard College. 1876–1880

It felt like the universe was conspiring when LeBron James, who was in town to lead his team, the Cleveland Cavaliers, against the Boston Celtics in the NBA's Eastern Conference Finals, used a Sharpie to write the words "The Man in the Arena" on his sneakers. When I told this to an old friend in Cambridge, a former point guard for one of the earliest Harvard women's teams, she surprised me by reciting the entire Roosevelt quote from memory:

It is not the critic who counts; not the man who points out how the strong man stumbles, or where the doer of deeds could have done them better. The credit belongs to the man who is actually in the arena, whose face is marred by dust and sweat and blood; who strives valiantly; who errs, who comes short again and again, because there is no effort without error and shortcoming; but who does actually strive to do the deeds; who knows great enthusiasms, the great devotions; who spends himself in a worthy cause; who at the best knows in the end the triumph of high achievement, and who at the worst, if he fails, at least fails while daring greatly, so that his place shall never be with those cold and timid souls who neither know victory nor defeat.

If all these coincidences and connections were any indication, this dead president was very much alive. The great nature writer John Muir once wrote: "When we try to pick out anything by itself, we find it hitched to everything else in the Universe." This, it seemed to me, was particularly true if the thing you picked out was Teddy Roosevelt. On our very last night in Boston, Noah and I attended the seventh game of the Conference Finals, rooting for a Celtics team that couldn't quite hit enough shots to defeat the Man in the Arena.

That had all been fun, but it was still just prelude. Libraries and dorm rooms and even arenas were not what the trip was about. It took three full days of driving to get to where we needed to be, a place where we could finally sleep out of doors under the stars. Badlands National Park in South Dakota is hardly an obscure destination, with approximately one million tourists a year ticking it off their lists. But we had managed to find a little piece of it to call our own. After we unpacked, I climbed atop an orange-pink hill of rock, about twenty feet up, and stared out at gigantic sand doodles of stone, spires, and pinnacles, and at a roseate rim, a great wall of sculpted rock, that was lighting up pink and yellow and red as the sun dipped. Having spent so much time in Utah, I was used to rock rising and twisting in any strange hoodoo shape that rock might want to twist. But what was different was all the grass between the rock. Here were the otherworldly shapes of Utah amid a bright green carpet. Green shone out among the striated white and dull pink and yellow needles of rock and below the great curving amphitheater of stone that arced along what I decided must be a river below. And all the grass of course helped explain all the bison that grazed in the foreground below the rock statuary.

I cracked a beer, and sitting there, atop my pink hill, I began to feel immensely happy about being back in the West. After a thousand miles of farms and flatness, small towns and suburbs, here we were. I was filled with a sense of giddy possibility. Noah climbed up on top of the rock to join me. He nodded out at the view of sculpted rock.

"It's almost like the whole ride through the East and Midwest was just buildup," he said. "It's like the incline on a roller coaster that takes a while to get to the pinnacle, but once you hit this place, there are all kinds of crazy loops and turns and spins."

Before the sun set, we decided to find the river. We began a long walk down trails pioneered by bison. The grassland was drier than it appeared from a distance, the cracked ground looking like it was made of buffalo chips (which it sometimes was). Cacti grew in grass only interrupted by islands of peanut brittle rocks. Based on the curving architecture of the wall above it, Noah had imagined a rushing river, and when we got to it, finding only a muddy brown trickle, he said, "That's disappointing." But then he added: "If there were more water it wouldn't be the West." Yes, grasshopper, I thought, you are learning. He had just been told in the shorthand of our walk the same disappointing story that has been told repeatedly to hopeful Easterners over the last couple of centuries. The promise, the dream . . . and then the stark, arid reality.

The true highlight of our trip to the river was seeing a fat porcupine waddling away from us, in no great hurry, into the brush. Then, when we got back to the camp, I walked to where I could look back up at the ridge and saw that the bison were still there. Earlier that day we had watched bighorn sheep on a ridge, and they had seemed to be holding both their poses and their heads up while atop the highest rocks. "Skylining" it is called. While their profiles weren't quite as dramatic, the same could now be said of the bulky black shapes silhouetted above us. My xB was right there with them, proudly displaying itself, a modest car that turned out to be a show-off.

After a quick dinner, Noah headed for his tent. He was a friendly but shy kid, tall and thin with a mop of blond hair, who had majored in math. He had a nice smile and an easy manner. We had been very close his whole life, and during summers at the beach people sometimes mistook me for his father. His own father and my sister Heidi had divorced when he was ten. From when he was born I had a running joke with Heidi that when he was an adolescent I would take him on an initiatory mushroom-fueled spirit quest in the desert. This road trip wasn't quite that. But it was something.

Noah had settled in his tent, but I decided to sleep outside on my pad. Our first night in the Badlands began with a gentle breeze and a blazing orange moon rising over the sand doodle rocks. I quieted my mind and listened to the deep respiration of the earth. At first it seemed to be shaping up to be a spectacular night for sleeping, but it was foolish of me to expect the weather that we dozed off with to be the weather throughout the night. At various times I was awakened by coyotes yipping and the spectacle of the moon being revealed by a fleet of black and ink-blue clouds, and later to a light rain and building winds that set our tarp luffing like a sail. I woke to birdsong but had slept through what Noah showed me on his phone had been a blazing sunrise.

Happily, though the cameras on our phones worked, the signals didn't. I spent the next morning occupied not with business dictated by the device that often ran my life, but with a lone buffalo that had wandered close. I drank black camp coffee and took field notes as it grazed. Aged solitary individuals like the one I was watching, who keep apart from the herd, were once called "Lonesome George"s. I studied the burl and huff of the huge animal as he shook his head to rid himself of two blackbirds on his back. The bulk was all in the massive shoulders. Despite that power, and his sheer size, he walked almost daintily down what must have been his regular morning path to his grazing grounds. In just this way buffalo, in herds that sometimes could reach a million animals, created deep grooved paths that acted as the earliest roads in this part of the world. Fur, like leg warmers, covered his front legs, but his back legs were bare. His back was sand- and dirt-encrusted, the cracked skin not unlike the cracks in the strange pink-orange mound I was sitting on. His twitching tail kept time. He snuffed in the grass. He took a long satisfying piss.

Noah sat down with me. We didn't talk, but I like to think that he was feeling something close to what I felt: how truly miraculous it was to wake to this scene. No people in sight, no planes overhead. A buffalo grazing in front of us. A reduced wild but a wild still. This great grunting presence near camp boded well. For what? For our trip perhaps. For a future beyond our compromised now.

While I didn't want to do it—not on that glorious morning, not on our first full day in the West—my mind couldn't stop itself from going where it often went when I was faced with one of nature's glorious spectacles. My capacity for enjoyment is fairly high, but I, like the rest of us, have taken a large bite out of the apple. I, *we*, know too much.

We know, for instance, that these lands used to be *covered* by buffalo. Some have estimated as many as sixty million roamed North America before Europeans arrived, though recent estimates suggest that the number was closer to thirty. Either way, this means, according to buffalo advocate Daniel Brister, that "in terms of biomass, North America's bison comprised the largest concentration of animals known to exist." And then the gruesome and inevitable punch line that comes with any such bison refresher course: while there were still millions of buffalo in the 1860s, there were twenty-three buffalo left in the wild by 1902. To which you may respond: *Are you fucking kidding me? Twenty-three? How could this happen?*

A very short answer—the cattle industry, the railroads' incursions into the West, an Eastern and European taste for buffalo robes, a taste also for their very convenient meat, multipurpose industrial and commercial uses for hides, and finally, a belief that would prove founded: that by killing off the buffalo our westward hurtling country could also kill off the Indigenous people who had been inhabiting the land, and who depended on the buffalo for, well, pretty much everything.

It might be easy to also point a finger at Roosevelt for this near extinction, and he certainly isn't blameless. His business was cattle after all, a direct competitor for the same grazing land, and the first thing he wanted to do when he came west was shoot a buffalo. But Roosevelt hunted and killed maybe two bison in his life, while Buffalo Bill, according to Brister, "bragged of killing 4,280 buffalo in an eighteen-month period." The entire near-extinction happened in a blur: the majority of the animals were killed in just one bloody decade. The 1870s were the peak years for the slaughter, with millions of dead buffalo left to rot on the plains, some shot just for fun by tourists in passing trains, and soon enough what had been the realm of giant shaggy beasts became the realm of cows.

* * *

The riddle we have to answer, the essential mystery we have to solve, is how some rich kid from Manhattan, born with the silverest of spoons in his mouth, becomes the buffalo's savior. The answer has implications for us all.

Luckily, we don't have to solve this mystery alone. The transformation we are describing is also the basic plot of two of the best biographies ever written about Roosevelt: *Mornings on Horseback*, by David McCullough, and *The Rise of Theodore Roosevelt*, by Edmund Morris. Published within two years of each other (*Rise* in 1979 and *Mornings* in 1981), both vibrantly tell the story of how Roosevelt became Roosevelt. They are influential works that Morris himself, in his summation of the many Roosevelt biographies, including his own, says began a movement away from either hagiographies or hatchet jobs and "marked the beginning of a more objective reassessment" of TR. "Objective" is one word for them, though I prefer "stirring" and "contagious." Maybe even "rip-roaring." Both biographies present a robust Roosevelt, full of contradiction and fire, and it is no knock on McCullough's excellent book to say that I give the slight nod to Morris's. While obviously meticulously researched, *The Rise* provides much more than a year-to-year, sometimes month-to-month, account of young Roosevelt's life. We also get a sense of the hyperactive energy, the manic but simultaneously deeply focused mind of the young TR. Best of all it can rub off on you. "The richness of Roosevelt's knowledge causes a continuous process of cross-fertilization to go on in his mind," writes Morris. It is not unpleasant, in fact it is rousing and energizing, to spend time with a mind like that. Before you know it, you are connecting historical events to present ones and maybe even looking up the Latin name of the bird you saw on your way to work. There is a briskness to the book, to the taut sentences, an energy not unlike Roosevelt's own.

Both books tell the origin story of the man who many later will call TR. But this hero is first called "Teedie" and is far from heroic. Small, sickly, tortured by asthma, he worships his leonine father, Theodore Sr., also known as Thee, a man who looms like a great planet in the youngster's universe and whom his son will call "the best man I ever knew." Theodore Sr. strolls through the streets of 1850s and '60s New York like he owns the place, which he pretty much does. *His* wealthy father, and his wealthy father before him, and so on and so forth, are part of a family line that extends back two hundred years to when New Amsterdam was first settled. Thee, bored by mere business, spends his time doing good: cofounding institutions like the American Museum of Natural History and the New York Orthopedic Hospital. He is broad-shouldered, big-hearted, charming, and slightly scary in the eyes of his small son. For he is not just the best man Teedie ever knew but the only one whom he will ever admit to being afraid of. Thee is what a man should be like: not small and sickly and awkward.

Thee's beautiful bride, Martha or "Mittie" Bulloch, hails from the South, which will prove more than a small problem when the Civil War breaks out two and a half years after baby Theodore is born. But while the household will revere the Republicanism of Lincoln, Theodore will relish the stories of derring-do of Mittie's blockade-breaking and swashbuckling Confederate relatives, and will conflate these with the beloved adventure stories that he begins to read omnivorously. To be a hero! To be a big man! These are his dreams. And, importantly: To be a *fighter*! It is to his great shame that the biggest man he knows, the father who he calls Great Heart, opts out of fighting in the war, hiring a replacement soldier like many of his wealthy peers.

Though all things masculine are romanticized by the boy, it would be wrong to think he evolves in an all-male world. His older sister Anna, called "Bamie," is his great confidante, supporter, and friend, and will remain so his entire life. His mother, a Southern belle who will devolve toward invalidism, will cart her sick son along with her to the sanatoriums she visits. He is homeschooled and has few friends not named

Roosevelt, but within the family, in the society of Bamie and his younger siblings Elliott and Corinne, he can shine in his own way. His memory is a flytrap, and as well as reading stories he tells them, craving the spotlight from the start.

We can imagine a small invalid boy, clinging to his mother while both loving and fearing his father, feeling helpless in the larger world but wanting to be like the heroes in his books. But in the meantime he is wrapped in blankets, carted off to sanatoriums, pampered and feared for. Why? Because there are moments, hours, nights, when he simply can't breathe.

This is the first of the two key childhood story lines that emerge from the great Roosevelt biographies. McCullough writes of the boy's chronic asthma:

> The sensation of an acute asthmatic attack is that of being strangled or suffocated, only infinitely more complex . . . the agony is total, unlike say, smashing a finger in a door, where the pain is concentrated at one point. And the largest part of the agony is psychological—inexpressible terror, panic.

It is this disease that marks Roosevelt's childhood and that much of his character seems to be a reaction against. The frightened boy vows to be brave, the small boy vows to be big, the uncertain boy, living at the whims of illness, vows to take control. The disease stays with the boy as he becomes a young man, the famous moment occurring when he is almost twelve, grown taller now but still scrawny and prone to terrifying bouts of breathlessness. The father, the composed and powerful father who must also be so frightened and overwhelmed by fear that his first-born boy might die at any moment, comes to him and utters the famous words: "Theodore, you have the mind but you have not the body, and without the help of the body the mind cannot go as far as it should. You must *make* your body. It is hard drudgery to make one's body, but I know you will do it."

In saying this his father is of his time, and is taking the advice of the boy's doctors. But how exactly does one *make* one's body? The boy must build up his chest, must lift weights and strengthen his arms, must become, in effect, more *manly* and therefore expel his disease. And of course, the story goes, the boy immediately vows to do so and sets right to it with a kind of upbeat fanaticism. It is a great story, a tale of a boy remade into a man, a tale of willpower, Roosevelt as a sort of upper-crust nineteenth-century Rocky Balboa.

Of course it is not so simple. The asthma continues, and according to Kathleen Dalton's fascinating reappraisal, 2002's *The Strenuous Life*, it will continue the rest of his life. It is hidden from the public in much the way his famous cousin, Franklin, will later hide his polio. This is a life-long pattern of Roosevelt's: to charge ahead in the face of illness. When he is warned of heart trouble by his doctor at twenty-one, and told to slow down and live a quiet life, he ignores the advice outright. His name will become synonymous with vigor, though an argument can be made that this vital man, plagued not just by asthma but by malaria, leg infections, heart trouble, and the small matter of an assassination attempt, could still be called, in at least one sense, sickly. But his many ailments and injuries don't stop him from throwing himself, sometimes wildly, into physical activity.

If the response to his father's injunction is immediate, the results come slowly. Though he sets right to lifting barbells and straining on the gymnastic bars, there is a lag time, of many years in fact, before others will notice the thickening chest and stronger arms. As TR wrote of his attempts to learn how to box: "I was a painfully slow and awkward pupil, and certainly worked two or three years before I made any perceptible improvement whatever."

But the lack of results is not due to a lack of effort. Effort, and the idea of it—and of willpower—will become lifelong themes, a story he tells himself. Maybe the most important story. It is vital to the man he becomes, even if we believe, as more and more modern scientists and thinkers tell us, that the whole idea of "will" is a fiction. His near contemporary and his future teacher at Harvard, the great psychologist William James, has written of willpower that whether it exists or not is ultimately unimportant, since our experience of it is real, and therefore we should act as if it does exist. Theodore doesn't need to perform any such mental gymnastics. *Will exists.* It is how he has expunged weakness, and fear, from his life. It is the rock he will build himself on. And even if we don't believe in will, there is something to this. It may be a delusion, but it is a delusion that helps get things done. And it is a delusion that helps one change.

For our purposes, to solve our riddle, it is important to note that this stress on getting stronger is also married to an emphasis on being in the open air, mostly while going on cold coach rides with his father (though, to complicate things, the cigar smoke his father blows on him is also thought to be salutary). What is key here, for the future conservationist, is that nature and physical hardiness start to become intertwined. Morris writes of this evolution: "Glorifying in his newfound strength, he plunges into the depths of icy rapids, and clambers to the heights of seven mountains (one of them twice on the same day). Along with this physical exuberance, he develops a more studious interest in nature."

It is an interest that will prove crucial to the creation of our first and greatest environmental president, that will lead quite directly to the fact that we still have buffalo to observe in the Badlands. While asthma punctuates his life, there are periods in between for play, for reading, and, more and more, for the study of natural history. His is a curious mind, self-centered at times but always ready to reach outward, and no biography of Roosevelt is complete without describing the pivotal moment when he first sees the seal.

He is seven years old walking up Broadway to the market when he spies the large dead seal laid out "on a slab of wood." "This was a turning point, an epiphany," Michael Canfield writes in *Theodore Roosevelt in the Field* of the moment Roosevelt saw "the type of magnificent animal he had previously encountered only in the dusty books of his family's library." He studies the seal carefully and then visits it the next day to study it some more, this time measuring it and taking notes, and then returns "day after day." The seal is a glimpse of a distant watery world, and the study of it and its mysteries leads to the creation of the Roosevelt Museum of Natural History, the youngster's collection that will include the seal skull along with turtles, snakes, and, eventually, hundreds of specimens of stuffed birds.

It is not just a sense of wonder that the boy finds in nature. Ambition rises like heat off the lined pages of the natural history notebooks he begins to keep. While it goes without saying that the young man is ferociously ambitious, it is interesting that the earliest manifestation of that ambition is tied to the natural world. If asked what he wanted to be when he grew up, the boy who studied the seal would not have answered a statesman or soldier or author or even president. Like his hero, Charles Darwin, he wanted not just to be a naturalist but a naturalist in the field, and he set about tackling this goal with what we would come to know as typical Rooseveltian focus and energy.

It is an unusual combination but will prove a vital one. We associate nature lovers with passivity, with going with the flow. But passivity doesn't save parks. What was being created in that strange chemistry set of self that was the young Teedie would turn out to be just what the increasingly industrial nation would need in the coming century. His father, who loomed so large in his psychic life, was a proponent of the idea of "muscular Christianity," which was popular at the time. No more scrawny, meek Christ for him and his generation. It was time for a more manly Jesus, and it would be no mistake that "Onward, Christian Soldiers" would later be the theme song of the Bull Moose Party. The younger Roosevelt was never particularly religious. But what was forming in him, as a seed that wouldn't sprout for many years, was something that we might call muscular environmentalism.

* * *

My nephew, despite himself, was becoming a sort of expert on Theodore Roosevelt. During the two thousand or so miles of driving we had done already, we had been listening to books on tape, specifically biographies of or books by Roosevelt.

When I asked him when we started driving if he had read any good books recently, he replied, "*The Tao of the Dude*," which, he explained, was a compendium of the wisdom of the bathrobe-wearing, White Russian–drinking slacker from *The Big Lebowski*.

That was his idea of a real hero, and he had quickly grown sick of hearing about the hyperactive, un-Dude-like Teddy. He would grow much sicker. By the end of the trip I was pretty sure that he would be happy to never again hear the phrase "manly vigor."

"We are kind of opposites," he had said at one point in the drive, somewhere between Cleveland and Chicago, of himself and the twenty-sixth president.

Certainly they were physical opposites. At six-foot-four, long and lanky, Noah could have been the exclamation point to Roosevelt's period. And verbal opposites, too. Roosevelt fired off sentences all day long. Noah could go for hours without saying anything while we drove, and could go longer if I didn't feel the occasional need to fill the air with words.

The president and my nephew do have one area of physical overlap. Noah also suffers from asthma. When we hike he keeps his inhaler handy. Teddy had no such luxury.

There is a sweetness to my nephew, and he has a fine aesthetic sense, something that I noticed in his awed appreciation of the rock formations surrounding our Badlands campsite. But his is a relatively passive nature, while one can imagine TR spitting out the word "passivity" as if he'd tasted a rotten peach.

Teddy had exhorted us from the Scion's tinny speakers as we drove across the Midwest. He warned against "ignoble ease" and "the weakling or coward who babbles of peace," and those who do "their puny bests." To the modern ear the words sounded sexist and homophobic. Good qualities were always "manly," bad always "effeminate." No one should be "mollycoddled." We should "sink from no strife."

After a while I gave up trying to put Roosevelt's comments in the context of his own time or otherwise justify what he was saying. To a recent college graduate like Noah, who had not yet landed a job, how could the words not sound like *scolding*? It must have been like hearing an angry commencement speech over and over. I had an easier time forgiving Roosevelt, even when he came off sounding like an angry Tony Robbins. I felt beyond judging: I had come to believe that anyone who created energy was useful. For a long time I had used figures like TR as whetstones to shape myself. It wasn't ease I was after. It was something more, a kind of secret, that, despite his belligerence, I knew Teddy held. I had read recently in the Morris biography that Roosevelt believed in "the fellowship of the doers." That was one secret society I would like to join.

Even when he sounded most extreme, I remembered that we had common ground, and that was the ground itself. The American land. The places that my nephew and I would now be entering that would have been so different without the millions of acres TR had saved.

*   *   *

During our time in Badlands National Park, I saw not just dozens of buffalo but a prairie falcon, a horned lark, several bobolinks, a few killdeer, a blue grosbeak, bluebirds, and a flock of yellow-rumped warblers. But the main bird that had been serenading us since we arrived was the main bird that had serenaded Teddy when he came to the Badlands 130 years before: the meadowlark. Roosevelt considered this uplifting creature with the bright yellow chest and black bib *the* bird of the prairie and wrote about it in a fairly brilliant passage that touches upon the subjective way that most of us judge birdsong. In words so different than the bellicose and dated sentences that unsettled Noah, he wrote of the variety, length, and richness of the bird's song but then qualified what he'd said, admitting that the appeal of the music was in part because it

> comes laden with a hundred memories and associations: with
> the sight of dim hills reddening in the dawn, with the breath of
> cool morning winds blowing across lonely plains, with the scent

of flowers on the sunlit prairie, with the motion of fiery horses, with all the strong thrill of eager and buoyant life. I doubt if any man can judge dispassionately the bird songs of his country; he cannot disassociate them from the sights and sounds of the land that is so dear to him.

Roosevelt was one of those lucky human beings for whom the music of birds is life's soundtrack. He had an excellent ear. In this way he was like his fellow connoisseur of birdsong, the famous birder and field guide creator Roger Tory Peterson, who stayed in bed one day while the rest of his eager birding party headed out at dawn. When they came back and bragged of seeing forty-two species, Peterson told them he had heard forty while lying in his bed. This was Roosevelt, too: though he loved the colors and flight of birds, his bird world started as and remained an aural one. He would compare the song of the nightingale with that of the hermit and wood thrush as if comparing symphonies: "The serene ethereal beauty of the hermit's song, rising and falling through the still evening; under the archways of hoary mountain forests that have endured from time everlasting; the golden, leisurely chiming of the wood thrush, sounding on June afternoons, stanza by stanza; through sun-flecked groves of tall hickories, oaks, and chestnuts; with these nothing in the nightingale's song compares." (Entirely unsurprising is the fact that he preferred the song of the *American* bird to the European one.)

Back in Cambridge, I had spent a morning studying one of Roosevelt's youthful bird notebooks in Houghton Library. The first thing I read was a journal that he kept during his family's months-long boat trip down the Nile in the winter after he turned fifteen. The title of the journal was *Remarks on Birds 1874*, and in its pages the automobile and the atomic bomb had not yet been invented, though the pyramids were only a whisper younger than today. In a light pencil script and a looping but legible hand, the fifteen-year-old told the story of the birds he encountered along the Nile. I read about an Egyptian Plover, a beautiful little creature, sleeker than the plovers we see on the shores in the U.S., with a sharp black mask, cap, and bib, and tawny undersides. Or, as the teen-aged would-be scientist put it, the plover, also known as the ZicZac or Crocodile Bird, was a "marked and conspicuous bird" with "a very erect carriage" that is "*the* bird of the Nile." More specifically he noted: "Head with a slight occipital crest. Upper mandible somewhat decurved, no groove on the sides, nostril oval, situated at the base. . . . Tarsus longer than middle toe . . . under tail coverts nearly as long as a quail." The sex of the bird, and the exact length of its wingspan, bill, and tarsus, were also noted. As well as close observation, the entry contained both po-etry and fun. He described plovers as "watchers," and their "office of the watcher" was to, however unintentionally, "warn" cranes and larger birds that hunters and other predators were creeping near. They did this with a shriek-like call that "would scare a blind donkey let alone a wild animal."

You could argue that for Theodore Roosevelt it *all* started with birds. The mystery of them, this flying other, this daily delight that lives among us but that so few seem to really see. Theodore saw them. As a young teenager he would continue to study birds with the care and precision of the naturalist he dreamed of becoming. And they would transport him, as they tend to do, with their fluttering, their flight, and, of course, their music. Birds would provide Roosevelt passage to a larger universe, and it would be through them that he would start to learn about the world be-yond himself and his family. If he really did ever get out of his time, out of his head, out of his self, out of his prejudices, it would be due at least in part to his empathy with things that fly. They unlocked the door. They helped show him how small it is to only think of the self, the human.

And, for this eventual author of forty-seven books, the beginning of his writing life was directly tied to birds and nature. This passion was there from the beginning, and it would stay with him until the end. While president, he would famously rush into a cabinet meeting with important news, and ask his expectant cabinet: "Gentlemen, do you know what has happened this morning?" They did not, so he told them: "Just now I saw a chestnut-sided warbler—and it is only February!"

Many birds would die in the service of young Roosevelt's quest.

Because he was not just closely observing these birds, but shooting and stuffing them. The avian genocide he wrought, the likes of which had not been seen since John James Audubon (another hero of his), was done in the service, he told himself, of science, and in this he was no different than many other ornithologists of his time. He was aided in his mission by two gifts that were given to him not long before the trip to Egypt: glasses and a gun. The gifts worked in unison, the glasses opening up a world of color and detail for him while also making him a better killer.

As I closed the notebook, I found myself briefly judging the long-gone boy, but then I questioned my questioning. As a bird lover in the twenty-first century, would I have shot birds to study them in the nineteenth? I don't know. I do know that throughout his life, tempered by age and urged on by prominent naturalists like John Burroughs and John Muir, Roosevelt shot fewer specimens while still observing keenly, and that he felt a lifelong intimacy with birds. And if his numbers in the deficit column are great, they are a thousand times balanced out by what grew out of this intimacy: his creation of dozens of federal bird reservations, starting with Pelican Island in Florida; his prosecution of poachers; his fight against species extinction; and his lifelong efforts to raise awareness of the creatures whose migratory paths run across the globe like a beautiful network of wires.

Still one might wish that the boy, like the man who came after, had had a little less of a taste for blood.

*   *   *

It was early afternoon when we said goodbye to Lonesome George and the other bison. It took several trips to pack out our supplies and tents. We got our first close look at our buffalo-blessed car, and noted that the bison had not just left streaks of dirt along its side and flattened the rear-view mirrors, but had given it a very distinct odor that you could smell even inside the car, like a kind of musky bison air freshener. That smell would stay with us for days.

"Gone forever are the mighty herds of the lordly buffalo," Roosevelt wrote in *Hunting Trips of a Ranchman,* "never before in all history were so many large animals of one species slain in so short a space of time. . . . The extermination of the buffalo has been a veritable tragedy of the animal world." He was a realist about the many causes for this extermination: "The incoming of the cattle-men was another cause of the completeness of their destruction. Wherever there is good feed for a buffalo, there is good feed for a steer or cow; and so the latter have penetrated into all the pastures of the former; and of course the cowboys follow." What he was describing was the great cataclysmic alteration of the plains, and later, the West itself. It was a cataclysm that continues to send ripples forward to the present, when almost a century and a half later more than a third of the land in the contiguous United States is used for grazing.

If Roosevelt was aware of the way cows displaced wild animals, his melancholy also extended to the impermanence about his own ranching life, his sense that more people coming west meant fewer animals, less freedom, more fences: "For we ourselves, the life we lead, will shortly pass away from the plains as completely as the red and white hunters who have vanished before our herds. The free open-air life of the ranch-man, the pleasantest and healthiest life in America, is from its very nature ephemeral. The broad and boundless prairies have already been bound and will soon be made narrow."

His vision was, and would remain, a mix of realism and idealism. He saw what was coming, saw the inevitable losses, knew certain things couldn't be stopped. But he vowed to hold on to what he could. And it was through those vows, and their fulfillment, that he would hand down a gift to the future.

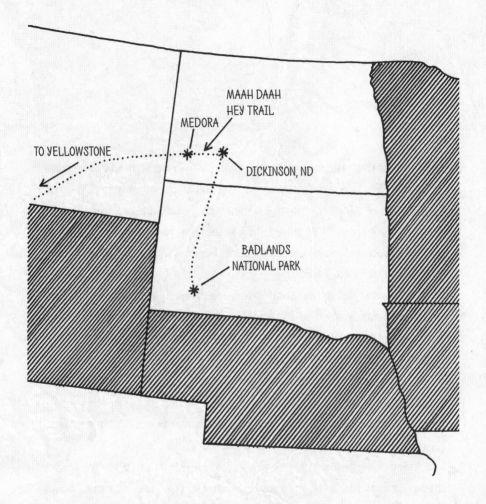

* * * CHAPTER TWO * * *

Teddyland

lmost since the moment young Mr. Roosevelt stepped off the train in 1884, and certainly after his rise to the presidency in 1901, the town of Medora, North Dakota, was built on him. The Medora that Noah and I explored, 117 years later, had transformed into a kind of Theodore Roosevelt theme park. Disneyland with TR as Mickey Mouse. Call it Teddyland.

If Noah was sick of the man before we arrived, in Medora he found himself surrounded by him. South Dakota had given us a taste of Teddy, but by traveling to this part of North Dakota we had entered the belly of the Rooseveltian beast. This fact became obvious on our first day, during lunch at the bar in the Little Missouri Saloon and Dining Room, when I eavesdropped on a stockbroker from New York and a bearded motorcyclist discussing our Rough Rider president over beers. The biker made his politics clear when he said that the NBA player Steph Curry was "un-American" for not going to the White House to celebrate his team's championship, but both men agreed that TR was "the best president." The stockbroker retold the famous story of the French ambassador swimming the Potomac with TR. During his administration Roosevelt would take the members of his so-called tennis cabinet, including his secretary of state, secretary of the interior, and Gifford Pinchot, chief of the Forest Service, on what he called their point-to-point walks, "not turning aside for anything—for instance swimming Rock Creek or even the Potomac if it came in our way." The rule on these walks was *over*, *under*, or *through*, but never *around*. Another rule was that the swimming was often done while naked. The French ambassador, Jean Jules Jusserand, was a member of that group, and he was with them one day when, before swimming the Potomac, the tennis cabinet members all took off their clothes to ready for the swim. Someone from the group called to him, "Mr. Ambassador, Mr. Ambassador, you haven't taken off your gloves." The ambassador replied: "I think I will leave them on; we might meet ladies!"

The biker laughed when the stockbroker repeated the punch line, though after taking a bite of his burger, he said he already knew the story.

The proof that we were really in for something strange came after our lunch at the saloon, on the way back to our campsite. That was when I saw a sign on the side of the building with a giant representation of Roosevelt's signature on it, and, thinking it a library, pulled into the parking lot. It turned out to be a career and life skills center for Medora's summer employees, but, curious, we went in anyway. Then, on the way to the men's room, I ran into Theodore Roosevelt. He had his wife Edith with him, and a tall boy who turned out to be their son Quentin. I stopped to shake their hands.

Theodore, who was wearing a brown vest, brown-and-white cowboy kerchief, and, of course, spectacles, said he was *dee*-lighted to meet us. Edith, in a blue dress and bonnet with a red band, nodded demurely. They were off-duty and likely there for some work-related reason, maybe to fill in unemployment forms for all we knew, but they politely stood in the hallway with us, claiming to be thrilled as I told them about our Roosevelt-related adventures. It turned out that our new friend was not the only TR impersonator around, and that in fact the dean of them all, Joe Wiegand, who had performed for George W. Bush in the White House, was in town. Though this might have relegated our Roosevelt to JV status, I didn't detect any envy, and in fact he told me that he and Wiegand were friendly and saw each other at the impersonators' convention every year. I complimented him on his imitation of TR's voice and mentioned that back at Sagamore Hill I had heard a recording of a speech by Roosevelt. Which led to a deeper discussion of TR's voice, cadence, and mannerisms. It was this Teddy's belief that the president's voice was not quite as high as reported in many of the biographies.

"In the recordings, when we hear that falsetto, you are really only hearing the overtones of his voice," he said. "On the old Edison cylinders, the wax cylinders, it was higher pitch so his voice comes off as squeakier than it was."

He recited a little of the "Man in the Arena" speech, and I commented on the way he nailed the rhythm. It was impressive, almost uncanny.

"Yes, he speaks in a kind of chopping way, and they say he would bite off his words, so that the words came out explosively."

"Someone in the 1880s called him a conversational Gatling gun," Edith said.

"Especially on his Ps and Ts," Quentin added. "If he had been talking into one of today's mics, it would have constantly popped."

They seemed genuinely excited to be talking shop. We discussed the fine points of Roosevelt's characteristic gesture of chopping down with his hand as he spoke, which I had read TR may have unconsciously nicked from the charismatic minister Dwight L. Moody, whom he had seen preach as a boy.

"Was it more of a slap or a kind of karate chop?" I asked.

"Usually it was more like a slap or a fist, up and down, something to let the audience keep rhythm. Though, who knows, maybe sometimes it could be a karate chop since he studied jujitsu with the Japanese ambassador's son."

While we discussed Rooseveltian gesticulations, Quentin was sizing up Noah. They were about the same height, with Noah at six-four maybe a half inch taller, which meant the kid was much taller than the actual Quentin. The boy looked at my nephew through professional eyes.

"I think you could play a young Lincoln," he told Noah.

He looked Noah up and down and nodded, saying: "Yes, lawyer Lincoln. You could pull it off."

Later Noah said that he had always heard that Lincoln was ugly, and wondered if the kid had been insulting him, but I assured my nephew that it was a compliment.

*　　*　　*

Biographers of Roosevelt focus on two main origin stories, the first detailing a change of physiology, the second of geography. But to get from one chapter to the next the young TR would have to travel through the land of death and suffering. The years before the move west were years of his first triumphs but also years of struggle and tragedy. These were the forge in which his character was shaped. As agonizing as asthma had been, it was a series of losses of those he loved that would push Roosevelt not just westward but toward extremes of immersion in work and wilderness.

For all his efforts to make his body, the teenaged Theodore remained something of a runt. And a fop. The young man who enters Harvard College in 1876 is a strange creature who dresses like a dandy and at first has few friends. He still dreams of being a naturalist, and his apartment at 16 Winthrop Street, a half mile from Harvard Yard, is filled with birds, salamanders, turtles, and the stink of arsenic in which he bathes specimens. As Michael Canfield writes in *Theodore Roosevelt in the Field*: "Roosevelt's idea of a college housing residential environment was different than most of his classmates, as few would have considered live specimens, bird skins, and shotguns to be homey."

If the homeschooled boy seems a little peculiar to his classmates, he does not lack for confidence. Some would argue he has an overabundance of it. His geology professor, tired of his relentless questions, stops the lecture he is giving to address him directly, saying: "Now look here, Roosevelt, let me talk. I'm running this course."

In those early years people are always underestimating him. During hunting trips to Maine with local guides Bill Sewall and Wilmot Dow, the two men who will later run his ranch in the Badlands, these hardened woodsmen assume the boy won't be able to keep up. But he impresses them, never giving up no matter how strenuous the hike or climb. Back in Cambridge he pursues his first love, Alice Lee, the beautiful daughter of a wealthy family from Boston's Chestnut Hill, with the same tenacity and certainty with which he does pretty much everything. He gradually makes friends and joins the Porcellian, the snootiest of the snooty Harvard clubs. His grades, too, succumb to his will, though his interest in natural history as a career will begin to fade for a couple of reasons. For one, his professors don't share his vision of the naturalist as a dashing figure in the outdoors, and their classes have begun to shift, along with society itself, toward a more strictly scientific study of nature. For another, "Field Naturalist" doesn't seem like the appropriate title for the future husband of a wife from high society.

In his sophomore year, he will suffer from the first of the great cataclysms in which the harder metals of his character will be formed. His beloved father will fall ill and die at forty-six. What is it like to have someone who you hold above all else, who is the largest planet in your universe, suddenly gone? Edmund Morris writes of the diaries in which the son expresses his grief for the loss of the father: "They give the impression of a sensitivity so extreme it verges on mental imbalance." "Sensitivity" may not be a word we usually associate with Roosevelt. But all of the frantic movement, and the hurling of self into action, will be at least in part a reaction to the acute loss and misery he will too often experience as a young man. The pain, too much, must be exorcised.

All that restlessness will compulsively drive this most driven of men. Roosevelt could rightly be said to have had at least half a dozen careers over his sixty years of life, among them writer, soldier, scholar, explorer, and naturalist. He will remain an accomplished amateur at the last of these, despite his childhood dreams, and the career the newly married college graduate will ultimately embrace, after a year at Columbia Law School, will be the one he will become best known for: politician. At twenty-three he is elected as a New York assemblyman and heads up to the capital in Albany. His reception there is not unlike his reception at Harvard: he is seen as an odd duck, a fancy dresser and something of a snob in the rough-and-tumble world of state politics. He is ridiculed at first for his clothes and his airs and his squeaky voice. While he will continue to have his critics, most will be worn down by his persistence, his energy, and his charm, and within two years he will become the head of his party in the assembly. Again, he doesn't lack for confidence. From the beginning he has something of the Old Testament prophet about him, and there is always a moral element to his speeches. He rails against all that is corrupt, machine politics, and, more and more frequently, the rich, his own class. Politics is a dirty business, and many of his wealthy relatives frown upon his interest in it, but it is through the pursuit of politics, and his attempts at reform, that Roosevelt begins to glimpse a class of people beyond his own and, for the first time, begins to understand their struggles. That is, he begins to grow.

A born reformer, he would have no doubt made his mark if he remained in the East. What is less certain is whether he would have embraced conservation as he did. He takes his first hunting trip out to the Badlands while still a New York assemblyman, and it has a strange effect on him. He feels something inside lift as he walks among the twisted rocks and along the winding river. It's amazing how quickly the place manages to wedge its way inside him. But while he loves the place from the start, it will take tragedy to spur him to actually move there.

It happens almost exactly six years after his father's death. His beloved bride Alice dies of Bright's disease, just two days after delivering their first child. That same morning Roosevelt's mother, Mittie, has died in the same house. A large black X fills his journal the next morning, with the words "The light has gone out of my life."

Six months later, with his newborn daughter Alice safely cared for back east by his sister Bamie, the twenty-five-year-old Theodore Roosevelt, who has lost his father, mother, and wife in rapid succession, will find himself living in the strange, often eerie wilderness of rock and grass that is the Badlands.

*   *   *

While visiting Medora Noah and I camped near the Maah Daah Hey Trail, just a couple of miles outside of town. A friend had told us about the spectacular views along the trail, and it would prove the perfect way to get to know both Medora and the land around it. The ninety-six-mile-long trail runs along a hundreds-foot-high rock ridge that follows the Little Missouri River, winding north and passing by Roosevelt's Elkhorn

Ranch, dropping into the Dakota Grasslands, and ending at Theodore Roosevelt National Park. Maah Daah Hey means "grandfather" in the language of the local Mandan tribe, and for centuries before Europeans came these grasslands were home to the Mandan people. The Lakota and Oglala Sioux, the Assiniboine, Blackfoot, Hidatsa, Arikara, Chippewa, Crow, and Oglala also lived here. As usual in this country, layers of loss and the bones of gone people fertilize the land. More recently, the unprotected parts of the landscape nearby have been populated by thousands of fracking pumps, courtesy of the boom that turned North Dakota into an oil supplier to rival Texas. That frenzy has died but left the usual scars. And while boom has lately turned to bust, the search for oil continues, and a new refinery has been approved just three miles from the borders of the Theodore Roosevelt National Park itself.

The Maah Daah Hey, which is administered by the Forest Service, and patched together out of federal, state, and private lands, is not unusual in the way it has been created. When we think of public lands, we often think first of national parks. But it isn't that simple. John D. Leshy, a land expert and former general counsel for the Interior Department, believes that the trouble starts with the name. The truth is that when we debate "public lands" today, most of us don't know what we are talking about. Which is understandable. According to Leshy:

> There is no standard definition, legal or otherwise, for the term "public lands." I use it to mean those lands owned by the U.S. that are generally open to the public and managed for broad public purposes. They are overseen by four federal agencies— the National Park Service, the U.S. Forest Service, the Fish and Wildlife Service, and the Bureau of Land Management. They carry many labels, including national parks, forests, wildlife refuges, monuments, wilderness areas, and conservation areas.

It is the variety of the preserved landscapes in this country, particularly in the parts of the country west of the Mississippi, that make it still, despite all the threats and diminishments, what Wallace Stegner called a "geography of hope." Feel like camping but don't want to pay the admission fee at a park? Just look on your map and find some forest reserve land, the national forests or grasslands that usually abut parks, and put up your tent for free. It isn't hard: there are approximately 193 million acres available for you to do this on.

In fact almost 640 million acres in this country, or 28 percent of the total land, is federally owned. The national parks, all combined, make up 52.2 million of those acres, but most of those acres are the province of two federal agencies, the Forest Service and the Bureau of Land Management. Landowners and campers in the West know the so-called BLM, which manages a whopping 247 million acres, well, though few Easterners have heard of the agency. The BLM, along with the Forest Service, manages its lands along a "multiple use" philosophy that includes grazing, mining, road-building, lumbering, drilling, and fracking. But it also includes actual and potential wilderness areas. This, as you can imagine, sets the stage for conflict.

From the beginning the prime directive of both of these organizations, and of the BLM's predecessor, the General Land Office, has been utilitarian, but there have been sporadic and brief uprisings, like near the end of the Clinton administration in 1999, when it seemed like the BLM might embrace a larger, more conservationist ethic. That ember has since flickered to the point of nearly dying, but there is some hope left in the fact that *we* own these lands and that, ultimately, through our lawmakers, we can decide what to do with them. The practical obstacles to changing the course of these organizations are multifold and historically imbedded. And yet it is reassuring: over a quarter of this country is in the public's hands. This complicated patchwork of lands is Roosevelt's legacy, as is his influence on how we think about these lands.

If Roosevelt handed us down a gift—a vision of the natural world where large swaths of land would be left as they were—where is that vision today? Can it still guide us? In our crowded, cluttered virtual world, does it still matter? We pay lip service to nature, but too often it is just a stage on which to take selfies; meanwhile, those who fight to save it have been reduced to just one more caricaturable interest group. And with so much else to save, mere "landscapes" fall further and further down our priority lists. Nature rears its head through ever more fierce storms and fires, reminding us it is still here, but we seem quite adept at burying our heads in the virtual sand. The idea of loving a place, of fighting for it, begins to seem quaint in this overwhelming and always busy world.

I believe the larger vision starts with something smaller. Theodore Roosevelt never lost touch with the world he was trying to save. He loved particular *places*. Even in the corrupt halls of Washington, in the midst of daily crises and piles of work, he found time to return to a more primal way of being, frequently heading out to do some "scrambling and climbing along the cliffs" at Rock Creek, which in those days "was as wild as a stream in the White Mountains." This is one reason to reach out, to reach back, to Roosevelt. He might have been the busiest man in the country, if not the world, and his interests, and responsibilities, were so many and varied that you would think that the natural world would hardly retain any pull on his attention. But he didn't forget; he never forgot. He was many things, but he was always an animal who loved to prowl and explore and who knew his territory. I believe this still matters.

This is one of the places he prowled and it, despite the threats, is still a place of deep beauty and strangeness. Each morning of our stay I climb up to the ridge to drink my coffee and sit in a dramatic saddle of rock, taking in sunrise views of the undulating grasses and winding Little Missouri. It isn't hard to understand the appeal of a landscape that Roosevelt said "*looked* exactly like Poe's tales and poems *sound*."

One morning when I was hiking up the trail to my dawn spot, where I could watch the sun come up on one side of the great rock spine and the Little Missouri on the other, I noticed a strange tumbling and tumult in a juniper tree. Out of the tree flew a small raptor—a prairie falcon I think—screeching off by my head. It was gone in a flash, but it left something bulky and hawk-like behind in the juniper. But not *exactly* hawk-like. A ball of feather and muscle seemed to somersault down the tree and hang upside down, and as I got close I could see it was an owl. It appeared to have some small prey in one talon, which may have accounted for the falcon's assault and maybe for the owl's tumbling act. It continued to hang upside down and then, when I was less than ten feet away, straightened itself and stared right at me with big black eyes. It was not as large as a great horned owl or a snowy, but it was not small. It had distinct black rings around its eyes (and I would later identify it as a short-eared owl). It stared at me for another second before flying off.

For a moment I felt myself jolted out of my life, my own habitual cycles of doubt and worry and obsession with my own small world. It was a kind of momentary and happy shock, a re-setting, and I thought: "This is what nature can give us." A reminder of a world beyond ourselves. Something we cannot get on our computer or phone.

We may not know it, but we crave these moments and we want to preserve them, perhaps as much as we want to preserve the land. There are better reasons to want to save the world, of course, for the sake of the biosphere and the animals in it. But there is also something valid about this more selfish sort of urgency. We go to nature and away from the human world because we are longing for something authentic. We turn away from the phony, the fake, the artificial, in hopes of finding the real. We are searching for something solid, something not of our time, something not dependent on the fashions or politics of the day. Henry David Thoreau might have said it best in these famous lines from *Walden*:

> Let us settle ourselves, and work and wedge our feet downwards through the mud and slush of opinion and tradition, and pride and prejudice, appearance and delusion, through the alluvium which covers the globe, through poetry and philosophy and religion, through church and state, through Paris and London, through New York and Boston and Concord, till we come to a hard bottom and rocks in place which we can call *reality* and say, This is and no mistake.

Roosevelt found his hard rock here in the Badlands. A reality removed from the show of politics and the pain of loss. A reality of which he could say *this is and no mistake*.

It is admittedly a little harder to do so today. In a world where we are rarely alone with our own thoughts, wedging downward is a challenge. The town of Medora is a case in point. It supports itself by feeding off the carcass of Teddy, exists in that self-conscious state that plagues not just us these days but many of our landscapes. For instance, if I decided to hike a quarter mile up the trail from where I saw the owl, I would find myself no longer looking down at a spectacular riverine scene of water and cottonwoods, but at the wilds of the Bully Pulpit Golf Course.

*   *   *

"I have always said that I would never have been president if it had not been for my experiences in North Dakota," Roosevelt will write later in life.

But while he immediately falls for the Badlands, it takes those who live there a little while to get used to him. Just as at Harvard, just as in the Maine Woods, and just as in the New York Assembly, Theodore Roosevelt is underestimated at first. And why not? The tenderfoot is always regarded with suspicion, and this Eastern dude looks like he has the tenderest of feet. For starters, he still doesn't appear to be that strong, and his glasses are the subject of ridicule. He will clearly not be tough enough to make it here. His two main helpers, Bill Sewall and Will Dow, know otherwise. They have watched him in the Maine Woods, watched him push his weak body until it became strong. They have seen what his new neighbors don't know yet. That Roosevelt will never give up.

The neighbors learn. For one thing they quickly see that the newcomer, for all the fun he seems to have, never shirks when it comes to work. He builds his ranch and herds his newly bought cattle with the same energy that he does everything. His biographer Edmund Morris writes of how he proved himself to other cowboys during those early Medora days: "It soon became apparent that Roosevelt could ride a hundred miles a day, stay up all night on watch, and be back at work after a hastily gulped

3:00 A.M. breakfast. On one occasion he was in the saddle for nearly forty hours, wearing out five horses and winding up in another stampede."

His capacity for hard work would never fade, later proving as true for the presidency as for ranching. In the West he learned to respond to the challenge of large tasks in an almost animal way. It would be fair to say he *loved* work, and in the Badlands he worked harder than he ever had, driving cattle, sleeping on the ground, hunting as well as ranching, putting on muscle. Gradually, the tanned, tough, barrel-chested ranchman began to exorcise the Eastern dandy. Of course there was a self-consciousness to the experience, as if he were suddenly living inside the adventure books he had read as a child. One of the books that he wrote about that period, *The Wilderness Hunter*, captures the flavor of the time. Here is a passage describing a night camping with his horse Manitou:

> Afterwards I kindled a small fire, roasted both prairie fowl, and put the other by for breakfast; and soon rolled myself in my blanket, with the saddle for a pillow, and the oilskin beneath. Manitou was munching the grass nearby. I lay just outside the line of stiff black cedars; the night air was soft on my face; I gazed at the shining and brilliant multitude of stars until my eyelids closed.

The romance is so powerful that we have to remember that the life was more complicated than the myth. Readers of the Roosevelt story rightly see his time in the Badlands as a heroic and exuberant chapter, but his best biographers remind us of the event that preceded this period: the death of Alice. Which means that a lot of what he is doing in the Badlands is grieving. Grieving and forgetting. Driving the pain of his wife's memory out of his mind as hard as he is driving himself. Punishing himself, exorcising through exercise. It is possible that for all his "dee-lightfuls" and other expressions of exuberance, what he really wanted at the time was a kind of oblivion. And for all his vaunted bravery, there is avoidance here. One of his most famous utterances is "Black care seldom sits behind the rider whose pace is fast enough." But what or whom is this rider riding from?

His political future was uncertain. Before heading to the Badlands, he had gone to Chicago for the Republican Convention, where he opposed the nomination of James Blaine. When Blaine won the nomination, and Roosevelt flip-flopped and stuck with Blaine and the Republican party, some saw it as his political death warrant, the young moralist caving to political expediency. As far as he knew, his days as a politician were over.

And what of poor gone Alice? Her namesake daughter left back in New York with Roosevelt's sister Bamie, and her own name never again mentioned publicly by Theodore, even in his autobiography. Is this really courageous? Or just a quashing of the sensitivity that torments him? Of course we don't know what was going on inside. He had lost something beautiful and so he came to someplace beautiful. Maybe he thought of her while camping alone, under the melancholy rocks, far from his public places and his public persona. Or maybe he just thought of killing things, for he was hunting fanatically. We will never know. For all his love of writing about himself he was far from confessional. What we are left with are the public utterances; the private thoughts are all speculative.

In *A Strenuous Life*, Kathleen Dalton does a fine job of deconstructing the TR myths while respecting the decency and courage of the man. "Escape and flight from pain provided familiar devices to protect himself from his own strong emotions and from unpleasant facts he wanted to avoid," she writes. And: "Roosevelt preferred heroic themes to psychological reality in the stories he told about his life." This was particularly true of his time in the Badlands: "As he headed west to lead 'the wild, half adventurous life of a ranchman,' Roosevelt entered the 'hero land' of his favorite literature in order to become a hero himself. He outfitted himself in buckskin cowboy garb and made sure he was photographed in it."

Dalton makes the case that not just overcompensation but fear played a part in his glorification of manliness. Meekness and turning the other cheek might have worked for the Christian savior, but he, following his father's lead, preferred a slightly more vigorous religion.

Christians should be strong, physically and morally, fighters for righteousness against sin and immorality. For a frail boy with a powerful father it had been imperative to not be weak. This was drilled into his psyche not just by his father but by his times. The frontier would soon be declared closed by both historian Frederick Jackson Turner and the U. S. Census Bureau, and there was great fear that Americans would now become overcivilized, soft, effete. This must be battled at all costs, and in Roosevelt, as in many of his peers, this urge flowed into another trend: the romanticizing of nature and the fear, for the first time, that what was valued in the natural world could be lost.

These self-myths were part of the grid through which TR saw wilderness, a complex grid that included his fervent belief in "manly vigor," his love of animals, his love of killing animals, and a deep sense of American exceptionalism. Roosevelt carried all this mental and intellectual baggage with him when he headed west. But I want to pause and move beyond psychoanalyzing, or at least complement it with something else that I think was equally important. That is the place itself. With its strange, melancholy rocks and its variations of vastness and claustrophobia, with its winding river and frozen nights and blazing days, and its ground that was "rent and broken into the most fantastic shapes, partly by volcanic action and partly by the action of water in a dry climate." Something inside him responded to the vast, strange landscape, his whole self vibrating like a tuning fork.

Again, no one can know his private thoughts. But I do know the experience of having a place ring some bell inside me, and having it bring out thoughts and feelings that I have had nowhere else. In these cases the land provides a kind of dual stimulus: a prod to go both inward and outward. And unless all TR wrote about the Badlands was false, he knew the experience of being in the so-called natural world on the deepest level. There are those who would dismiss this as due to his being a "nature romantic," and he certainly was, but I think it's more than that. He did not love this place because it was fashionable or just because he had some book-learned idea of nature's glory. He loved it because he felt it inside, at his root. He loved it because it was here he felt most whole, his best, and because, in the end, how he felt was beside the point. He loved it precisely because it wasn't about his feelings at all; it was about the fact that there was a whole world beyond him and that world, lo and behold, was even more interesting than he was.

On a simpler level, the Badlands gave him a change of place and a change of focus. For who would want to stay back east in a land associated with political uncertainty and dead wives and mothers? But it was more than change of place, more than novelty, more than stimulation. When he said the place transformed him, he wasn't lying. He didn't stay in the Badlands for very long, but he was there long enough to both experience something and to create a self-myth out of that something.

There would be consequences for this country, as well as for himself, in his finding something so resonant in the Badlands. Something that would lead to the saving of this and many other wild places. It's a fairly simple formula really: our love of places leads us to protect them. Conservation as a kind of chivalry. His time in the Badlands also fed his sense that America was special and that the specialness started with the place itself. The fact that our land was exceptional and the fact that we were went hand in hand. He would hold on to this belief his whole life, and if it was inherently chauvinistic, it was also what ultimately made him such a champion of the land.

*   *   *

Before we drove into Medora the other day, Noah and I first stopped in the nearby town of Dickinson. I was there to see Sharon Kilzer, the project manager of the Theodore Roosevelt Center at Dickinson State University, which houses the world's largest digital archive of all things Roosevelt. Sharon and I met in a church turned coffee shop and passed an engaging hour caffeinating ourselves and chatting. This, too, as she pointed out, was in the Rooseveltian tradition. A coffee fanatic, TR actually coined the phrase that would become Maxwell House's tagline: "Good to the last drop!"

Sharon brought up something that, for all my Teddy obsessing, I had not been thinking about: Roosevelt as friend. It had started back in his tight-knit family, with Bamie and Elliott and Corinne, but it had continued all his life. Though Teddy loved Teddy, he had plenty of affection left over for others. You can imagine a driven politician and writer having little time for others but this was not the case. Sharon talked about the deep and long friendships that Roosevelt had, one with his Harvard classmate, the pioneering writer of cowboy westerns Owen Wister, and another with Isabella Greenway, who became the first U.S. congresswoman from Arizona.

"He had these warm, rich friendships," Sharon said. "It was so eye-opening to me when I read his letters. Friendships that were deep and sustained despite everything else that was going on. That's what first made me fall in love with him. Not just that he was this great man. But that he could be such a good friend."

On the other hand, she was not so in love with TR the killer.

"Look, I come from a hunting culture. Everybody owns guns up here. It's part of what I grew up with. But what he did was too much. I call it extreme hunting. A lot of it was the way science and collecting was at the time. But not all. He had to be working out interior aggression and angst."

Before we said goodbye, we walked over to the Dickinson courthouse and took pictures with the life-sized statue of Teddy that stood out front. It was here, in Dickinson, that Roosevelt had hand-delivered three boat thieves to the authorities back in 1886.

That event had new meaning for me. Back at Houghton Library in Cambridge, after I had returned the birding journal of the fifteen-year-old Roosevelt's trip down the Nile, the librarian handed me a second journal, which, as it happened, recorded Roosevelt's capture of the boat thieves. The sentences told a terse adventure story, the now twenty-six-year-old Roosevelt describing how he tracked down and captured at gunpoint three thieves who had stolen his boat from the banks of the Little Missouri on his Badlands ranch. Twelve years had passed since the previous journal, but while the skinny boy had grown into a muscular man, his handwriting had evolved in the opposite direction, atrophying into something smaller and crimped:

March 1886

Wednesday 24.
Thieves stole boat: started to build another to go after them.

Thursday 25.
Went after deer; saw nothing.
Boat being built. River very high; ice piled on bank several feet.

Friday 26.
Boat building.

Sunday 28.
Bitter cold.

Monday 29.
Furious blizzard.

Tuesday 30.
Weather milder. Stayed in boat with Sewall. [Illegible to me.]
downstream of thieves. Camped below Le Con. Shot three prairie
chickens.

Thursday April 1.
Shot whitetail deer. Dow shot another. Confined the three boat thieves.

Sunday 4.
Hung up on ice.

Monday 5.
Worked down a couple of miles till ice jam again.

Wednesday 7.
Worked down to C Diamond ranch. 2 prairie chickens.

Thursday 8.
Road down to Killdeer mountain. Walking for a—for wagon which I
had.

Friday 9.
Walked captives to Killdeer Mountain.

Saturday 10.
Drove captives to Captain Brown's ranch.

Sunday 11.
Drove captives to Dickinson & gave them to sheriff.

What is missing from this bare-bones account? Quite a lot. While the stolen boat belonged to TR and had been on the shore of the Little Missouri near his ranch, it was actually Bill Sewall and Wilmot Dow, the former Maine woodsmen who were now running his cattle ranch, who built the new boat he would pursue the thieves in. Roosevelt was busy hunkering down to write his biography of Missouri senator Thomas Hart Benton. When the three men began their pursuit, pushing off into the ice-clogged Little Missouri, TR brought along a copy of Tolstoy's *Anna Karenina* and the writings of Matthew Arnold to entertain himself in between bouts of derring-do. Once they had caught and captured the three thieves at gunpoint, the six men continued down the nearly frozen river together, until Roosevelt, having secured a wagon, escorted the thieves on the forty-five-mile trip to the nearest town, Dickinson, while Dow and Sewall continued downstream in the boats to the town of Mandan. The captives rode to Dickinson in the wagon driven by a local ranchman, Roosevelt warily walking behind the wagon the whole way, on guard and rifle in hand, not sleeping for the better part of two days and ripping his feet to shreds.

There is one important addendum to this adventure, an addendum that fills out the picture of the nouveau Westerner. His actions were brave, heroic even. But the event had not been recorded for posterity; no photographs had been taken. So, a week later, Roosevelt had three of his ranch hands, including Dow and Sewall, pose for a photograph of him pointing a gun at them, assuring that the adventure was properly immortalized.

* ⋆ *

The twin origin stories of the young Roosevelt have been told for many generations now. *He makes his body and expels asthma. He goes west and becomes a man.* Whether or not these myths are true—that is whether or not his transformation was due to willpower or geography or some other combination of genes, fate, physiology, luck, and privilege—they are myths he himself believed and was happy to retell. In his autobiography he presents a perfect "Before" picture, one that might fit in an old-time Charles Atlas ad:

> Having been a sickly boy, with no natural bodily prowess and having lived much at home, I was at first quite unable to hold my own when thrown into contact with other boys of rougher antecedents. I was nervous and timid.

But of course implied here is the "After" part of the same advertisement. The part where the skinny kid who gets sand kicked in his face builds up his muscles and comes back to confront the bullies. "He cast himself as a hero in the many stories he told about himself," Kathleen Dalton writes. And that hero would train himself to no longer be nervous and timid, to no longer be bullied, in fact to later give us a perfect Charles Atlas ending by punching a bully who had been shooting up a Western barroom and dared to call him "Four Eyes."

The story is worth pausing for. Roosevelt was out looking for lost horses thirty-five miles west of his ranch when he stopped in to eat at a bar/dining room in the small town of Mingusville in what was not yet the state of Montana. There he encountered a "shabby individual in a broad hat with a cocked gun in each hand" who was "walking up and down the floor talking with strident profanity." (Not profanity!) This individual insisted that "Four Eyes" buy the rest of the bar drinks, and crowded close to TR with his guns still out, threatening. Roosevelt pretended to go along, rising to order the drinks, but then, as he stood, he, by his own account, threw three quick punches, a right to the jaw followed by a left and another right. The man managed to fire his gun, missing everything and everyone as he fell, and then hit his head on the corner of the bar and was knocked out cold. Teddy the Harvard boxer was now playing out his fantasy in the Wild West. He took the man's guns while the other patrons locked him in a shed. Roosevelt passed an understandably nervous night: "I got dinner as soon as possible, sitting in a corner of the dining-room away from the windows, and then went upstairs to bed where it was dark so that there would be no chance of any one shooting at me from outside. However, nothing happened. When my assailant came to, he went down to the station and left on a freight."

All through his life, the man famous for shouting "Bully!" had little tolerance for them. Whether he was one himself is a more complicated question, but clearly he was not afraid to fight when it came to righting what he perceived as wrongs.

It is during the Badlands years that we most vividly see that unusual combination of qualities that will lead to his saving so much of the American land: his relish of the natural world and his readiness to fight.

* * *

My mornings walking the Maah Daah Hey ridge above our campsite filled me with deep and reliable delight, and an appreciation for a landscape that was new to me, a land of twisting rock and endless grasslands with a view of distant mountains. I stared out at the grasslands, carved and segmented by the winding Little Missouri River, and one morning I watched a bald eagle flying over the river, its strong wings rowing muscularly.

Being in nature had always done something to me that I have never been able to accurately describe despite thousands of sentences attempting to do so. But appreciating nature is one thing, fighting for it another. Though many of my heroes have been activists, even the word "advocacy" fills me with unease. It reeks of protest signs and petitions and, worst of all, meetings. My attempt to counter this feeling, to put my money where my mouth is, was one of the reasons I'd come back to Roosevelt. The idea was to use him as a prod, a spur.

I knew he had something direct and relevant to say to our times, something that might surprise those who saw him merely as a fighter. In his essay "Longitude and Latitude Among Reformers," he described his route through the political world as similar to hiking along the top of a ridgeline not unlike the one I now found myself walking every morning. On either side of the metaphoric ridge were two things he disliked equally. On the one side he despised the *merely successful*. He would be disturbed to see the way this shallow valuation has continued and grown: our national glorification of results whatever the means. Commercialism for its own sake was despicable to him, and the power that corporations and the rich had gained appalled him. But the other side of the ridge was equally unappealing. This was the domain of the dogmatists. It was here that he encountered extreme do-gooders and pushers of causes who ultimately harmed those causes because their minds would not open to any vision but their own. His dislike of the first side was idealistic, his dislike of the second practical. You could say that one was what he disliked about the political right, the other about the left. The one pushed him toward supporting issues like economic justice. The other helped him get things done. Efficiency for selfish gain was an evil. Efficiency toward a greater good was admirable.

For all his dislike of impractical reformers, he saved his greatest wrath for those who were ambitious without morals. He wrote: "Success is abhorrent if attained by the sacrifice of the fundamental principles of morality. The successful man, whether in business or politics, who has risen by conscienceless swindling of his neighbors, by deceit and chicanery, by unscrupulous boldness and unscrupulous cunning, stands toward society as a dangerous wild beast."

That he spoke those words emphatically goes without saying. That is one of the central paradoxes of Roosevelt. His lifelong growth, his wide and deep reading, his openness to new ideas and compassion for those not as lucky as himself—these all seem like the very definition of magnanimity. He was, to a degree few other presidents were, a scholar, writer, and thinker, and was often able to see beyond himself. But he was also a fierce advocate, and advocacy itself, while absolutely necessary, requires a certain smallness, a tightening of focus, a reduction of world-view. It sometimes even requires fighting as if you can see nothing of value in the words of your enemy.

Which was exactly what I was struggling with. I wanted to become, after a lifetime of Hamlet-like equivocations, an advocate and activist. Which was a hard thing for me to say let alone do. It meant giving up one of a writer's main tools: the ability to see all sides. But if there was one thing I was going to put my chips down on in this world, one thing I was ready to fight for, it was nature and wilderness.

I had heard the criticism: environmentalism is elitist, fraught with a dark colonial history, and our thinking about "nature" has been formed from historic sources that are not always so pure. That might be true, but so is this: I love my family, my work, my friends, but nature, the possibilities of a world that includes the world beyond the human, is my other. My something more. If the environmental fight has grown in-creasingly foggy and complex since Roosevelt's day, and if global warm-ing has changed the climate not just of the world but of the fight itself, I now found myself returning to that initial desire: to save land, to save places, to save things beyond myself. There are other things to do in this world, perhaps better things, but that is what *I* want to do. And maybe that is what I had come to Roosevelt to ask. How do you grow beyond yourself and learn, but still be small and focused enough to fight? How to embrace a muscular environmentalism?

Answers were emerging as I learned more about Roosevelt's life. Proceed with your contradictions intact but proceed *briskly*. Anyone or anything that creates energy is important. Avoid the dogmatism of ex-tremism on one side and the lure of mere success on the other. Know that it is not the critic who counts. If you take a stand, half the people will be standing against you. It is okay to be hated; no one was able to brush off vitriol quite like Roosevelt. But know, too, that it is okay to step

out of the arena when the fight is done, to shake hands with your oppo-
nent, to turn your attention away from advocacy to more private arenas.
Remind yourself frequently what you are fighting for.

Leave it as it is. The fact that over the years we have learned that this
"is" is more complicated than we first imagined does not render this
phrase impotent. *As it is* is enough. I am not sure that it is possible for
humans to evolve so that they can have, in more than occasional spasms,
a sense of love and responsibility toward this miraculous, multifarious
world we are born into. But I know that, more than a specific policy,
what I am trying to fight for is a worldview or maybe more accurately
the mere hope of a worldview, that sees ourselves as less special and less
unique while simultaneously seeing how much more there is out there
beyond ourselves, how profoundly interesting and vital the "it" is that
we are all part of. I don't expect myself, or any of us, to feel this every
day, when we are busy at work, or even when we, in our unhurried moments, have time to consider our own lives with less urgency. But if we
can glimpse it occasionally and hold on to that glimpse, and then use
that glimpse as a starting point for a way of seeing a larger world, then
that is enough. And as it happens, luckily, nature or the so-called natural
world are very good places to get those glimpses.

What we call largeness in an individual—meaning magnanimity and
generosity—is dependent on seeing clearly just how small we really are.
Which gives me part of my answer: I need to argue for magnanimity. To
battle for the large. While not losing sight of my own smallness.

*   *   *

Noah was getting a little tired of Teddyland, as well as the army of ticks
that had invaded our campsite, and was eager to head to our next stop.
He had never seen Yellowstone but had heard stories, mostly from me,
of elk and bear and wolves.

On our last day in Medora we betrayed the Roosevelt imitators we
had met on our first day by going to see their rival, Joe Wiegand, perform. Halfway through the show, to our surprise, *our* Quentin strode on

stage. This was the boy we'd met when we chatted with fake Teddy and fake Edith, and, as it turned out, we were there to witness his very first professional performance. It was rough, but promising, and though he was hampered by nerves and a bad microphone, he powered through.

The story Mr. Wiegand narrated for us, in Teddy's voice, centered on Medora's influence in Roosevelt's life. Wiegand argued that while American exceptionalism was always part of the equation with TR, something more interesting was also evolving during his time here. If his Elkhorn Ranch was to become "the cradle of conservation," it was because it was in the Badlands that Roosevelt's already fine-tuned appreciation of the land grew. The Badlands *made* him in many ways. He stared out at the twisted rocks and winding river and he became *more*.

It was a vision that Roosevelt hammered out in the Badlands. A vision first glimpsed in the sight of the seal on Broadway and the flight of a plover in Egypt. He had found something in the eerie rock formations and ship-like buttes and great grasslands and endless mountains. It was this thing he had found that would result in the saving of large swaths of that wilderness that otherwise likely would not have been saved.

As usual, he was not quiet about what he had discovered. Articles poured from his pen celebrating the vast spaces and vibrant animal life. Books would follow, including *Hunting Trips of a Ranchman* and *Ranch Life and the Hunting Trail*, both of which, gore aside, contain passages of moving nature writing. His culminating multivolume historical work saw its beginnings here as well: *The Winning of the West*. But first, perhaps most importantly from an environmental perspective, came a stream of articles that focused on conservation, preservation of forest reserves, and the large and threatened animals within those reserves. These same themes would lead to his founding the Boone and Crockett Club in 1887 with George Bird Grinnell, the editor of *Forest and Stream* magazine and a fellow warrior against wildlife destruction. The organization they founded, and that Roosevelt then became president of, would be the first of its kind to successfully lobby Congress, helping push through an act protecting wildlife in Yellowstone, as well as founding the New

York Zoological Society, which would lead to the Bronx Zoo and its fight to preserve the buffalo.

These were also the years when he married Edith Carow, whom he had known since childhood, and who would provide a strong, smart, and cultured counterbalance to his more excessive personality for the rest of his life. Edith would take over the care of young Alice from sister Bamie and would have five more children, four boys and a girl. Their home would be Sagamore Hill on Oyster Bay in Long Island, where the ever-growing brood would swim in the waters, run in the woods, wrestle and play on the lawns, led by their boyish father, and where Roosevelt would find a sanctuary from his relentless travels and troubles. While he birded all around the world, there was nothing like his home birds.

Family and nature were intertwined, as were advocacy and nature. On a smaller scale the work he did as president of the Boone and Crockett Club would prove a template for his work as the first truly environmental president of the United States. But of course, this being TR, that was just one of the many fields he was plowing. With his return east he got back to politics, first with an unsuccessful run for mayor of New York and then, after supporting Benjamin Harrison's run for the presidency in 1888, three years as the civil service commissioner in D.C. President Harrison, a hunter who had grown to love Yellowstone, was open to TR's appeals to preserve, and would use the Forest Reserve Act, passed by Congress in 1891, to put aside millions of acres.

As civil service commissioner, Roosevelt fought a spoils system, and entrenched corruption, with a ferocity that would soon become familiar to the rest of the country. When he took over as a New York City police commissioner in 1895, he became famous for his vigilant oversight of the force, staging surprise late night inspections of police on the beat, and sometimes finding policemen asleep or drinking in bars.

His job prowling the poorer sections of New York City made him a champion of the downtrodden, but his next assignment highlighted him at his most combative. After having campaigned heartedly for William McKinley for president in 1896, he was rewarded with the post of assistant secretary of the navy. Since the older and less-ambitious secretary, John Long, was often gone from Washington for long periods, Roosevelt took charge. That meant much sword-rattling and hunger for conquest, in particular an eagerness to get into war with Spain over Cuba. When this did come about, he immediately resigned his position and vowed to enlist, despite the fact that he was closing in on forty years old. He wanted to be in the thick of the fight, partly, his sister Corinne thought, to compensate "for an unspoken disappointment in his father's course" during the Civil War.

That this bellicosity, and even jingoism, could coexist inside one breast with compassion and intellectualism might surprise us. But, as the country at large would learn, boisterous contradictions were the rule when it came to Mr. Roosevelt.

And there he was up on the stage in Medora, contradictions intact, exuberantly telling us the story of his life. Noah said he enjoyed the show, even though by now he knew most of the story by heart. Afterward, I went up and talked with Joe Wiegand, still dressed as Teddy. I asked him if he knew Dr. Sean Palfrey. Palfrey was the faculty dean, along with his wife, of Harvard's Adams House and the great-grandson of Theodore Roosevelt, his mother being Teddy's son Kermit's daughter. During the year my daughter Hadley was born I had filled in for another writer as a lecturer at Harvard, and my wife Nina and I had the honor of staying in the Adams House apartment of the great Irish poet Seamus Heaney, who was away that term. That spring I would sometimes put Hadley to sleep by pushing her stroller over the courtyard's cobblestones. But the greatest honor of that semester was when Sean Palfrey invited us into their house and allowed us to rock Hadley in the cradle that Teddy had rocked in as a baby.

Now I told Wiegand the news: the Roosevelts were making a comeback in politics. Sean's son, Quentin Palfrey, was running for lieutenant governor of Massachusetts.

When we finished talking, I went to find Noah and discovered that he had been cornered by the other Quentin, who was talking about possible roles for them both, as if they were a fledgling Vaudeville team.

Quentin clearly wanted a friend his own age in town. He told Noah that he had learned there was an opening for a young Lincoln in the town's daily patriotic musical.

Noah looked amused and a little flummoxed, so to distract Quentin I showed him a picture from my phone of his namesake, Quentin Palfrey.

He studied it for a minute, through the lens of his profession as always, before speaking.

"Hmmm," he said finally. "Doesn't look like a Roosevelt. Looks more like an Eisenhower."

After we left, I reminded Noah that now that he had graduated he was going to have to get a job.

"You sure you don't want to stay here and try out for Lincoln?" I asked.

He shook his head.

"There are worse jobs," I said.

After the show we headed back to pack up our campsite. Noah shook ticks out of his sleeping bag. An hour later we left Medora and pointed the car southwest toward Montana.

I didn't know it at the time, but it would turn out that in doing so we were once again following Teddy. Our next stop was Yellowstone, and the route we took to get there, through Montana to the town of Gardiner, the gateway to the park, was more or less the route of the first significant campaign tour ever taken by a sitting president. That was in the spring of 1903 when Roosevelt launched a fourteen-thousand-mile journey in a private train, a grand tour of American cities from the East to the West and back. The early climax of the trip, which would later take him to Yellowstone, Yosemite, and the Grand Canyon, was his homecoming in Medora. There he shocked people by remembering their names from twenty years before.

"Most all of you are old friends," he said during his short speech. "With some of the men I have ridden guard round the cattle at night, worked in the round up, and hunted, so I know them pretty well. It is the greatest possible pleasure to me to come back and see how you are getting along."

* * *

In the end, TR's Medora epoch was not quite as upbeat as Joe Wiegand and others make it out to be. As Roosevelt himself predicted, ranch life proved ephemeral and its end was abrupt. The winter of 1886–1887 was a bad one in the Dakotas, the "Winter of the Blue Snow," and when the record snows finally thawed they revealed thousands of dead cattle, including more than half of Roosevelt's herd. He saw the carnage with his own eyes, corpses on a dreamland turned drear nightmare-scape. That winter gave him a harsh lesson in the precariousness of living in the West. Disaster could strike at any moment.

He had first seen the West through the eyes of romance, but he left with a heavy dose of reality. It would have profound implications for TR's future politics. You had to know a land if you wanted to save it.

The raw wilderness he celebrated in his books and speeches turned out to be more complicated than he had first imagined. If Roosevelt's idea of nature remained big, bold, and wild, it was also tinged with this ever-present possibility of loss, even before the final winter. What drove him to preserve was both his love of wild places and wild animals and his fear of losing them. We are all the beneficiaries of the latter anxiety.

Roosevelt bought his cattle ranch in 1884. For all the pleasure he took in being a ranchman, he knew he had come too late. The great herds of buffalo were already gone, and so, too, the rest of the big game. This changed him in a subtler way than his embrace of ranch life would. He saw with his own eyes what extinction meant, saw how quickly human beings could destroy not just landscapes but other animals. He was still a sportsman, but this was not sport; it was slaughter. And for all the gusto that would fill the stories of his time in the West, his accounts are laced with melancholy. He knew he was living in a relatively empty world where the question was how to make the best of what was left.

It is a question we are still asking today.

Theodore Absorbed

He hunches down behind the hummock so he can see the herd but they can't see him. His breath comes out as clouds in the cold, but it is not his own breath he is focused on. He watches as the chests of the grazing animals rise and fall.

He is that boy again. Seeing the seal for the first time on Broadway. Collecting for the Roosevelt Museum. Of course he is no longer that boy. He now has the world on his back: it is no exaggeration to say that he may have more responsibilities and cares than anyone else on the planet. Just in the last week he has been preoccupied with a precedent-setting anti-trust lawsuit against the Northern Security Company, fighting for digging rights for the Panama Canal, and working out an arbitration award for the miners involved in the coal strike that ground the country to a halt the previous winter. But not at this moment. All that matters now is the great herd of elk in front of him covering the valley in Yellowstone. The hooves clomping down nervously. The breaths of vapor. The massive racks of the bulls. The noises of nuzzling and snorting. In this moment he understands that for the ungulates in the meadow the getting of food is every bit as important and urgent as any human concern is to his own kind. Disguised under piles of thought and custom, humans have convinced themselves that their urgency is more urgent. It isn't. He sees that.

He has fallen hard for Yellowstone, his country's first national park. It is already thirty years old at this point, which makes it a model for the other monuments and parks he has been busy creating as president. At more than two million acres, it touches three states, filling the northwest corner of Wyoming while spilling into Idaho and up into Montana. It is most famous for its geysers, like Old Faithful, but these bore the president. What interests him are the animals. The elk and the wolves and bears and pronghorn antelope and the last herds of buffalo. Anxiety mixes with wonder. He deeply fears the loss of places like this, knows that something vital will be lost in the country he loves if wilderness is reduced to smaller and smaller patches. What would happen to an America without wilderness? He expunges the thought and focuses on the sea of elk.

He studies an individual through his field glasses, then lowers the glasses to take in the massive whole of the herd. How many elk are on the snowy field? Thousands. Innumerable. But that's not true, is it? As soon as he thinks this, it stands as a challenge: he will count them! He is the president of the United States but he is still the boy with his bird collection. He counts groups not individuals, but he is careful not to exaggerate, to be scientific, precise. He wants the number he reports when he returns to camp to be impressive, but reliable. He scribbles the estimate on a piece of paper and puts it in his pocket.

For once he is still. For two thousand miles he has been hurtling forward, the center of a nonstop show. He has no complaints: he is quite up front about the fact that he likes being the center of attention. But he likes *this* more, or maybe he just likes it *differently*. He has left both his Secret Service and the disgruntled members of the press behind back at the north gate of Yellowstone, not allowing them to follow him on this two-week retreat from the world. And he has also left behind the fourteen-thousand-mile train trip that he has been in the midst of, a trip that began in Pennsylvania and will stretch to California and back.

That trip has been a strange juxtaposition of the private and public. Mostly public, of course. The year is 1903 and he is in his third year as president. He is in the midst of a campaign for reelection, though technically it is not *re*-election. The president seems to embody confidence, but he is keenly aware that in 1901 it had been a bullet, not the ballot box, and the assassination of President McKinley, not the American people, that had brought him the presidency. Before this trip, in past elections, it had always been considered unseemly for a sitting president to actually campaign. He didn't care. He wasn't going to sit idly—to sit *still*—while his fate was decided. The reason he had always liked rocking chairs was because, unlike other chairs, they *moved*. And in response to the looming election, and his anxiety about it, he would move, too.

He started his trip in Harrisburg, Pennsylvania, and less than a week later he was blitzing South Dakota—Sioux Falls, Yankton, Scotland, Tripp, Parkston, Mitchell, Woonsocket, Alpena, Tulare, Redfield, Aberdeen, Frederick—before crossing the border into North Dakota to stop at Ellendale; the next day he spoke in Edgeley, Fargo, Casselton, Tower City, Valley City, Dawson City, and Bismarck. The handy metaphor was to compare Roosevelt to the locomotive he was riding across the country, and plenty of newsmen did. His gift was not just for self-promotion, but to get others to buy into the myth. He still wasn't trusted on Wall Street or in Washington, but the American people had begun to embrace him. In every small town in the Dakotas people would remember the day they saw the president and would tell their children, who would tell their children. They would never forget the explosive voice, the flashing teeth, the chopping arm. The president of the United States had come to them!

Then his long-awaited homecoming in Medora. It was a whirlwind of hands shook, babies kissed, and names remembered, and it wasn't until the next stop, in Yellowstone, that the trip took a private turn. While up until then there had been several speeches a day, there would now be a glaring gap between his short speech to the crowd in Gardiner and his famous dedication of the Yellowstone Arch in the same town sixteen days later. It was time for Roosevelt to embrace his other self, and so, in the midst of a campaign whistle-stop tour, a camping trip broke out. Before Yellowstone, every moment of the trip had been recorded by reporters, but now they found themselves left behind. Only John Burroughs, the country's most famous nature writer, remained with him. He was there because he was Roosevelt's friend but he would also serve another role: TR's handpicked Boswell. Tall and white-haired, Burroughs, whom the president had nicknamed "Oom John," carefully recorded the entire trip: the day they face-planted while skiing, the time the president didn't wait to wash the shaving cream off his half-shaved face in his hurry to see some "mountain sheep" descend a steep slope—"The shaving can wait, the sheep won't!"—and most of all their shared obsession with birds.

"Throughout the trip I found his interest in bird life very keen, and his eye and ear remarkably quick," Burroughs would write. "He usually heard its note as quickly as I did,—and I had nothing else to think about, and had been teaching my ear and eye the trick of it for over fifty years."

As they tramped through the snow in Yellowstone, chasing birds and observing animals, Roosevelt and Burroughs were also embroiled in a controversy that involved, of all things, nature writers. Just a month before their trip Burroughs published a piece in the *Atlantic Monthly* called "Real and Sham Natural History." The article called out sentimental writers who anthropomorphized their animal characters. With Darwin's ideas ascending, the close of the frontier, and the creation of parks like Yellowstone, and all the other forces that influenced Burroughs, Roosevelt, and their generation, people were turning more and more toward nature, and that also meant toward nature books. These were hot commodities, which of course Burroughs didn't mind. What he minded was writers claiming to be good naturalists while describing crows teaching school or wolves killing themselves after their mates died. While he loved a good story, he wanted the science to be tight, accurate, and grounded, and he deplored what he called the "yellow journalism of the woods." It was one thing to lionize a president, but don't do it to a lion. He despised both those who fabricated their experiences in nature and those who gave animals characteristics they did not possess. As did Roosevelt, who had trained hard to be specific and scientific as a young man while working toward becoming a naturalist. It would be four years later, during his second term, that the president would come strongly to his friend's side during this fight, in an article that gave the controversy its name: "The Nature Fakers."

As for Roosevelt himself, he passes Burroughs's test with flying colors. The nature writer will later exclaim over the president's "keenness and enthusiasm as a student of animal life, and his extraordinary powers of observation," and add: "Nothing escaped him, from bears to mice, from wild geese to chickadees, from elk to red squirrels; he took it all in and he took it in as only an alert vigorous mind can take it in." Burroughs particularly admired the fact that when the president wrote of what he saw, he, unlike in the stories he told about his mythic self, kept things unsentimental, unexaggerated, and scientifically accurate.

The article that rebuts the nature fakers will actually be written in the form of a self-interview, and in it TR will say: "I don't believe for a minute, that some of these men who are writing nature stories and putting the word 'truth' prominently in their prefaces know the heart of the wild things."

*   *   *

Every night around the fire, shadows playing off the snow, Roosevelt tells stories.

Burroughs will remember:

> While in camp we always had a big fire at night in the open air near the tents, and around this we sat upon logs or camp-stools, and listened to the President's talk. What a stream he poured forth! And what a varied and picturesque stream!—anecdote, history, science, politics, adventure, literature; bits of his experience as a ranchman, hunter, Rough Rider, legislator, civil service commissioner, police commissioner, governor, president,—the frankest confessions, the most telling criticisms, happy characterizations of prominent leaders, or foreign leaders, or members of his own Cabinet; always surprising by his

candor, astonishing by his memory, and diverting by his humor. His reading was very wide, and he has that rare type of memory which retains details as well as mass and generalities. One night something started him off on ancient history, and one would have thought he was just fresh from his college course in history, the dates and names and events came so readily. Another time he discussed paleontology, and rapidly gave the outlines of the science, and the main facts, as if he had been reading up on the subject that very day. He sees things as wholes, and hence the relation of the parts comes easy to him.

The night before he sees the elk Theodore tells his favorite story. "One night he entertained us with his reminiscences of the Cuban war," Burroughs will recall. Sitting around the fire, TR remembers everything from that day, describing "the look of the slope of Kettle Hill when they were about to charge up it, how the grass was combed and rippled by the storm of rifle bullets that swept down it."

The story he tells is one he will tell again and again, particularly as he gets older, and it will grow longer and more lavish over the years. It will become the central legend of his life, the story on which his other stories are built. As much as he loves nature, and his family, it isn't time spent in the wilderness or the birth of his beloved children that he will rank as the peak of his existence. No, his crowded hour, his great moment, the story he will tell until it becomes threadbare, and in many ways the story that will catapult him to national prominence and the presidency, is the charge up San Juan Hill.

*   *   *

Just five years before he studied the elk, just three years before he became president, Theodore Roosevelt at last went to war. It was a moment that, in his bellicose heart, he had long awaited.

The sinking of the USS *Maine* precipitated the Spanish-American War, though the cause of that sinking was never definitive. It didn't matter to Roosevelt, who was already clamoring for a fight, and the war, theoretically fought for Cuban independence, was really about the bitter end of one colonial empire and the new dreams of another.

By going to war himself Roosevelt finally had the chance to clear the family name, doing penance for the fact that his father did not fight in the Civil War, but he was almost too old. Already assistant secretary of the navy, close to forty, it made no sense to quit his post to fight in Cuba. There was really no place for him anyway, no role, no regiment. But of course he did what he always did: he created his own. Of the forty-seven books he wrote, all are nonfiction, but when it came to his own life he was a brilliant novelist. He spun stories and then made them true.

The first part of the story was the creation of the Rough Riders. He assembled, from east and west, from the cowboy ranch lands to Ivy Leagues, his very own regiment. He brought them to Texas to train, and though for once in his life he demurred and refused to accept the command of the regiment, ceding that to his friend, Colonel Leonard Wood, there was no question that they were *his* men. These men, who captured the public's imagination even before the first gun was fired, were almost like parts of his own complex and contradictory personality: cowboys and Harvard graduates, sheriffs and Indians, toughened cops and even, God help him, a Yale man or two. He was never more part of a team than with the Rough Riders.

But he was also, as always, separate. And not just because he was an officer. If eyewitness accounts and his own self-mythologizing stories are to be believed, he really was alone at one point, leading the charge up Kettle Hill, the Spanish Mauser bullets whizzing by his head, exhorting others to be brave and follow. As the bullets flew, and the men took cover, he rode back and forth on horseback, snapping orders.

When he told the story to Burroughs, he admitted he had been afraid. He knew he looked pale that morning, but conquered his own fear of charging into gunfire and then set to conquering his men's fears. "Get up, men, get up!" he called to them before the famous charge began. More bullets flew past and his men still lagged behind and so he went back to cajole them.

His glasses fogged over, his horse balked at a fence, and he was forced to dismount, but upward he charged. By the time he reached the top, a berserker's frenzy had come over him, and, after years of killing every other sort of animal, he finally killed his first human being, the Spaniard who "rose out of the trenches and deliberately fired at him at a distance of only a few paces." In fairness he had no choice: that Spanish soldier was one of three who jumped out from behind the barricades and turned their guns on him, and he shot back.

The charge up Kettle Hill would have been enough to gain him glory, especially since he had brought more than one hand-picked reporter along for the ride to Cuba, but, as always, he pushed things further. If the first charge was his bravest moment, it was the next surge that would become the greatest legend in a legendary life. The Battle of San Juan Hill. Every schoolchild would hear of it. It was a tale that would grow with each retelling. As Edmund Morris writes, "The farther Cuba dropped away, the brighter it shone the memory."

But if Roosevelt was a nonstop self-mythologizing machine, he was also self-aware and could laugh about his own flaws. In a book review of Roosevelt's *The Rough Riders* in *Harper's*, Peter Dunne, taking on his popular persona, "Mr. Dooley," suggested that a better title for the book would have been *Alone in Cuba*. Roosevelt, rather than being offended, stole the joke and, in a bit of creative nonfiction, turned it into a story in which a young woman tells him that her favorite book of his is *Alone in Cuba*.

*　*　*

This, his single day of real solitude, watching the elk, will stand out from all the rest of the hundred days of his grand tour of the country. For the moment he is away from all the squabbles, all the controversies, all the fights. He has already been here for hours observing the herd, but he can't bring himself to leave. He doesn't want this time to end.

The animals ignore him. They don't care that he is president. They nibble at the snow for water and nose below it in search of dead grass and brush. The males have retained their great racks into winter, but will be losing them soon. The new buds of their antlers will then grow, covered with velvet. They will also be shedding soon; he can tell by the scruffiness of their light brown coats. He watches for another hour. Then another. The way these animals walk and graze and stand is so stately that it is hard to remember the speed with which they can move when needed or the wild energy they expend during rutting season. His own movements slow with theirs. He focuses in on one bull as it stands and chews, staring off with its black eyes. He estimates that it is five feet high at the shoulder, likely around seven hundred pounds. He admires the fine rack with its six tines. The points glisten in the sun.

Famously restless, he finds himself at peace. He is a man with many selves, but perhaps during this long day of cold and observation, it occurs to him, for a moment at least, that this self, turned outward, is truly his best one.

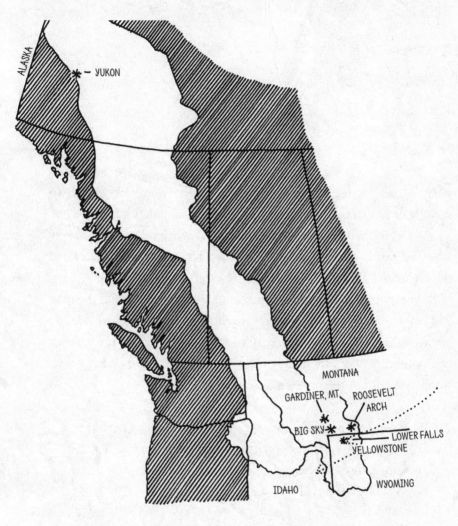

ALASKA

* — YUKON

MONTANA

GARDINER, MT   ROOSEVELT
                ARCH

BIG SKY *   *

            * *   LOWER FALLS
            YELLOWSTONE

IDAHO   WYOMING

CHAPTER THREE

Complicated Nature

On the day he gained San Juan Hill, Theodore Roosevelt also gained national and international fame. From then on he was forever in the spotlight, a place he was deeply fond of. It is unlikely he would have ascended to the presidency had he not ascended those Cuban hills.

It is easy to mock his bluster now, but you can't deny that the man had courage. Luck, yes. Privilege, certainly. But courage above all. The virtue without which, as Samuel Johnson said, no other virtue is possible. Without it, ideas are merely ideas. We all *believe* things. That is fine. Roosevelt *acted*. As Henry Adams wrote:

> Power when wielded by abnormal energy is the most serious of facts. . . . Roosevelt, more than any other man living within the range of notoriety, showed the singular primitive quality that belongs to ultimate matter—he was pure Act.

This is a book about Roosevelt's environmental triumphs, not his military ones. But had he not gained larger power, the land he saved would have been of a smaller order; he would have just led the Boone and Crockett Club, not the country. It was through exercising the powers of the executive branch that Roosevelt would take the big, bold strokes that would preserve what was left of the American wilderness. It was through being president that he could really enact his vision of a still-wild world, saving parks, national monuments, national forests, and bird and game reserves. And it would be the first, and perhaps the only, time in our history when wilderness and wildness were truly national priorities, never far from a president's mind despite all the other pressing business of the world.

It would all hinge on accident. And tragedy. His charge up San Juan had led to the governorship of New York in 1898, and then in 1900, Roosevelt reluctantly agreed to run as William McKinley's vice president after Vice President Garret Hobart died. When McKinley was assassinated early in his second term, Roosevelt was appropriately solemn, but, as his daughter Alice pointed out, deep inside he was thrilled about the prospect of being in charge. Many years later Alice was asked by a reporter about this moment, and when the reporter suggested that it was "a terrible moment of sadness" for her father, she laughed and said, "Are you kidding?"

Whatever his reaction, it is fair to say that Roosevelt delighted in being president. In fact, the presidency would prove less oppressive for him than it had or has been for almost everyone else who has held the job before or since: he once described it simply as "fun." The youngest president ever, he loved good work, big work, the shouldering of heavy loads, almost as much as he liked romping freely up trails and swimming rivers. "His activity is tireless," John Burroughs wrote. "All the relaxation he needs or craves is a change of work. He is like the farmer's fields, that only need a rotation of crops. I once heard him say that all he cared about being President was just 'the big work.'"

That big work would famously include busting trusts, negotiating the end to a coal strike that threatened the country during the frigid winter of 1902, and the construction of the Panama Canal. But it would also include, from the beginning of his presidency, a concern for wilderness and public lands. And "concern" may be too tame a word here—"love" may work better. This was a president who loved American land, particularly the land that belonged to all of us. And, as it would happen, when Roosevelt left office seven and a half years later, there would be over two hundred million more acres of it.

As president he started relatively slowly. His would prove to be the work of education as well as conservation, particularly since the meaning of that word was known to few in Congress or the country. "The idea that our national resources were inexhaustible" was commonly held, he wrote later in his autobiography. And yet "there was no real knowledge of their extent and condition." At times he grew impatient with a sluggish and obstinate Congress, filled with characters like Joseph Cannon, who was speaker of the house for much of TR's time as president, and who declared: "Not one cent for scenery." *Scenery* of course would have been said with a sneer. Roosevelt responded with a flurry of executive decrees. For instance, realizing there was no law preventing him from simply declaring a place a wildlife refuge, and enraged that poachers were killing egrets and other birds for the feathers that adorned the day's fashionable hats, he created the Pelican Island National Wildlife Refuge, an island that is now part of the Everglades Headwaters National Wildlife Complex. This would be the first of many refuges and sanctuaries so declared. And those places were not just declared but defended: another early move was bolstering the then almost nonexistent protection given to our parks and public lands, sometimes recruiting tough guy enforcers from the ranks of his Rough Riders to battle the poachers.

When it comes to land that is preserved, it is common to say that it is "saved." Henry David Thoreau might be our most quoted author with regard to wildness; John Muir might have inspired generations of environmentalists; Rachel Carson awakened the modern environmental movement; and there are many more heroes in the roll call of environmental achievement. But if we accept the popular nomenclature, there is, practically speaking, no greater savior than Theodore Roosevelt. As well as creating five national parks and eighteen national monuments, he set aside fifty-one federal bird reserves and four national game preserves, and of course created the United States Forest Service and one hundred and fifty national forests. He did so relentlessly, in the face of much criticism from people who didn't just question what he was doing but could barely comprehend the why of it, and he did it while opposing the most powerful commercial and corporate interests of his time. He did it in the face of an increasingly reluctant Congress.

He not only fought the battles but he had to practically create the arena they were fought in. Few, outside of an elite circle, could even comprehend the logic, the profit, the advantage—there had to be one, right?—in simply *setting things aside*. If we think of politicians as having one eye on the polls, here was someone making a stand against interest groups for an issue that was not only unpopular but that until recently had not existed. His job was not just saving the land but creating the vision and language for why we should.

* * *

What would Theodore Roosevelt make of the mess we are in now? What would he make of the warming climate and dying species and what we have done with the wilderness he left us? He would still fight for the wild of course, that was *his* nature, but he would find that the fight is not as simple as it once was.

If it was a realistic assessment he was after, his beloved Yellowstone National Park, and the 22.6 million acres that constitute the Greater Yellowstone Ecosystem, would be a good place to start. Here he could see all that we have to fear, and all that we can still hope for. He would find resurgent wolf packs roaming the woods and miles-long traffic jams, a thriving buffalo population feared by neighboring ranchers for a disease it has never spread to their cows, grizzlies coexisting with the crush of tourism, the same steaming geysers he once saw but the melting glaciers he didn't. And he would also find that this beloved place had become the center of a debate about what wilderness is and isn't, where it is going, and whom it belongs to.

Over the course of three days Noah and I found the same. We witnessed a grizzly bear mother trying to corral her two romping cubs as they leapt over logs and climbed trees, but to do so we had to do some leaping and climbing of our own, fighting our way through a traffic jam and then a jostling crowd of our fellow gawking humans. Another cold morning we watched several dozen buffalo at the Gibbon River as they slowly woke, blowing out spittle and clouds of breath, before going about their business of sipping river water, nuzzling each other, and grazing breakfast. Yellowstone is home to the largest herd of bison on public land, more than four thousand now, and the only herd in the world to have roamed the same area since prehistoric times, and to not be interbred with domestic cattle. But let them wander across the park's border and they risk being shot by stockmen who fear that they will transmit the disease brucellosis, which can cause pregnant animals to abort, though there has not been a single documented case of this transmission to cattle in decades. Elk, too, are thriving, with ten to twenty thousand grazing in Yellowstone's high-elevation grasslands during the summers. But when it's time to migrate, they better pick the right direction, as big game hunters, Teddy's progeny, wait at the park borders for a legal kill.

The news is either great or terrible depending on whom you talk to. Yellowstone is tourist hell; Yellowstone is a wilderness paradise. The evidence supports both theories. The greater ecosystem is staggering in its size, bigger than any wilderness in this country outside of Alaska, and all the big predators are back, the wolves and mountain lions returning from complete extirpation in the area. But private lands and a burgeoning human population encircle the park, making it more and more what it has always been, an island, and islands, as evolutionary biologists like to tell us, are where species go to die. What could be more ridiculous than asking big animals to politely respect the park's borders by not migrating?

Meanwhile the glaciers in Grand Teton recede, the temperature rises, the pine bark beetles, no longer frozen out by the long winter, chew through and kill trees. A great thriving rebounding wilderness, with wolves being taken off the endangered species list and grizzlies possibly being next, is also a precarious one. There's even a potential scenario where humans don't play our usual role as the chief eco-villains: a volcano, let alone a potential super-volcano, would wipe out the majority of the grizzlies, wolves, and elk in the Lower 48. This sounds a lot less farfetched when you are walking through a landscape that seethes steam and blows boiling water.

Watching Noah watch big animals for the first time was a pleasure, but if the buffalo and the elk herds were impressive, the car herds, herds that we were very much part of, were staggering. In fact we were coming to Yellowstone during the busiest year on record, and for the first time more than four million people would visit. *Four million.* This was not the Yellowstone of Burroughs and Roosevelt, and, except for rare moments, we spent more time in traffic jams, gas stations, and gift shops than in nature.

The first night, after arriving in Gardiner exhausted from our long drive, Noah and I ate a dinner of bison burgers at a bar by the Yellowstone River. There we met Aidan Campbell, an effervescent nineteen-year-old who is a friend of the family and already a fairly Rooseveltian figure herself, a veteran of many Alaskan camping trips, who was spending the summer working as a rafting guide on the Yellowstone after completing her freshman year at Yale.

After dinner, we took a short walk over to what has become known as the Roosevelt Arch, which marks the park's northern entrance. This was where TR gave his first speech after his furlough with John Burroughs in Yellowstone, and he did so in a dedication of the then only partially built arch. In a warm-up for his Grand Canyon speech, he spoke of our need to preserve the "great national playground" for our children's children, though he snuck in some more utilitarian comments about irrigation and forest reserves, too. Words from that speech adorn the top of the arch: "FOR THE BENEFIT AND ENJOYMENT OF THE PEOPLE."

Some of today's troubles are ones Roosevelt could not have foreseen. Not just climate change but pressures that he, always a cheerleader for procreation and increasing the American population, couldn't have anticipated. Strangely but prophetically, he also spoke on the day of the arch dedication about the need for *good roads* in the park. Well, we can't always be prescient: "carriage roads" he called them, but car roads they quickly became. And cars followed by the millions.

While being caught in wildlife traffic jams, as my fellow tourists posed with the elk and buffalo in the background, I wasn't reminded of other times in wild nature, but of the Van Gogh exhibit I had gone to in New York, standing four deep in a mob of people, craning my neck in an attempt to glimpse something beautiful. The metaphor can be carried further, much further, as that is exactly what Yellowstone felt like to me: a museum. A museum that held works of beauty from long ago, curated for the curious and the many.

*   *   *

Leave it as it is.

It is a good phrase. A strong phrase.

But it, like Theodore himself, requires some deconstructing for our time.

When TR declared "leave it as it is" at the Grand Canyon and expressed a similar sentiment about the other national parks and monuments he would save, the "is" he had in mind was one that has been called into question of late. Some recent environmental scholars believe it was somewhat mythic, if not entirely fictional. The "is" for Roosevelt, and for the other conservationists of his time, John Muir included, was a pristine ideal of an *unpeopled* nature, of a place that existed without us— that is, without humans—an empty Eden. But this was not the North America that Europeans found when they landed. This was not the "is" that was.

What Europeans found was a land where human beings, in numbers much larger than we were once taught as schoolchildren, had been living, loving, procreating, working, and dying for thousands of years. Though there were plenty of places that we would consider "wild" and relatively unpopulated, many of the lands we would come to call "wilderness" were in fact landscapes that humans had manipulated and manicured by farming and fire for hundreds of generations. They were also lands that were extensively used as hunting grounds, summer grounds, winter grounds. If you wanted to call this—human beings working in a sustainable fashion with the animals and plants they lived amid—"pure," you could. But what you couldn't call it was uninhabited.

A couple of influential books on this subject have come out in the last twenty years, *Dispossessing the Wilderness* by Mark David Spence and *Conservation Refugees* by Mark Dowie. They argue that in our romanticizing of nature as a place apart, a place without people, we have created a kind of willful amnesia about the people who were actually living here when Europeans landed on this continent. Obviously the first settlers were aware that the woods were anything but empty. Spence argues that up until the Civil War, Americans thought of "wilderness" as being virtually synonymous with "the place Indians were," that the presence of Indigenous people was part of what *made* a place wild. Back then the country could be thought of as virtually infinite, and the Indians existed "out there," but as America pushed onward after the Civil War, the Indigenous people were no longer seen as part of wilderness but as the enemy, the thing in the way. And at that very moment, two coincident and not unrelated movements were growing. One was the idea that Indians belonged on reservations. The other was that we needed to preserve some of the wilderness we were spilling over onto, and that we should do this by creating parks.

Both of these newly conceived places were segmented off from the rest of the land, like islands, and to those doing the segmenting it was clear that Indigenous people, forced onto one type of island, should be forced off the other. "Reservation" was in fact the general name for both the places the country wanted to put Indians and the forest reserves and other "saved" lands that were being set aside. The motivations for the two movements, intertwined and obvious then, seem strange and ironic a century and a half later. With the frontier closing, our romance with big monumental nature grew, as did the fear that our national vigor was fading. Wouldn't we shrivel and grow weak and overcivilized (and somewhat European) without wild lands? "To protect wilderness was in a very real sense to protect the nation's most sacred myth of origin," writes the environmental scholar William Cronon in his groundbreaking essay

"The Trouble with Wilderness." He adds: "The myth of wilderness as 'virgin' uninhabited land has always been especially cruel when seen from the perspective of the Indians who had once called that land home. Now they were forced to move elsewhere, with the result that tourists could safely enjoy the illusion that they were seeing their nation in its pristine, original state, in the new morning of God's own creation."

Yellowstone, our very first national park, was a prime example. Created in 1872 by Congress and signed into law by Ulysses S. Grant, it became a template for all parks to follow. The story we were told about Yellowstone, and that we told ourselves, was that it was an "empty" place, the superstitious Indians supposedly spooked by the geysers, but as Spence argues it had long been the hunting grounds of many tribes. The same was true of the tribe that gave Yosemite its name, but in John Muir's eyes, and Roosevelt's, what had been long inhabitation was viewed as encroachment. Muir liked his nature solitary, and while he marveled at the majestic views, he famously found the local Yosemite Indians "dirty." You didn't live in wilderness. It was where you went to get away from where you lived. To a place empty of people. A place that matched the increasingly refined and romantic notion of what nature was.

Where does this leave us today? For some it has led to a questioning not just of the history of our parks but of their present value. Rather than consider them as being what Wallace Stegner, citing Lord Bryce, called "America's best idea," they are now painted by some as poorly managed biological islands, tourist traps where Native people were expelled and where a false Edenic ideal of nature is promoted.

In *As Long As Grass Grows: The Indigenous Fight for Environmental Justice, from Colonization to Standing Rock*, Dina Gilio-Whitaker distills this view of the history of the parks: "When environmentalists laud 'America's best idea' and reiterate narratives about pristine national park environments, they are participating in the erasure of Indigenous peoples, thus replicating colonial patterns of white supremacy and settler privilege."

*   *   *

It is not just scholars and Native writers who are critical of parks today. Parks have also come under attack from an informal group of thinkers, dubbed variously ecopragmatists, neo-environmentalists, green post-modernists, and ecomodernists, who consider themselves proponents of pragmatism over a more romantic view of nature. They tell us that wilderness has always been a human construct. They have little use for parks or coffee table books about nature. Preservation, which was the great cry not just of Roosevelt but of the environmentalism of the 1950s, '60s, and '70s, leading to the Wilderness Act and a flurry of en-vironmental protections, has lately become something of a dirty word. Some see parks and other reserves not just as museums but as an ineffec-tive focus for our environmental battles. Their thinking is that in a world of 7.5 billion people, in an age that has been dubbed the Anthropocene because of man's impact on the earth's environment, merely putting land aside will do little to stave off the worst impacts of climate change, slow down extinctions, or help us adapt to a changed world. To believe that we can simply put huge swaths of land aside is naïve, and even when we do, it quickly becomes apparent that that land, far from being wild, must be managed. This management becomes more pressing in the age of climate change, when habitats are shifting, leaving species stranded.

Their argument continues: there is no real wilderness and we should just come out and admit it. The age we live in is called the Anthropocene because nothing, not even the atmosphere, is beyond the human. The earth is a ruined thing, and the old ways of fighting that ruin, through parks and preservation, have not worked. In fact, the old-school way of thinking about nature, the mystic love of the wild found in the work of Henry David Thoreau and John Muir, is of little relevance in our new world. We must embrace new ideas and new technologies if we are to provide the resources to feed nine billion humans. Nature is dead, and the earth isn't a wild place, but a garden. And like Candide, we must cultivate our garden. We must manage what earth is left.

If that sounds a little depressing, this argument continues, do not fear. Wild nature may be dead, but natural ecosystems are surprisingly resilient. Capitalism and technology, far from being the enemies, are allies in this fight. Humans got us into this mess, and humans (and their ingenuity) will get us out. This, they tell us, is not Roosevelt's Yellowstone or John Muir's Yosemite. This is not Ralph Waldo Emerson's transparent eyeball. This is a new nature, and it is time to wake up to it.

While trying to give these ideas the consideration they deserve, I will admit to some impatience. To go fully down this line of thought twists me into knots of indecision and, at times, can lead me to something close to a panic attack. But they challenge me, too: Am I simply clinging to an old romantic narrative, and worse, a romantic narrative based on a lie? Add the doom of climate change to the mix and why fight for wilderness at all?

Steeped as I have been in Roosevelt's life and work, I bristle at the concept that preservation is dead and that humans can invent our way out of this one. To me it reeks of the perfectibility of man, of the idea that we, and our gizmos, can solve everything. But while I don't like the idea, I have to admit that it is no longer possible to regard Yellowstone in the manner that Roosevelt did. I, and the four million other visitors, and our millions of cars, make that impossible.

In the midst of my panic and anger I reach for something concrete, for anything solid to hold on to. Yellowstone, for instance. "FOR THE BENEFIT AND ENJOYMENT OF THE PEOPLE" is what the sign above the arch says. But Roosevelt's secret agenda was to preserve the park not just for the people but for the thousands of animals and plants and lichen and fungi. I am reminded of my friend Dan Driscoll, who battled for years to have bike paths put in along the Charles River in Boston, but whose secret agenda, an agenda that would prove largely successful, was to return native plantings to the riverbanks. He knew this wasn't a perfect solution. He accepted that as limited creatures ours were only limited and partial steps. "We are all hypocrites," he told me. "But we need more hypocrites who fight."

Seen from a car Yellowstone can seem like a disaster. But the carica-ture of the park is not the park. Only 1 percent of Yellowstone is made up of roads; 99 percent is the realm of the elk, bear, wolf, and cougar. Ac-tual wild animals. That's what Roosevelt loved about Yellowstone, not the geysers, and that's what he wanted to save. And he did, or rather, *we* did. I remind myself that there are 4,500 bison, 500 wolves, and 10,000 elk who don't care what the ecomodernists think.

*   *   *

We can and should be critical of Roosevelt and his contemporaries for their expulsion of Native people from the national parks and monu-ments. It was part of a greater genocide, our original national sin. Wear-ing the blinders of his time, Roosevelt not just accepted but promoted the ideas behind creating reservations and assimilation, while simulta-neously promoting parks as places to play and as belonging to all of us.

But while we are being critical of Roosevelt and others for not step-ping out of their time, we should not fail to step out of our own. Take one step back and we can see a crowded, fractious world of *Homo sa-piens,* battling as always for power, status, resources. But take another step back and the picture is less anthropocentric and even more dire. At this very moment, every second of every day, we are guilty of our own brand of biocide, destroying not hundreds or thousands but millions of creatures that we share this planet with. This is no exaggeration. Barely a day passes when we don't wipe out a species, often a species that has never been categorized. We are killing the living world. We forget that we ourselves are just one sort of animal, though an animal that seems hell-bent on wiping out all others. We are the Borg on *Star Trek* assimi-lating all. This is not just morally indefensible, and species murder, but it is very likely species suicide for us. Climate change, sure, that is part of it. But so is the larger destruction of the biosphere and most of the animals on earth.

This is where Roosevelt, whatever his flaws, remains relevant. Over a century ago he got it in a way most of us still do not get. He saw where

we are heading. While Roosevelt was limited by the myopia and racism of his time, his training as a young scientist, combined with days
in the wild, seems to have occasionally freed him from a larger limita-
tion: anthropocentrism. The inability to see beyond the human. It is this
belief, that all of the great creation revolves around man, that is dooming
the planet.

It may seem funny to say about a man who was by all accounts con-
fident to the point of conceited, but Roosevelt possessed a larger humility. Call it "species humility." Studying and hero-worshipping Darwin as
a young man certainly didn't hurt. He understood that we *Homo sapiens*
are just, in E. O. Wilson's words, "a fortunate species of Old World
primate." And for all his self-centeredness and egotism he seemed to
understand this primary insight: that the world is more important than
we are.

We are right to question Theodore Roosevelt. But we are also right
to question our questioning, particularly on the subject of preservation.
As with TR, so with the parks and monuments he championed. Parks
work. Whatever its limitations, and murky history, Yellowstone remains
the largest wilderness in the Lower 48 states and the one place where
all the large mammals that were here when Europeans first came to this
continent still roam with at least relative freedom. While the wolves were
reintroduced by humans, the mountain lions, which had also been wiped
out in the park, reintroduced themselves. Secretive and stealthy, they slid
into the back spaces of the millions of preserved wild acres. Which means
that Yellowstone once again has its three great carnivores, the most charismatic of the charismatic megafauna: mountain lion, grizzly, wolf.

While acknowledging that it was once the native hunting ground
of tribes, we need to put this in the context of the times and remember what the realistic alternative to preservation might have been. It is
unlikely it would have been happily allowing Indigenous people to go
about their business. The rapacious pace of westward movement brought
with it a force that downed forests, despoiled rivers, stripped vegetation, and killed animals, a force that is still very much with us. Tribes

in Yellowstone would have been mowed down as surely as tribes in the Badlands. The hunger of settlers surging west rivaled that of locusts descending on a field. And in many cases the eviction of Native peoples occurred not because of the creation of parks, but before the parks were even created. The choice, then, was not between a park and a Native settlement or hunting grounds, but between parkland and private land.

What if parks had not been created? There was no obvious reason they should have been. After all it had never happened before in any other country. Where would we be then? While parks and other preserves might have been wrongly romanticized and, to some extent, built on false principles, they were, on a practical level, an attempt, an often desperate attempt, to stop our hunger from despoiling our last beautiful places. And whether or not our parks are "America's best idea," the idea of putting land aside, of not developing it, was inspired. Ecomodernists can sneer at parks if they like, but without them and the habitats they provide, thousands more species would have been lost. If it was an idea mired in the prejudices of its time, it was also one that looked beyond those prejudices toward the future.

*　*　*

I believe that the park ideal, the public land ideal, still has something great and bold in it. We need to acknowledge its historic flaws and current limitations. But if we reimagine it, we can make it newly relevant for our own times.

Among those who have resisted the techno-postmodern vision of nature, and who have clung to a bigger, bolder idea of saving the land, are some visionaries who see Yellowstone itself, not as the end-all or jewel of the park system, but as just the beginning, the starting point, of a great migratory route north. This route would connect the continent's first national park, Yellowstone, with the continent's second, Canada's Banff National Park, which is more than five hundred miles to the northwest. But it wouldn't stop there. It would keep going for almost another two thousand miles, right up to the Yukon. This project is called the

Yellowstone to Yukon Conservation Initiative, or Y2Y, and it is just the kind of park that Roosevelt would have loved. Big, bold, wild. A half million square miles where wolves, elk, caribou, bear, bighorn, and bison still live and freely migrate thousands of miles to the north and south. As inspiring as the place is, the idea is equally so: evidence that boldness still exists in a limited and reduced time.

I visited Banff, in the Canadian province of Alberta, the year before our trip, and for me it was a paradise of moments: Standing next to a full-racked elk by the river as the snow came down on both of us. Watching a striptease of snow clouds moving on and revealing jagged mountain-tops. The wet and glistening back of a soaring raven. The deep blue of a high-elevation lake.

In Banff I spoke with Harvey Locke, a jack of all environmental trades and founder of the Yellowstone to Yukon Initiative. Harvey was a vision-ary in the most basic sense: he had seen what others hadn't and then he had shaped a story out of it. That story, of a big wilderness that allowed wild animals to continue to migrate and evolve but that didn't exclude human beings, was one that had sparked the imagination of many and that has had surprising success in the almost thirty years since it was first told.

"The story grew out of the science," Harvey told me. "Parks were a brilliant idea, and without parks we would have not just lost land but species. Parks work. But conservation biology began to teach us that parks could be improved on. Parks were islands. For species like wolves and bears, who can migrate thousands of miles, parks are not enough. Conservation biologists taught us to think on a continental scale. We began to think of connecting the parks, the islands, and creating great pathways. Y2Y grew directly out of that idea."

For all the talk of the ecomodernist critics, only one way exists to preserve biodiversity and large species, and fend off further extinction, and that is not just conserving large swaths of wild land but connecting those swaths. Large animals thrive in wilderness, not labs. Preservation may be a dirty word, but all the technology and market analysis in the world cannot rebuild what billions of years of evolution created. Connectivity of wild lands is an idea TR would have understood instinctively and delighted in, and for some it has become a rallying cry. While Roosevelt was keenly aware that preserved land was a resource to eventually be *used*, he was one of the first to understand that big animals need big land. His dark experience in the Badlands had taught him well. You can't protect species unless you protect habitat.

While our current president talks of building a wall on our southern border, Harvey Locke and Canadian environmentalists, working with the Canadian and United States governments, have been making a pathway north. The path includes eleven national parks, national forests, wildlife refuges, provincial parks, wilderness lands, and increasingly, private lands. Dozens of overpasses and underpasses allow animals to cross over and under major highways, connecting one wilderness area to another. These are vegetated and wooded bridges that arc over the roads, and equally green passages that tunnel below them, and after some initial hesitation, animal migrants are warming to them. We are offering them a path and they are taking it.

Over the last twenty years the amount of land saved in the Y2Y corridor has increased by thirty million acres, and support has grown despite corporate campaigns to depict the movement as economically harmful to the humans who live in or near the preserved areas.

The concept of growing and connecting parks in our reduced and virtual age, rather than shrinking them and exploiting them, seems as absurd to some people as the concept of parks themselves once did, but the idea of big nature has the value of exciting our imaginations, of being something we can picture. What if, instead of packing it in and saying *the world is screwed* and cultivating our tiny gardens, we turn it around and embrace the idea of not giving up on the wild. If parks were our best idea, maybe connecting parks could be an even better one.

The Y2Y picture is not all rosy of course, with the usual incursions from extractive industries, and governments, particularly the one south of the Y2Y border, attempting to strip away the environmental safeguards that big conservation depends on. But for the postmodern theorists who doubt whether or not wilderness still exists I would recommend a week in the backcountry of the Y2Y, hanging out on a mountain ridge in the snow with grizzlies and wolverines. They would learn quickly that the earth is still wild.

*   *   *

Noah and I spent our days in Yellowstone and our nights at my friends Tom and Sue's house in Big Sky, an hour from the park. Tom suggested another job opportunity for Noah.

"I thought of a great way for someone to make money up here," he said. "Someone could buy a bear costume and stand right outside the gate at the west entrance. While the people are sitting there in traffic you could charge five bucks for tourists to take their picture with a bear. You'd make hundreds of bucks a day."

Noah laughed and considered it for a minute. He liked the idea much better than playing Lawyer Lincoln in the Medora musical. But once again my nephew demurred.

Our hosts in Big Sky were unceasingly generous. One night after a sumptuous dinner they told me that they'd had relatively high hopes when Ryan Zinke became interior secretary since he was a self-avowed outdoorsman and had been relatively open-minded as their congressman here in Montana. But those hopes had been dashed. As well as his work to reduce Bears Ears and Grand Staircase-Escalante, Zinke had been revealed to be somewhat of a nature faker. Or at least an outdoorsman faker.

When Zinke first came into office, the writer, and former army engineer, Elliott Woods wrote a brilliant and scathing profile of him for *Outside* magazine. Woods asked Roosevelt's grandson, Ted Roosevelt IV, about Zinke:

What did Roosevelt think of Zinke's constant comparisons of himself to TR?

"Pretty soon people are going to come to the conclusion, as I have, that he's not a Teddy Roosevelt Republican and he's misappropriating the legacy," Roosevelt replied. "People are going to say, 'This is fraudulent.'"

Woods continued: "It could be said that the Zinke doctrine is not multiple use but maximum use. In pursuit of President Trump's energy agenda, he's pledged to throw open the gates to development on public lands on a scale that has not been seen for decades, if ever."

Woods concluded that TR would have been "extremely disappointed" with Zinke, but as damning as that thought might have been, the final image of the article, and the one that has stuck with me and many others, had to do not with environmental policies but with fishing. Woods concludes:

> As Zinke and I casted over the ice-cold water, I noticed something funny about his setup. He kept struggling to strip line out of the bottom of the reel. For a while, I thought he was simply having trouble concentrating on our conversation while casting. No, there was something wrong, and when I asked him to stand for a portrait, I finally saw what the problem was. He had rigged his reel backward, so that the line was coming out of the top of the reel. Every so often when he went to strip line out, he would grasp air where the line should've been.
>
> Seems like an inconsequential thing, but in Montana, it's everything.

*   *   *

Noah and I had come to the park at the height of the season.

"Maybe we should visit again some other time," he said.

He didn't know it, but he was echoing TR.

People, myself included, complain about the overcrowding that tourism brings. And they—we—have a point. But if relative solitude is what you are after, there is a simple enough solution: *go at the wrong time*. Roosevelt might have praised roads during his dedication at Yellowstone, but he also buried a secret in that speech: "Incidentally, I should like to point out that sometime people will surely awake to the fact that the Park has special beauties to be seen in winter, and any hardy man who can go through it in that season on skis will enjoy himself as he scarcely could elsewhere." And there it is. Go to Yellowstone in January, try Cape Cod in February, and head to the desert in the dead of summer. "No one but a lunatic goes to southern Utah in July," people told me when I lived in Colorado. That's why I started going then. If you really want a sense of being out in it, and being out in it alone, wrong-foot the seasons. By the way, weekdays help. And rain. And the dead of night.

We can quibble all we want about whether or not wilderness still exists. But I know wildness does. Back in the park with Noah it wasn't a bear or cougar that did it to me but something much more common. We were standing at the top of Lower Falls, the spectacular torrent of green-blue water where the Yellowstone River abruptly drops three hundred feet. We were staring down into the spray when suddenly something lifted up, seemingly out of the falls itself. It was an osprey emerging from below the waterfall, rising through the spray like an apparition, its black-and-white patterns distinct, before flying off to perch in a nearby pine. Wildness is defined by surprise, and even though I have long known and studied ospreys, seeing one suddenly, in this new context, hit me like an electric jolt.

Ospreys are the animals I know best, and theirs is a story that has been interwoven with my life. Sleek and black-masked, these raptors peer down into waters from as high up as a hundred feet and then hurtle downward to snare fish with their talons. Evolution has fine-tuned them over millions of years into perfect fishing machines. For years I studied the birds, watching them at their nests and while they hunted, and in some ways it is the best thing I ever did. It made me see, and really believe, that there are lives that are in every way as passionate and important as human lives. Humans who strive for money strive no harder than ospreys do for fish. The longer I studied the birds, the fonder I grew of them.

Yet I grew up in a New England devoid of ospreys. A bird that took millions of years to evolve was all but wiped out in a single generation. They had been extirpated throughout much of the Northeast, and much of the world, thanks to our post–World War II use of the chemical insecticide DDT, which was liberally sprayed to control mosquitoes. The chemical had killed the mosquitoes, but it had also worked its way up the food chain from the insects to the fish to the ospreys. The birds had died a cruel death: the chemical thinned their eggs so that when a mother sat on her brood she would crush them.

But the story does not stop there. A group of citizens on Long Island, having read Rachel Carson's book *Silent Spring*, decided to fight back against the spraying of DDT on their marshes. In the early 1960s they formed a group that would eventually become the Environmental Defense Fund and would embrace the motto "Sue the Bastards." The first time they did, they filed a case against the local Mosquito Commission, and the spraying stopped. Other groups did the same around the country. Laws were passed.

As a young man living on Cape Cod, I rarely saw any ospreys. I moved away for more than a decade, and when I came back one of my first sights was of an osprey nest at the end of the jetty near my house. Ospreys were everywhere. Large, powerful birds diving for fish, building great shaggy nests, filling the air with their high-pitched cries. Now, while many bird populations have plummeted, osprey numbers have soared.

Humans often fuck up. But sometimes humans do things right. Seeing the birds flying around a landscape they had once been exiled from was a cause for celebration. It felt like hope embodied.

Now think of the wolves roaming Yellowstone, running the ridgelines hunting elk, their packs growing in number. Think of the restoration of balance in the ecosystem as the wolves thin out the elk herds, which lets the aspen grow full again and the river thrive. The pulse of wildness returned to the park. Hope may be overrated as fuel for our environmental fights. Desperation may work just as well. But the infusion of wildness into the wild fight can't be scoffed at.

*   *   *

In my travels over the last twenty years I have sought out new ideas
yoked to old ideals, ideals that I would call *Rooseveltean*. What I have
been surprised by is not the lack of but the abundance of these ideas,
and how often I come across people who have dedicated their lives to
the preservation of the wild. Scientists, environmentalists, ranchers,
fishermen, writers, outfitters, rangers, politicians, hunting guides, activists, and thousands of concerned citizens.

Karsten Heuer is one of those people. In the spring of 1998, the
young wildlife biologist set off on a twenty-one-hundred-mile walk
up the spine of the Rockies, traveling from Yellowstone to the Yukon
as a way to celebrate and honor the Y2Y initiative. During his hike he
watched herds of caribou running through the snow, encountered grizzlies and black bears face-to-face, and had the rare pleasure of seeing a
wolverine in the wild. When I spoke to him, after Harvey Locke put us
in touch, I knew I wasn't talking to a nature poseur or theorist.

"The big inspires us," he told me. "But it also allows us to see the
small more clearly. One of the best things about the story Harvey told,
the Y2Y story, is that it puts the smaller fights, the local efforts to conserve land, into a larger continental context. This gives incredible weight
to all of our efforts to save land."

I thought of how that worked in my own life. How tackling something that was part of something big inspired and kicked me into action
in a way something I regarded as small did not. Urgency was another
motivator, and saving land, particularly land that is connected to other
land, is even more urgent now than it was when Karsten made his long
walk. Scientists tell us that with climate change, many North American
species will naturally migrate northward. And if there is a finite line, nowhere to migrate to, the species will expire. Karsten pointed out that
this didn't just mean buffalo and grizzlies, but plant and tree species,
and lichen, the basis of all life. Adaptability is key. And it is up to human
beings to save the land that makes adaptability possible.

I had read Karsten's book, *Walking the Big Wild*, and I mentioned that when he had undertaken his walk larger mammals had been reluctant to use the underpasses, and even some of the overpasses, which had been built to help them migrate.

"That's a perfect example of adaptability. Of the resilience of species. The longer the overpasses have been in place the more they have been used by migrating animals. We have evidence now that female grizzly bears pass the knowledge of using these overpasses on to their cubs."

Human beings, including ranchers who might be threatened by Y2Y, have also proven to be adaptable.

"I think it's less polarized in Canada than in the States. With the generational turnover on a lot of ranches you see the change. There is an openness to not just reach for the rifle. Liberal values are more prevalent in the younger generations and they understand the importance of preserving public lands."

That sounded good. It also sounded quite unlike what was going on in the States, particularly the headline-grabbing stories of armed ranchers laying claim to public lands. Karsten and I agreed that any vision of wilderness had to include the human beings who lived in or near that wilderness. In fact, together we came up with a list of things that wilderness would have to be as we thought and worked toward the future:

Big
Inclusive
Connected
Adaptable
Realistic

"And necessary," he added. "We must do this *now*. There is no time left."

Most of us go about our lives ignoring the fact that we are gobbling up wild lands and driving species toward extinction. It is natural not to want to think about these things; we have plenty else to do, and who wants to have a panic attack about the state of the world? I know we humans aren't built to respond to large, long-term problems, that it's actually a Darwinian adaptation for us to focus on the short-term problems, but stay with me here. Maybe we *need* to have a panic attack about this. Maybe it's worthy of panic. Maybe we shouldn't stay calm and carry on. Maybe instead we should freak out a little bit. Freak out and think about what this really means.

Reports from our top climate scientists tell us our time is running short. The conclusions of the latest Intergovernmental Panel on Climate Change paint a grim picture of drought, heat waves, rising seas, dangerous storms, failing crops, climate refugees, and erratic weather that will disrupt ecosystems and human life all over the earth. This is not a scenario for the future but the stark reality we are beginning to face right now. Roosevelt, always not just environmentally passionate but morally high-handed, would not have equivocated. Remember he wanted to be a scientist when he was young. I can't help but think of what he would do now as president. *Here is what our scientists are saying,* he would exhort. *And here is what we need to do. Now!*

Are we beyond even believing that our world can be saved? Wilderness has inspired this continent since our beginnings, our wild lands a wellspring of the art, ideas, and ideals that have defined us. But do the story of the osprey, the story of the wolf still matter? In our cynical, virtual, and ever-warming world, can the idea of wildness still stir hope and excitement? As we crowd and contaminate this planet, wild places have never been more vital. They offer a vision of a different world, a world where a kind of paradise might still survive amid what feels more and more like dystopia. This vision of hope has always been there, and, while battered, beaten and under assault, it is there still. It is a vision some of us cling to when the human world seems close to hopeless, and it is a vision most clearly seen in our continent's large wild lands.

If our parks seem tame when we drive through them, we need to remember that creating parks was once a *wild* idea. Wild as in out-of-the-blue, fresh, new, dangerous, out-there intoxicating. Wild as in people thought the idea was crazy. It is hard to remember this in a time when parks seem like museums, drone-patrolled and knowable by Google maps. But if you put on a backpack and head into the backcountry, you may discover that these are great, startling, beautiful, and wild museums.

Theodore Roosevelt was one of the first to make an appeal to us to think of our children's children. That appeal might now seem stale. But let's try to wake it up, shake it out, shock it back to life. Take a second and think about what it really means. If we behave poorly, the gifts of nature we have now will not be handed down to our grandchildren. It is only thanks to the gifts of our grandparents and great-grandparents that we have the wilderness we do. In this way the generations are interwoven and alive.

Scientists now tell us that our situation could not be more dire. They tell us we have just twelve years left, as of this writing, until we have ruined the planet for our children and their children. What if we really believed that? And why *don't* we believe it? What would we do differently? How would we live differently?

If we believed, really believed, what our scientists are telling us, wouldn't we drop everything else and do whatever we possibly could to resist exploiting, denuding, and destroying our wilderness? Wouldn't we do this with an urgency we have never felt before, as if our lives depended on it, for the simple reason that they do?

We are like a bad student who has blown off work all term and now is forced to pull an all-nighter. Preserving land is not some antiquated idea that plays no role in the current fight. We need some places that are not shattered, fracked, and torn apart. We need to let places heal not just to save our present but in the hopes of a future different from the one scientists tell us is coming.

As I look toward the future, I don't want to abandon the past. What TR left us with, on top of the gift of the land itself, was a story of wildness. It's a damn good story, one that has worked quite effectively for over a century. As we have discovered, there are flaws in the story, some due to the times he lived in and some due to his own biases. Roosevelt is dead, and so he can't revise his story. That is up to us. We need to tell a new story about wilderness for a new time. With any luck we can tell a story half as inspired as his. We likely won't. But we must try. We owe it to the land and to the animals and to ourselves to try.

BITTERROOT
MOUNTAINS

BIG SKY

YELLOWSTONE

JACKPOT, NV

SNAKE RIVER

COTTONWOOD
RANCH

MUIR
WOODS

YOSEMITE

CHAPTER FOUR

The Cowboy Problem

t isn't just how we view wilderness that has grown more complicated over the last century, but how we view the president who helped create our country's central vision of wilderness.

The story I have laid out is straightforward. Teddy goes west and learns about himself and the land. Teddy vows to conserve the land and understands how fragile it really is. Teddy sees in the demise of the buffalo a lesson in how humans can impact the nonhuman world.

So far, so good. But then we hit a little hitch. No, not a *little* hitch. In the same passage in *Hunting Trips of a Ranchman* where TR writes movingly of the passing of the buffalo, we also find him, a few paragraphs later, adding that there is at least one *good thing* about the extinction of the great herds. And here it is:

> Above all, the extermination of the buffalo was the only way of solving the Indian question. As long as this large animal of the chase existed, the Indians simply could not be kept on reservations, and always had an ample supply of meat on hand to supply them in the event of war; and its disappearance was the only method of forcing them to at least partially abandon their savage mode of life. From the standpoint of humanity at large the extermination of the buffalo has been a blessing. The many have benefited by it; and I suppose the comparatively few of us who would have preferred the continuance of the old order of things, merely for the sake of our own selfish enjoyment, have no right to complain.

In *The Winning of the West*, Roosevelt wrote: "The truth is, the Indians never had any real title to the soil." It's easy to find plenty more damning quotes. Roosevelt's attitude toward Indigenous peoples was torqued by his imperialistic vision of a shining America spreading across the continent and then the world. Native people were an obstacle, which was one reason his breed of Americanism did not include the original Americans. He did grow to believe that the "square deal" that he thought all Americans deserved should be extended to Indians, but he never evolved far beyond the idea that the goal should be their assimilation into the larger culture. There's not much of a way to defend him except to suggest he was "of his time." But even that falls flat. If we are going to give him credit for being prescient on environmental issues we have to admit that on Native American issues he was anything but.

I have noticed a somewhat standard move made by his biographers. The biographer brings up something that Roosevelt did or said, usually something appalling to our modern ear—and most often involving killing or bloodlust or craving for empire—and then either counterbalances it with something positive, puts it in the context of the times, or simply moves briskly on. Forgive and forget. I know I am guilty of this, too, in particular in my insistence that we have historical empathy. But here we must pause.

Here we must look directly, without flinching or excusing. Roosevelt was of his time, but he was also an exemplar of his time. Manifest destiny, our epic national rationalization, was already a half century old when Roosevelt came into power. It was part of his belief system. As much as he put America first, the real ideal for him, the role model, was England and her empire. This ideal led to the building of the Panama Canal, the expansion of executive power, the growth of our military. Though his time as president was a peaceful one, he fully supported expansion at every turn, from Hawaii to the Philippines. On top of believing that we had the right to conquer and cultivate the West, he would later go as far as regretting that we hadn't taken Canada. This was a man who would evolve and would always treat *individual* Indigenous people decently—who would

consider the Native American members of the Rough Riders his brothers and would be a major factor in the return of the buffalo to the plains,
presenting a herd of six to Quannah, a Plains Indian chief. In the same
essay I quoted above he wrote: "The Indians should be treated in just the
same way that we treat white settlers." The problem was not Indigenous
people themselves, but that they were in the way.

That the entire country had already indulged in a similar rationalization, and built their new world on the blood of those who had lived
here before, does not get Roosevelt off the hook. How could such a deep
reader and prolific writer, a student of history and speaker of multiple
languages, a world traveler and world citizen who conversed with kings
and tribal leaders and prime ministers, be so chauvinistic and limited as
to think one nation was more special than all the rest? Had he forgotten
the lessons of Rome? (More likely, he saw Rome, along with England, as
potential role models.) Here was a man who was capable of great empathy and who had flashes of seeing outside of himself, but who could not
let go of his belief in American exceptionalism. It is a belief that can be
hard to shake and that still grips some a century later. But to hold hard
to this belief, to not let go at all costs, means to ignore or displace certain
bloody realities. It is the very ideal of American exceptionalism that so
often has gone hand in hand with our unexceptional behavior.

My instinct now is to make excuses for TR. But I won't, not for the
moment. I will just let this fact sit here, cold and ugly. It is us after all. It
is our history.

*   *   *

This land. This blood-soaked beautiful land, laced with human history
but also having its own stories separate from the human. True, Yellowstone was clogged with cars, but as soon as we pushed off we left the
crowds behind. Angling down from Montana through Idaho, you can
still remember the vastness of this country. We followed the Snake River.
Mountains appeared, range after range. The Bitterroots. The Salmon
River Mountains, the Sawtooth Range, the Lost River Range. These are

just a few of the 114 mountain ranges in Idaho. Not 114 mountains, but 114 *ranges*. Jagged, jutting up, cutting into the sky. Blue-green marbles of lakes at their feet. Continents of clouds above, shifting as if by some sort of plate tectonics in the sky.

More than 70 percent of Idaho's land is public land. Think of it. Millions of acres that belong to all of us. We have done some things deeply wrong, true. But we have done some things right.

In Idaho there are more than twenty million acres of forest land, administered by the forest service, and more than twelve million additional acres administered by the Bureau of Land Management. Much of that was saved by Theodore Roosevelt, and in typically Rooseveltian fashion, his love of this landscape grew out of killing things in it. In the summer of 1888, in search of caribou, he headed into the wilderness of the Idaho Territories, land that two years later would become a state. He found no caribou but killed a large black bear. He also, while working his way through heavy brush, dense woods, thick bogs, and high mountains, found beauty. From the mountaintops he wrote:

> The view from the summit was magnificent, and I never tired of gazing at it. Sometimes the sky was a dome of blue crystal, and mountain, lake, and valley lay spread in startling clearness at our very feet; and again snow-peak and rock-peak were thrust up like islands through a sea of billowy clouds. At the feet of the topmost peaks, just above the edge of the forest, were marshy alpine valleys, the boggy ground soaked with water, and small bushes or stunted trees fringing the icy lakes.

He relished not just the sights but the sounds of nature:

> After nightfall, round the camp fire, or if I awakened after sleeping a little while, I would often lie silently for many minutes together, listening to the noises of the wilderness. At times the wind moaned harshly through the tops of the tall pines and

hemlocks; at times the branches were still; but the splashing murmur of the torrent never ceased, and through it came other sounds—the clatter of huge rocks falling down the cliffs, the dashing of cataracts in far-off ravines, the hooting of owls.

This trip, like so many of his experiences, would have a direct impact on his life and thinking, and on our country's politics. He never lost his vision of a wild Idaho. And as president he set to saving it. Douglas Brinley writes in *The Wilderness Warrior*:

On January 15, 1907, he created Caribou National Forest, about 200 miles east of Boise. The following year, on July 1, he virtually turned the state into one vast wildlife preserve, setting aside millions of acres in seventeen new national forests with his presidential pen: Pocatello, Cache, Challis, Salmon, Clearwater, Couer d'Alene, Pend Orielle, Kaniksu, Weiser, Nez Perce, Idaho, Payette, Boise, Sawtooth, Lemhi, Targhee, and Bitterroot. Seldom, if ever, had a hunt resulted in such a momentous conservationist gesture on behalf of wild creatures.

Though Roosevelt would sometimes act unilaterally, he did not act alone. From the beginning his great conservationist ally was Gifford Pinchot, who would be, in Roosevelt's words, "the man to whom the nation owes most for what has been accomplished as regards the preservation of the natural resources of our country." Roosevelt said that of all the men who advised him during his presidency, Pinchot "stood first" through a combination of "his tireless energy and activity, his fearlessness, his complete disinterestedness, his complete devotion to the interests of the plain people, and his extraordinary efficiency," and the fact that what he was doing, the work of conserving, was "breaking new ground." Pinchot was already chief of the country's Division of Forestry, but it was only after Roosevelt convinced Congress to shift the supervision of the forests to the Department of Agriculture, and put Pinchot in charge of the newly created Forest Service, that he began to flex his conservationist muscles to the point where critics began to call him "Czar Pinchot."

The two men worked well as a team. It would be easy, and glib, to see Roosevelt as an environmental Batman with Pinchot as his Robin, but as far as personalities went the roles would have to be reversed. Roosevelt, ever ebullient, was sometimes closer in spirit to Batman's expressive sidekick, while Pinchot, who seemed cold, removed, and somewhat fanatical, had grown up with the wealth of a Bruce Wayne. After graduating from Yale, he went to Europe to study forestry, a subject not taught at the time in the United States, and he came back with a mission: to bring the practice of American forestry out of the dark ages and in doing so preserve our natural resources.

There were clear philosophical differences between Roosevelt and Pinchot. The Czar didn't share TR's romantic view of nature. "The preservation of our forests is an imperative business necessity," wrote Pinchot. Forests and the resources therein were important for what they could "yield for the service of man." Pinchot walked a fine line with his forest reserves, preserving them yes, but also making them pay by leasing the land and logging it. More a conservationist, in the lingo of the time, than a preservationist, Pinchot would become a utilitarian icon. Later environmentalists would not look on him as fondly as Roosevelt did, and one of his favorite phrases, "wise use," would end up being turned against him as a kind of front for militant assaults on wilderness. While Pinchot was adroit at preserving forests at the same time as profiting from them, and at speaking the businessman's language while being at heart a conservationist, future leaders of the Forest Service would be less so, setting a precedent of use that was sometimes more rapacious than wise. The Forest Service, business-oriented from the beginning, would become increasingly dedicated to logging and increasingly in the pocket of logging interests.

But those were worries for the future. What Pinchot did in the first decade of the twentieth century was save the nation's forests from destruction. If that sounds like an exaggeration, consider these facts presented in Louis Auchincloss's short biography of TR: "Of 250 billion board feet of national timber, 40 billion were being cut annually and being replaced by only ten billion." At that rate our forests would have been wiped out in less than a decade.

Pinchot was efficient and stealthy in his steady acquisition of forest reserves. Roosevelt, as usual, preferred a more straightforward, barging-in sort of approach, declaring by proclamation. By 1907, Congress had had enough of both of their tactics. That year Senator Charles W. Fulton, a Republican from Oregon, backed by the usual cohort of ranchers and loggers and fellow Western congressmen (and sick of the damned public land that Roosevelt kept claiming), added a waiver to the Agricultural Appropriations Bill that read: "Hereafter no forest reserve shall be created, nor shall any addition be made to one heretofore created, within the limits of the States of Oregon, Washington, Idaho, Montana, Colorado or Wyoming." Roosevelt was cornered. The appropriations bill needed to be passed; there was no way around it. It had to be signed.

But before he signed the thing, the president huddled up with Pinchot, and drew up a list of land to be saved. The result of that huddling and discussion was the addition of sixteen million acres to the forest reserves. Remembering his long-ago hunt for caribou, these reserves included all the forests in Idaho. Once he had decreed those lands saved, he went ahead and signed the appropriations bill. He later gloated in his autobiography: "The opponents of the Forest Service turned handsprings in their wrath; and dire were the threats against the executive; but the threats could not be carried out, and were really only a tribute to the efficiency of our action."

For the enraged senators this sweeping action fueled their sense that they were dealing with a man who fancied himself more king than president. Perhaps. But at least he did what he did in the service of a vision, a vision that grew out of much study, thought, and experience. In fact, his actions were usually the outgrowth of a coherent philosophy, one that many disagreed with, true, but one that looks pretty good to his children's children's children.

What he finally achieved was monumental. Two hundred and thirty million acres. A decent amount of that land was forest land, which underwent a name change during the 1907 incident. Senator Fulton didn't like the *reserve* part in the name forest reserve, with its connotation of preservation not *use*, so the bill included a provision that changed the name from forest reserve to national forest. Whatever they were called, they became an important part of the Roosevelt legacy. This was Pinchot's territory, so the focus was and remains on resources and use, but the forests were, in their more utilitarian and less romanticized way, as important to the country and its future as our national parks.

* * *

Theodore Roosevelt owed his ascension to the presidency, in no small part, to the cowboy myth that he and his buddy, Owen Wister, helped create. A Harvard classmate, Wister exalted the romantic image of the cowboy in his immensely popular novel *The Virginian*, the first real Western, a book that was dedicated to Theodore Roosevelt. Roosevelt's own books did their part as well with *Ranch Life and the Hunting Trail*, *The Wilderness Hunter*, and *Hunting Trips of a Ranchman* painting a romantic picture of a simpler life in an increasingly crowded and industrial world. This relatively new myth was hugely successful, one that was quickly exported to the rest of the world. It is a myth built on conquest, blood, and, of course, on cows.

Roosevelt's own relationship with cows was complex. They were intertwined with his origin story on the Dakota ranch. But there were multiple ironies. Perhaps no one has unwrapped those ironies like the historian Elliott West, a distinguished professor of history at the University of Arkansas. West points out that while Roosevelt painted his life on the ranch as the opposite of the corporate model that had begun to dominate industry, it was actually an exemplar of that model. By the time TR headed west, ranching was already big business, relying completely on the biggest business of its time, the railroads, for transporting its product. While those who worked the land might have somewhat fit the picture of poor, romantic cowboys, those who owned the ranches were wealthy individuals and families, or, increasingly, multimillion-dollar corporations. Like many corporate enterprises of the time, ranching relied on government largesse, specifically on the millions of acres of public land that could be used for grazing. This was big business, right down to the slaughterhouses, which were this industry's factories.

"This was modernity defined," West writes. "Ranching was an industry, a nationalized arrangement of regional specialization, modern transport, and noisome factories. A ranch in the Dakotas or Wyoming was one part of a far larger system that in turn was part of the very economic order that Roosevelt and others found so alien and threatening to the life they imagined themselves living out in the West."

A capping irony, as West points out, is that, as president, Roosevelt would gain fame and stature for taking on the very corporate consolidations of power his own business exemplified.

West wonders whether Roosevelt, "looking back from the White House, ever experienced at least a slight shock of recognition that in his younger years he had been squarely in the middle of the process he was now confronting."

Whether he did or not, there is no way that Roosevelt could have wanted, or envisioned, the fact that the public lands he was creating as president would become ever more vast ranchlands, fiefdoms for not just ranchers and the rich but corporations. For all his romanticizing of the ranching life, Roosevelt grew to understand very well what cows had done to America's land.

What they had done was chew it up and spit it out. Or, more accurately, shit it out, as anyone walking along a Western creek or river could see. And they continue to do so to this day. One hundred years after TR's death over a *third of the land* in the contiguous United States remains pastureland, with a quarter of that being land leased by the government, and almost all of that land serving the mighty cow.

The leasing began under Pinchot, the pragmatist, who couldn't have known where it would lead. As for the results, there is no sense mincing words. The domination by cows of our public lands has been a complete and unequivocal environmental disaster. It has destroyed native plants, driven out native wildlife, and left a dry, cracked desert where tall grassy meadows once grew. Eastern media outlets, even liberal ones, make jokes about cow farts and carbon, while ignoring the much larger problem. If what Karsten Heuer and Harvey Locke are proposing is an environmental escape route, a green and wild path to the future, then cows are the sentries standing in the way. They turn green land to brown and devour the species that wild things thrive on. They block our escape.

We see the cowboy as a truly American figure, but cows were a European introduction and, if anything, have more thoroughly conquered this country than the humans who brought them here. The irony is tart: in their books, Roosevelt and Owen Wister unintentionally gave cover to the animals most responsible for denuding Western land.

The myth endures. Most people would greet the idea that cows should be kicked off what most Americans consider cowboy lands with bewilderment and amusement. No more home on the range? And the inevitable question follows: where will we get our steaks and burgers from? The simple answer: the same place you get them from now. Which is to say, not from anywhere west of the Mississippi. Less than 1 percent of U.S. beef production comes from Western public lands. Meanwhile the Bureau of Land Management leases around 60 percent of its 247.3 million acres for grazing. In other words, this sparse, dry landscape is far from ideal for ranching. You would think that at minimum the leasing process would pay for itself, but no. In his important book *Grand Canyon for Sale*, Stephen Nash writes: "Fiscal conservatives take note: as it happens, government administration of grazing costs the BLM about 6.5 times more money than the fees it brings in. In the most recently tallied year alone taxpayers would have saved somewhere between $50 and $80 million if private cattle vanished entirely from public land, by the BLM's own estimates." That is because the BLM, according to long-standing tradition, leases this land for a fraction of what it would cost to graze on private land. The beneficiaries are the ranchers, who despite their theoretical love of fierce independence, are dependent on government largesse. Ranchers fight any attempt to regulate their use of public land, and you can see why. They are furious that the old ways are threatened, and, perversely, they make the federal government, their benefactor, into the enemy.

The fight rages on. As Noah and I sliced through Idaho, following the Snake past the volcanic formations and lava flows of Craters of the Moon National Monument and Preserve, we had a decision to make. We were equidistant from the Oregon and Nevada borders. With public lands on my mind our choice was between Nevada, where 87 percent of its land is public, and Oregon, with more than 60 percent.

Dead ahead was the Malheur National Wildlife Refuge in Oregon, where a couple of summers before a rancher named Ammon Bundy and a dozen or so other so-called rebels had performed a little drama for the nation's benefit. Disguised as cowboys (some actually were ranchers, many weren't), they waved their guns and started bonfires and demanded that the federal government hand over the refuge since it was, they stated, unconstitutional for the United States to have claimed the land. Their armed takeover of the wildlife refuge had started as a protest over some locally imprisoned ranchers, who had just had their sentences for the crime of arson on public lands (to cover up illegal hunting on those lands) extended to the mandatory five years. But as became quickly clear the protestors' message was muddled, and their "local militia" had few locals in it, and when they appealed for snacks on Facebook the whole thing turned farcical. At least until the farce turned tragic and one of the militiamen was fatally shot by a state trooper.

The message the Bundys were trying to tell was confused, and relied on an extreme and extremely selective reading of the Constitution, but for the most part their story was a tried-and-true one, and one that has been played out again and again in the American West over the past century and a half. The story, in its simplest form, goes like this: we are taking back *our* land from the federal government. Leave aside for a moment the problem that they didn't actually own the land or that you and I own the public land as much as they do. Focus instead on the bones of the story, the same story told by the Sagebrush rebels of Reagan's time, by big-business ranchers in the 1950s, indeed by that minority of people who have been determined to "open up" the West to ranching, logging, and extracting from the very time that white people began to settle it. *We the people want our land back.*

To understand the ways in which Western myths of this variety undermine the region's best interests, there is no better place to turn than to Bernard DeVoto's magnificent 1947 essay "The West Against Itself," originally published in *Harper's* magazine. DeVoto, like Roosevelt, was a fighter, a bristling, energetic intellectual who loved to brawl, though he, born in Utah, was a Westerner who went east, not the other way around. In a vivid, aggressive, almost choppy style, DeVoto lays out his case. He warms up by taking on the extractive industries—mining, oil, and gas—summing up: "The West does not want to be liberated from the system of exploitation that it has always violently resented. It only wants to buy into it." He then turns his fury on the business "which created the West's most powerful illusion about itself and, though it is not immediately apparent, has done more damage to the West than any other: the stock business." He meant the big business of ranching, explaining that ranching's great era lasted from "about 1870 to the terminal winter of 1886–7," the very winter that TR's cattle froze in their tracks. While this was the end of an era, "the delusions of the era" have continued to dominate the industry ever since. Of those who perpetrated this myth he writes: "They thought of themselves as Westerners and they did live in the West, but they were the enemies of everyone else who lived there."

Why? Though tiny in number, the large ranchers grabbed water rights and foreclosed on small holdings. DeVoto, in a line that speaks to today, writes: "And, being Western individualists and therefore gifted with illusion, the little cattlemen have always fought the big ones' battles, have adopted and supported their politics to their own disadvantage and to the great hurt of the West." The hurt of the West began with the land and rivers that the cattle chewed up and destroyed by overgrazing, and with causing erosion to the point that Western rivers "have always been helping to carry the mountains to the sea." The cattle industry added little to the profit or health of Western communities, benefiting the few, but the myth of the cowboy helped sustain the business, so that "when you watch the Missouri sliding greasily past Kansas City you are watching those gallant horsemen out of Owen Wister shovel Wyoming into the Gulf of Mexico."

And then the kicker. The cattlemen, those great extollers of independence, owned less than 1 percent of the land their cattle grazed on. Who owned the rest? The American people and the federal government that the cowboys so scorned, though not enough to say no to leasing that American land for rates so cheap as to be laughable. Why were they—who were getting such a great deal—so angry? Maybe it was partly at the idea of relying on the rest of us, their benefactors. It isn't their land that they are fighting for but *our* land, and in DeVoto's ringing words:

> Cattlemen do not own the range now: it belongs to you and me, and since the fees they pay for using public land are much smaller than those they pay for using private land, those fees are in effect one of a number of subsidies we pay them. But they always acted as if they owned the public range and act so now; they convinced themselves that it belonged to them and now believe it does; and they are trying to take title to it.

DeVoto's essay culminates with perhaps his most famous line: "It shakes down to a platform: get out and give us money."

But there was an even worse alternative than socialism on the range. DeVoto writes: "A few groups of Western interests so small numerically as to constitute a minute fraction of the West" are "skillfully manipulating in their support sentiments that have always been powerful in the West—the home rule which means basically that we want federal help without federal regulation, the 'individualism' that has always made the small Western operator a handy tool of the big one, and the wild myth that stockgrowers constitute an aristocracy in which all Westerners somehow share."

And so it continues to this day. The Bureau of Land Management, our nation's major landlord with more than two hundred million acres, leases out our public lands at bargain basement prices to ranchers, who in turn let their cows chew up entire ecosystems. The Bundys rail against government socialism while making no mention of the federal subsidy that their families have been receiving in terms of grazing rights for generations. We the people subsidize the ranchers while they denude the American land, and then they turn around and fume about the fact that that land isn't theirs. And while they have benefited from this sweet deal, their ultimate plan now is the same as the plan DeVoto wrote about, "to get rid of public lands altogether, turning them over to the states, which can be coerced as the federal government cannot be, and eventually to private ownership."

The Bundy family's fringe beliefs were part of what turned the local ranchers in Harney County near the Malheur Wildlife Refuge against them. A close reading of what I will generously call their platform reveals the emptiness of their assertion that the federal government's claim to American lands is unconstitutional. It requires massive gymnastics of language and logic to even get to something close. In fact the birth of the United States coincided with a belief in public land, and that belief only grew as we moved westward. The larger problem is those who use the Bundys as pawns to support their agenda. These include Fox News and the corporations that would like very much for public land to become private. Stephen Nash writes: "No other factors look as powerful as the alignment of the stratospherically wealthy private interests with antigovernment ideology. Their campaigns are bankrolled by corporations and individuals that spend hundreds of millions of dollars on lobbying and political candidates—although the sources and amounts are now often hidden." And while local ranchers do still exist, they are outnumbered by corporate or absentee owners who "sleep in Los Angeles, not the bunkhouse." Cowboy hats, it turns out, often provide cover for the larger operations of corporations and those who would like to privatize public land.

What has changed in the seventy years since DeVoto wrote his essay? Well, the climate for one. The habitat of much of our public lands, which all species, including cattle, depend on, is in ruinous shape from a century and a half of grazing. Even the Bureau of Land Management, the agency that leases most of the land, admits that the land is subpar. This is bad in and of itself but even worse in the face of a warming world where the hope of species survival hinges on both healthy ecosystems and the ability of those species to move. Climate stressors are pushing species north. If we believe in the vision of migratory pathways that Karsten Heuer and Harvey Locke are putting forth, those pathways must be able to sustain wildlife and plants.

The choice is stark. If we accept that the climate is changing, and we want wilderness and healthy ecosystems, we need to battle against the splintering and push for unity and health, fighting against islands and for paths. This does not mean that the West can't still support millions of acres for grazing—it can. But a quick look at a map of the interior West shows that our vast public lands, while in bad shape, could provide migratory escape routes for our most stressed and drought-threatened species. And that perhaps this would be a better use for those lands than as the subsidized grazing fields of a few. If these are indeed *our* lands, lands that belong to you and me, we might consider asserting our collective will and, however strong the cowboy myth remains, putting forth the idea that these lands could be restored to health, and that there are things we the people value even more than the cow. That would be the real public lands rebellion, a new use for our lands that Roosevelt would have applauded. I don't want to gloss over the threats of both climate change and the "cowburnt" ecosystems. The situation is dire. But the fact that we even have a possible escape route is testament to the genius of the original vision of public lands.

If you think overgrazing is a small worry with everything else going on in the world, consider that, between the Bureau of Land Management, the Forest Service, and the Park Service, grazing is allowed on something like 379,200 square miles of public land. That is two Californias with a Maine and a Massachusetts thrown in for good measure. More than two Californias in our country especially reserved for cows.

It is enough land that, if managed correctly and allowed to return to relative health, it could avert, or at least seriously aid in the fight against, the extinction of hundreds of climate-threatened species of animals and plants. It is simple enough: healthy, native, and varied ecosystems have the best chance of surviving in an arid region that is turning hotter and drier with each passing year.

The idea that public land must be "returned" to the states that never owned it simply means that our great public lands would become the vast backyards of private interests and corporations. DeVoto paints a picture of states reclaiming public lands and turning them over to private owners. This is the route to a continued splintering of wilderness, to smaller and smaller islands. The alternate route is connectedness and the imagining of a great and healthy pathway. Restoration of those lands is visionary and may seem impossible in these times. But the proof that we could do it now is that we did the impossible in the past. No one had heard of national parks when we decided to create them. Wouldn't it be nice if a century from now someone said the same about migratory pathways and restored ecosystems along the continent's spine?

Why not? Or, more emphatically, why the fuck not? Why not try and save the world? What have we got to lose? These public lands allow us the possibility. They are like a secret that our predecessors whispered down to us.

True, a few cowboys would be angry at us if we told them their cows had to be restricted to the land they actually own, and they might even shoot at us. But maybe it is still worth it. The choice is ours. To reclaim the lands that we own or to shrug and walk away.

What would Teddy do?

I suspect you know the answer by now.

* * *

Reluctantly, Noah and I decided to cut south to Nevada instead of heading west to Oregon. My trip would go on for many more weeks, but my nephew's was nearing its end. He had to get on with the stressful business of life after graduation, and he would fly home to North Carolina soon. Our goal now was the same as Lewis and Clark's: the Pacific or bust. Before he left, he needed to stand on a beach in California. The fastest way to do that was to cut down into Nevada and then up through the Donner Pass.

We drove into a sunset that lit up the hills, and then we drove deep into the night. The next morning we woke to a new world. Bernard DeVoto was tough on everyone, as a rule, but when it came to Nevada he could be downright mean:

> The black lava is not the only reason why Nevada is the ugliest state, but would in itself suffice. (It is also the most corrugated state, though it is seldom thought of as mountainous and indeed has no spectacular mountains, since it ends east of the tremendous Sierra.) It requires a careful weighing of values to decide which of the Nevada deserts is most hideous.

I disagree, particularly when it comes to his assessment of the mountains. Nevada does not have the ranges that Idaho does, but its individual peaks shine with an otherworldly strangeness all their own. Also, it's the first state where Noah and I saw an animal that could act as the official greeter to the West: a coyote. It stared at us, then skulked across a field and under a fence. And if wilderness can be defined somewhat by the absence of humans, Nevada took the prize so far. Most of its three million people are clustered in cities—Las Vegas and Reno—and there are only eight states less densely populated. We traveled through long stretches without seeing a house or, for a good while, another car. Endless and relatively empty, but unlike the clichés about it, quite beautiful, a moonscape startling in its strange rock formations and deserts.

Though still buffalo blessed, our vehicle was not perfect. I have not mentioned it yet, but the gas tank of a Scion is, as far as carrying capacity goes, similar to the bladder of a middle-aged man. The road anxiously stretched toward the next gas station. We felt relief all around when we at last reached one, nearing dead empty for the car and dead full for me. Like so many Western oases, this one wasn't all that it promised to be. It would turn out that my credit card identity was stolen at the self-service pump, something I wouldn't learn until a few states later when the thief began ringing up charges.

Back on the road the world that Noah and I encountered was one cracking and crumbling from heat. For anyone who doubts that climate change is real, come on out to the Southwest. Just as farmers who live near the salt-killed ghost forests in my adopted state of North Carolina can't deny the rising seas, those who live here can't deny that the temperatures in the Southwest are rising year to year and that drought is a near constant. Water, always scarce in this arid world, has become scarcer. Stream levels are low, and a burgeoning population and decaying infrastructure make the lack of water even more painful. The winter before our trip had seen a far below average snowpack for most of the West, and a new term, "snow drought," was now being bandied about by scientists and locals alike. This refers to hard years that occur even when the annual precipitation climbs close to normal. The trouble is that in a warming world the precipitation often occurs as rain, not snow, and rain, unlike snow, does not stick around and gradually fill the reservoirs as it melts in time-release fashion. Snowpack in January means water in June. But, despite occasional aberrant years, we had better get used to decreased snowpack. Researchers at the Desert Research Institute in Reno report a "1,200-foot rise in the average snow level in the Northern Sierra over the last decade." The snow level is the point where rain turns to snow.

"Snowpack is crucial even in communities that rarely see any snow," the *Las Vegas Review Journal* reported in January 2018. "The Las Vegas Valley draws 90 percent of its water supply from Lake Mead, and nearly all of that water comes from snowmelt in the mountains that feed the Colorado River."

Public lands cannot singlehandedly save the day in the age of climate change. But they sure as hell don't hurt. "The Green New Deal" was making headlines as we drove, and by all means we should be responding in any and every way possible to the recent and overwhelming scientific reports that tell us we are in even hotter water than we thought. But in pushing the newest enviro flavor of the day we shouldn't forget the tried and true. The public lands provide what they have always provided us with, a vital buffer, which is especially true as the West grows hotter. "Much of Civilian Conservation Corps work in the original New Deal focused on public lands," a Western environmentalist friend reminded me recently. "Building trails, corrals, and fences for cattle and planting trees. A Green New Deal focused on restoring public lands could actively work to roll back harm from overgrazing." If we administer and manage them well, and with vision, our public lands can be a, if not *the*, key in our fight against climate change.

That is a big if. What our public lands should provide is a vast green counterbalance to the rabid energy consumption, and carbon emissions, that threaten the world. But they have dramatically failed at this, particularly in recent years. Which is due to the way these lands are administered and regulated. Right now, while the Bureau of Land Management lands continue to be denuded and degraded from grazing, both BLM and Forest Service lands have opened their arms to industry.

"Fossil energy extraction is the preferred tenant on America's public lands," writes Jamie Williams, president of the Wilderness Society. "For less than the price of a cup of coffee, developers can purchase and lock up America's favorite outdoor recreation areas and wildlife habitat for years so that oil developers and mining companies have sole access. That dirty secret means that public lands are a major source of the nation's climate emissions problem. In fact, if our public lands were their own country, its emissions would rank fifth in the world."

It is hard to overstate how dire the situation was that summer. Water was scarce in New Mexico and Arizona, and much of Colorado was on fire. California, too, was burning, though the year's most famous fire was still months away. Our own carbon footprints weren't helping matters, as we drove, stomping through the West like careless hikers clomping down on the crust of cryptobiotic soil. Spasms of self-disgust mixed in with my building other-disgust. As befits our species, we were to some degree self-aware, but we were also part of a larger swarm of humanity that was mindlessly overrunning, and warping, the world.

On we motored through the Nevada desert.

*   *   *

In recent years we have come to associate the cowboy myth with conservative politicians like Ronald Reagan or, more recently and to a lesser extent, former interior secretary Ryan Zinke and the Bundy family. But the cowboy that was Theodore Roosevelt had a few surprises up his sleeve, particularly when it came to public lands and to the ranching community he was once part of. By the time he was president organized movements had begun to fight back against the dangers of concentrated corporate wealth. Elliott West writes: "Roosevelt as president became the dominant voice in one of those movements, coined the New Nationalism, dedicated to matching and checking the concentration of corporate influence with an expanded regulatory role for the federal government. A special target in his presidency were the railroads, the very institutions that had provided the essential means for ranching as an early model of corporate power."

From the beginning, when he was chosen as vice president, political bosses, like Mark Hanna, didn't know what to make of TR and his strange mix of qualities. In *The Wilderness Warrior*, Douglas Brinkley writes:

> Famously, Mark Hanna once quipped that Roosevelt was a "damn cowboy," now only "one heartbeat away from the presidency." But the word "cowboy" would imply that Roosevelt was a rubber stamp for the stockmen's association for the Rocky Mountains, which he clearly wasn't. The reality, in fact, was far worse than Hanna contemplated. Roosevelt was a pro-forest, pro-buffalo, cougar-infatuated, socialistic land conservationist who had been trained at Harvard as a Darwinian-Huxleyite

zoologist and now believed that the moral implications of *On the Origin of Species* needed to be embraced by public policy. The GOP was in trouble.

Remember here that the GOP was Roosevelt's party, and that many of our most important environmental laws grew out of the Republican Party. In fact, right through Nixon's presidency the GOP was passing important environmental legislation. The big shift came with Reagan, wearing a cowboy hat of his own, and his interior secretary James Watt, who ushered in the more extreme assault on the resources that Roosevelt and Pinchot had sought to protect. In the time since, the cowboy myth has continued to be exploited to serve the corporate interests of the wealthy, an intentional stirring of anger over the loss of "freedom" and the fear of government control, in a manner that ultimately serves business interests. More importantly, it serves to destroy the very land being fought over.

Of course not all ranchers wear black hats in the fight over the future of wildness in the West, and not all cows block the path to a green future. The Bundys of the world are magnets for media attention. They are also far from representative of most Western ranchers. During his work on Y2Y Karsten Heuer found many examples of ranchers who were willing to adapt their practices and allow nearby migratory corridors even if it meant having large predators close to their livestock.

As Noah and I drove through the small town of Jackpot, Nevada, and down to the town of Wells, we were not far from a fine example of ranching that also took into account native plants, riverine health, and the idea that grasslands did not have to be chewed to the nub. Agee Smith of Cottonwood Ranch may not get the media attention that his fellow Nevada rancher Ammon Bundy does, but his vision of the future of ranching, like his land itself, is more resilient, sustainable, and healthy than Bundy's.

Smith, a fifth-generation rancher, had watched overgrazing lead to the destruction of his ranch's vegetation and reduce the health of the river and the number of fish and "began to wonder if I was in a business that was progressively becoming bad for the environment." But around 1996 he was introduced to the suspiciously New Agey-sounding idea of holistic resource management. It turned out to be less New Age than common sense. It stressed rotational grazing strategies and the idea that ecologically sustainable land is, in the end, more profitable land. Smith, along with three neighbors, formed what has become known as the "Shoesole" Group, and put the ideas to work on their private lands as well as the BLM and Forest Service lands that their animals grazed on. The result has been a return of native plants and native animals, specifically of sagebrush and the sage grouse, a flamboyantly wild bird (that anyone who has seen it dance will never forget). Smith points to how old ways can be married to new, rather than creating a false and warlike dichotomy. "I'm all for tradition," Smith recently told Dan Hottle of the Reno Fish and Wildlife Office. "But when we refuse to get out of our traditional boxes, it's the land that suffers."

His neighbor Steve Boies echoed this sentiment: "Managing holistically so that the cattle and wildlife can exist together is the easy part. Convincing people to work together toward a common goal for the good of everyone is the hard part."

* * *

As we think about public lands as yet another arena of conflict and parse human beings into categories—a crunchy liberal enviro over here and a crusty cowboy local over there—we forget how our public lands benefit all citizens. Until relatively recently, public lands were supported by both political parties and were a place and an issue for Americans to come together over, not be torn apart by. I believe that, for most of us, they still can be.

Many myths have grown up around our public lands, which account for almost a third of the nation's acreage, making them far and away our country's greatest resource (and financial asset). These myths and misconceptions were the subject of John D. Leshy's 2018 Wallace Stegner lecture at the University of Utah. Leshy, a land expert, frequent visiting professor at Harvard, and former general counsel for the Interior Department, explained that public lands, generally defined as lands open to the public and "managed for broad public purposes," were with us from the beginning, long before Yellowstone was declared our first national park. These non-private lands grew as our country did, most spectacularly in the arid and more recently acquired Western territories, which, in return for statehood, readily agreed to vast reserves being put aside in their own states. But even earlier than that public lands were central to our development. Leshy argues that our very first national crisis, before there was even a constitution, evolved out of a public lands debate: how should the newly acquired lands between the Appalachian Mountains and the Mississippi River be divvied up between the existing thirteen states? The decision to make this federal land and the property of the United States, not that of any one state, led to the ratification of the Articles of Confederation and, eventually, the U.S. Constitution, which granted the federal government much more power than the Articles of Confederation had. A common trope of the public land rebels is that it is unconstitutional for the federal government to own land; in fact the constitution was practically born of the embrace of public lands. With the Louisiana Purchase, and further westward expansion, the United States acquired more and more land. Leshy pauses here to correct some misconceptions. The first is that the states expected, upon admission to the union, that the federal government would cede its public land to them. There is not a "shred of evidence" to support this, says Leshy, and, in fact: "Leaders across the political spectrum—from James Madison to Henry Clay, Andrew Jackson, and John C. Calhoun—were absolutely opposed to the notion of ceding land to newly admitted states."

This would be the prevailing mood of the country for its first century, and it would not abate in its second. While we now sometimes think of public lands as a political war zone, the putting aside of more lands in the late 1800s was actually seen as a balm from war, an antidote, a common heritage after the tragic and deadly split of the Civil War. All Americans, the thinking went, could find solace and common ground in the great public lands of the West. That this thinking didn't include, as usual, the original Americans makes it shine less brightly in retrospect, but as Leshy points out: "How the U.S. acquired clear title to these lands from foreign governments and tribes is a complicated story and, especially where Indians are concerned, certainly one with a dark side. But it took place largely in advance of, and separate from, the movement to keep significant amounts of public land permanently in U.S. ownership."

Leshy dispels the myth that the putting aside of federal land did not occur until a hundred years after the nation was founded. What is true, however, is that after the Civil War the drive for more public land gained both new momentum and motivation. This was the world that Roosevelt grew up in, a world where the frontier was fading along with the wilderness and wildlife, and out of fear of these losses grew the first great efforts to preserve. It was also the moment when the federal government gave back significant land to the states to establish land grant colleges. In 1864 Abraham Lincoln had signed Yosemite into existence, and in 1872 President Grant created the "world's first national park" in Yellowstone. Far from splintering public opinion, these great parks would soon become a common point of national pride.

Then the fight for preservation really picked up steam. In 1891, Congress passed the Forest Reserve Act, which Leshy calls possibly "the single most consequential piece of public land legislation ever enacted." The Forest Reserve Act would be what eventually allowed Roosevelt to create the Forest Service and appoint Gifford Pinchot. This also gave the president sweeping power to create national forest reserves to "keep much of the nation's remaining public lands not suitable for conventional farming from falling into the hands of large corporations." Two important points are contained in this last phrase. One, millions of these acres were arid lands, desert or near-desert, that could not be farmed without the irrigation that only the federal government could eventually bring. And two, the intent was to keep the lands out of the rapacious hands not of individuals, but of corporations.

*   *   *

Noah and I finally reached the Pacific. To celebrate we threw a Frisbee around at Stinson Beach, just north of San Francisco, and then swam. Well, I swam. Noah was too low-key to celebrate in such an ostentatious fashion. It made me happy to have brought him there, though. My quiet millennial nephew. And while he didn't immerse himself in the ocean he did take a dozen or so pictures of it with his phone.

On top of seeing the Pacific, Noah would also, over the next day, mountain bike for the first time, and do a (small, safe, legal, uncle-supervised) dose of edibles in the form of a cookie. He claimed the last affected him least, though he did admit that the next day his cheeks hurt from laughing. If this wasn't the spirit quest I used to tease my sister Heidi, his mother, about, it was something. It seemed appropriately reckless—and Western.

Having visited the ocean, Noah and I had an important stop to make. That stop would echo a trip I took when I was not much older than Noah. My own first trip to Yosemite National Park, in 1987, did not elicit quite the ecstatic response I'd expected, at least not at first. Instead, I felt a sense of deep irritation at the huge crowds, and hustled with the take-a-number mob up the trail to Half Dome, jostling and bodychecking as if fighting onto a New York subway. Pissed off, I took to the hills. Or rather *we* did. My girlfriend and I headed to the backcountry, where we spent a couple of nights away from cars. There I finally found the Yosemite I was looking for. I had one of the best nights of my life, watching the light die while lying down on a large granite slab below a circle of swaying pines. It was a night of being in nature in a way I never had before, feeling the pulse of the granite below and the trees above. At that moment I knew that whatever I did with the rest of my life, nature would be at the core of it. I could feel the earth's respiration that night. I wanted Noah to feel something similar.

That was personal history.

But the Yosemite backcountry had also been the stage for one of the most important environmental meetings in world history. If Gifford Pinchot was the general of the more practical wing in Roosevelt's war for the environment, then President Roosevelt's campmate at Yosemite, during his stop there during the 1903 campaign tour, was the embodiment of the other, more radical wing. That campmate's name was Muir.

It has been called "the camping trip that changed America," and that may not be overstatement. Ditching his Secret Servicemen and the media just as he had at Yellowstone, Roosevelt headed off into the Yosemite backcountry with John Muir. The business of the United States, we are told, is business. No doubt that is usually true. But for a brief three-day window in May 1903 the business of the United States, or at least of the president of the United States, was nature.

The Yosemite Summit

The flames dance, shooting shadows off the canyon walls. Sparks fly over the snow. It is more bonfire than campfire, but there is no fear of it spreading. Not with so much snow on the ground. They have been trudging through that snow all day, and the feel of it is still in the air, the clouds gravid with the stuff, ready to come down again. There is an air of expectation, exhilaration even. Already tonight the bearded one has put on a show for the mustached one by setting fire to a dead pine. It went up like a giant piece of kindling. They both took pleasure in the crackling and the flames jumping from dry branch to dry branch, the two of them circling it, delighting in the leaping fire and the snap of pinecones and dead limbs that burst crackling into red and orange. And they both expressed their pagan appreciation in their own characteristic ways. One of them danced a jig; the other yelled "Bully!"

When this night is eventually retold as myth, the two men will be remembered as having been camping "alone." But alone means alone with two rangers, two mules, and a packer with a rhyming name built for a limerick: Jacker. As far as conversation goes, however, the two men might as well be alone. The others know their role. They are the audience.

Now sitting around the fire, the two men talk. And talk. The president, by force of long habit, guides the conversation with polished monologues—his clipped sentences snapping off like the pinecones bursting in the fire—that sound as if they have been revised at his desk. He shoots words like rivets. The prophet is no less a pontificator, and also, through habit, used to having the floor. For both of them listening means waiting your turn to speak. Sometimes they can't wait and so barge right in. "Both men wanted to do the talking," one of the park rangers in attendance will remember. Their words clash against each other like waves around a point.

Physically, they provide a sharp contrast. Roosevelt is the shorter and wider of the two, his face elastic as it follows his fast-moving mind. Muir, long and lean, wears the white beard of prophecy, and though he has deserted the Calvinism of his childhood, an earnestness close to fervor can still take hold of him. His cause, of course, is *nature*. He tells Roosevelt of his glacial theory for the landscape they have been hiking through, a theory that will prove fairly sturdy over the years, but he is also not afraid of laying it on thick. Muir wants to save this place, and he wants Roosevelt to want to save it, too.

"It is a holy place," the prophet says. "A church, a cathedral."

The president nods.

It isn't just their sentences that overlap but their languages, and one result of the night is that their future words, when fighting for the natural world, will intertwine ever more tightly as they plunder each other's vocabulary.

On the page both Muir and Roosevelt have their faults as chroniclers of nature, and both tend to break from clear description into rhapsodies, the prophet's of the purple variety, the president's of the bloody. Muir sings ecstatically about the natural world, full-throated paeans, celebratory paganism, but a paganism drenched in the language of religion. God still plays a major role. These sentences have inspired many, and I don't want to belittle them. But I am willing to make a radical statement: for my money the president is a better writer than the prophet. In fact I'll go further: the president is a better *nature writer* than the prophet. At his best this often unrestrained man can write with tight restraint, not unlike a certain macho writer, and fellow hunter, who will come along a generation later.

While the two men echo each other, they don't always overlap or even agree.

Last night, before this storm came in, Roosevelt delighted to the singing of a hermit thrush, but was puzzled by Muir's lack of bird knowledge. "I was interested and a little surprised to find that, unlike John Burroughs, John Muir cared little for birds and bird songs, and knew little about them," he will write in his autobiography.

Muir also has an irritating habit, perhaps to be expected of someone who writes his address as "John Muir, Earth-Planet, Universe," of trying to place small twigs in the buttonholes of the president's jacket. An impatient Roosevelt keeps brushing them away. Hippies won't walk the earth for another six decades, but here is their precursor.

But this hippie has nerve, too.

At one point, leaning in close to the fire, Roosevelt tells the story of a hunt for a grizzly. But Muir casually interrupts him. *Interrupts* the president. Interrupts *this* president.

"When are you going to get beyond the boyishness of killing things?" he asks as if addressing a misbehaving teenager.

For a second Roosevelt's face looks like it does when Muir tries to put those stupid twigs in his lapel, but then it softens.

"Muir, I guess you are right," he says.

Maybe Roosevelt doesn't really believe this, but he is not going to let any bickering spoil this grand night.

Despite the competition for verbal airspace, Muir will later write of TR on this trip that "I fairly fell in love with him." And why not? Taking a break from his day job as president of the United States, Roosevelt has put aside three days in the middle of his grand campaign tour of 1903 to hike and camp with Muir in the writer's beloved Yosemite. Back in March he wrote Muir to personally ask him to be his guide: "I do not want anyone with me but you, and I want to drop politics absolutely for four days and just be out in the open with you."

And so it has been. Two nights ago the president surprised all the grandees of San Francisco by ditching a party thrown in his honor and heading out into the park. Roosevelt later wrote: "The first night was clear, and we lay down in the darkening aisles of the great Sequoia grove. The majestic trunks, beautiful in color and symmetry, rose round us like the pillars of a mightier cathedral than ever was conceived even by the fervor of the Middle Ages." He slept on the ground that night but not in the dirt. One of the rangers, Charlie Leidig, put forty blankets down to create a "shelter bed" for Roosevelt. In his report on the trip Leidig wrote: "The President got just as deep into these as he wanted for warmth and comfort."

This morning they were up at 6:30. Yesterday's hike had the feel of an idyll. Today's did not. The blizzard started early. Roosevelt's one command to Charlie Leidig and the other guides was to "outskirt and keep away from civilization," and that they did. This meant avoiding the Wawona Hotel at all costs, since the president's party and the press were staying there. They hiked the Lightning Trail and crossed the South Fork River, then climbed the Empire Meadows Trail. The snow kept coming down and they took a cold lunch at Empire Meadows. The president never complained, though the snow got deeper and deeper. The official report reads:

> There was lots of snow as they crossed the Sentinel Dome; they took turns breaking trail through deep snow. In the Bridalveil Meadow the party plowed through five feet of snow. The president mired down and Charley had to get a log to get him out. It was snowing hard and the wind was blowing.

Leaving aside the image of the president of the United States "mired down" in snow, presumably like a hippo in a wallow, it is clear that today was something of a workout for a man no longer the athlete he was a decade before. It probably got the heart rate up of the sixty-five-year-old nature writer as well. After they worked their way through the meadow, Muir suggested they camp where they were, but Leidig pushed them on until they got here, protected somewhat by this rock wall beneath Glacier Point.

Now these two men, not exactly young, rather than curse their luck about the blizzard, seem to be having a great time of it. The storm rages and will continue through the night. Tomorrow morning they will wake covered with four more inches of fresh snow, which the president will of course delight in. *Bully* indeed. He will shake the snow off and stare up as the morning light shafts down through a canopy, the "spreading limbs of a grove of silver fir," those limbs now lined with white.

The fire crackles and dances. Despite their exhausting day, the two men talk late into the night. Muir tries not to come on too strong, though *too strong* is his habitual mode. In his extreme position there is an implied critique of the president's relatively moderate one. Not perhaps of Roosevelt himself but of a side of Roosevelt best embodied in the chief of his Forest Service, Gifford Pinchot.

Pinchot will come in direct conflict with Muir soon enough in the most famous environmental battle of the early twentieth century, the fight over the Hetch Hetchy dam in a valley near here that Muir deems every bit as beautiful as Yosemite's own. The Hetch Hetchy fight will set the template for so many of the century's other battles over dams, from Dinosaur National Monument to Glen Canyon, and will serve the purpose, despite the failure to save the valley, of teaching environmentalists how to fight. But the future can't possibly console Muir. Outraged, he will write these lines as he rails against those who would flood the valley for the dam:

> These temple destroyers, devotees of ravaging commercialism, seem to have a perfect contempt for Nature, and, instead of lifting their eyes to the God of the mountains, lift them to the Almighty Dollar.
>
> Dam Hetch Hetchy! As well dam for water-tanks the people's cathedrals and churches, for no holier temple has ever been consecrated by the heart of man.

Pinchot and Muir will line up on opposite sides for this fight, almost as if dueling. Muir famously attacking those temple destroyers. Pinchot sensibly arguing that the water is desperately needed for a city, San Francisco, recently devastated by earthquake and fire. And Roosevelt, writing with a heavy heart to Muir, will admit that this time he has sided with the human beings, or at least the many human beings and not the few who see nature as the temple that Muir assures them it is. This is the cold-blooded pragmatism of the politician. But despite this decision, made with deep regret, and unlike most politicians, Roosevelt will never let go of his idealism. Nowhere is he more idealistic than in his regard for wilderness.

Both of the men sitting by the fire will develop ideas about nature that will anticipate concepts that will grow later in the century. They have both glimpsed a biocentric world, a world beyond man. But they still view nature with chauvinistic overtones. Muir's tone brings a rhapsodic, religious, sometimes ecstatic sense that can leave many of us feeling let down by our own lack of reliably ecstatic responses when we are in nature. Roosevelt's prejudices are ones we have touched on before: that this is the *American* wilderness—bigger and better than other wildernesses—and its size and the fact that it symbolizes his country's inevitable rise in the world make it shine all the more. And don't ever forget that this is *manly* nature, a primal place where we can beat our chests, shed civilization's fetters, and exult.

Both men are trapped within the prejudices of their time, and as the years pass they will be criticized in various ways. John Muir will be called "a eugenicist" due to his association with fellow environmentalists who expounded racial theories about the "fall of the Nordic peoples." Muir's reputation will be tarnished by the fact he didn't want Indigenous people in his pristine Yosemite Valley, and that he opposed allowing the Havasupai to continue residing in the Grand Canyon, which they still do today. While both men drag their baggage with them, as we all do, and while both have mental grids that separate them from the world, they get out into that actual wild world more than most of us, and so sometimes see beyond or through—or without—the grid. When men of money talk of the "real world," these two laugh. *This* is the real world, this place of trees and birds and animal life, not the symbolic status-filled worlds of finance or culture. They both understand that wilderness, despite what we bring to it, is in fact a symbol of absolutely nothing. That it is exactly itself, beyond the halls and minds of humans.

And yet they also know that the way wilderness is perceived by humans has an enormous impact on how humans treat it. And they, with their books and bully pulpits, their speeches and large audiences, their intensity and conviction, their sometimes excessive verbiage, will do more to change and deepen this perception than almost any other two human beings of their time or since.

* * *

Gusts of wind blow snow down the canyon walls, grainy and skittering with a sound like the scurrying footsteps of mice, before breaking away from the wall and billowing outward. Those ghostly clouds join the smoke that moves randomly from one side of the fire to the other, stinging the men's eyes. Roosevelt still wears his jodhpurs and a thick wool sweater, with a bandana tied around his neck. He flaps his Stetson to keep the smoke away. Muir has wrapped himself in a big fur that covers an outfit that seems more fitting for teaching Sunday school than hiking through snow. In John Muir and John Burroughs, both white-bearded and black-suited, the president has collected a matching set of nature prophets, like salt and pepper shakers. Another gust of wind sends the flames sideways. Charlie Leidig throws a large branch on the fire and it crackles. Quickly the flames climb it from below and swallow it. Jacker is already asleep back by the mules. No moon can be seen through the clouds.

The fire itself, the dancing show of colors and jagged heat, the way it invites you to come close, to stare, is engrossing enough to quiet the two men for a moment. But then the quiet moment is over and they are at it again, going on about the need to preserve not just this place but places like it, and after that there is no gap in the talk.

Their conversation will have consequences. Roosevelt will immediately save the heart of Yosemite, and by presidential order stretch the California forests north to Mount Shasta, and create many other parks as well, and this, despite my gripes about all the cars and tourists (like me), is a great achievement. But if I suddenly appeared at the fire, a visitor from the future, I would be the bearer of disturbing news. I would tell them that the world is warming and that the beautiful trees that Muir worships are in my time threatened as never before by beetles, disease, climate, and fire. I would tell him that the human population of earth, which as we sit here at the fire is below 1.6 billion, will more than quadruple, to 7.6 billion, by the year 2018.

And yet, I would explain, despite our crowded, overheated world, we still romanticize the wilderness and the wild. I could choose to explain this thing called television and that the shows performed there often show men and women out in the wilderness, away from society. I might even attempt to lecture them on their own limits, on seeing beyond their time's prejudices, but perhaps not. Because if the president and the prophet are limited, if their times put blinders on them, what they are doing is also visionary. They are fighting back against the rise of the corporation, against the sort of self-interest that continues to rot out the core of our country today and that threatens the hope that we can be more.

They are also, I think, having fun. Their ideas are mingling, and they are laughing, even now as the fire dies. Charlie has set up the great nest of forty blankets for the president. The talk continues but slows. Even these restless beings must eventually rest.

Part of my job these days is to deconstruct TR, and I am well schooled in his limits and prejudices. But despite my efforts to view him at arm's length, and judge him with the necessary skepticism, how can I not be impressed by a president who hikes through a blizzard, loves a good fire, and will wake tomorrow happy that he is covered in snow? I may forfeit my membership card in the Biographers Guild by saying so, but can I help it if I, too, like Muir, am a little bit in love with him?

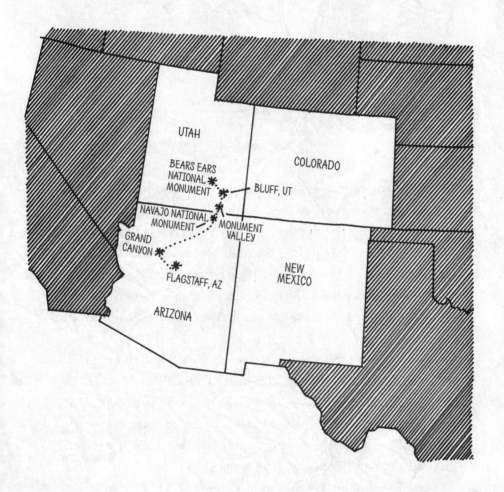

CHAPTER FIVE

Monumental

t was his favorite state so far. The canyons of Yosemite, the beaches, the edibles, the sun. All of these made for a great first visit to California for my nephew. But the trees were the highlight. Nowhere on earth do trees reach so high. In the Muir Woods we stared up and up at the trunks of those great grooved giants. Just to breathe among the redwoods is to understand why Muir himself often felt so exalted. For Easterners like my nephew the notions of size and scale are thrown all out of whack.

In my experience the best way to see the Muir Woods is to start in the morning and spend the day hiking out of the redwoods to the top of Mount Tam and then back down into the woods at twilight. This gives you some sense of the way the first people who found the woods experienced them, moving in and out of their intoxicating presence. Exhausted and mind empty, you can really see and feel the trees. The strip-barked madrones, the redwoods, the firs. Those trees do something to our brains, and I'm not saying that metaphorically. What TR knew by instinct we now know by science.

Noah and I didn't have time for a full-day hike when we visited Muir Woods, which Theodore Roosevelt declared a national monument in 1908. The place was crowded, but we managed to find quiet spots to stare upward through the branches at the light. And to appreciate what a miracle it was for the president to save almost three hundred acres of coastal redwoods just a short drive over the bridge from San Francisco.

Its proximity to an urban center was just one way in which Muir

Woods was an anomaly. Another was the fact that the land had been privately owned, by William Kent, a wealthy conservationist, who fought off public and private attempts to purchase it in the wake of the San Francisco earthquake of 1906. Land is particularly vulnerable in the wake of calamity, when human concerns are usually valued over all others, and the redwoods were coveted as a resource considered vital for rebuilding the ruined city. But Kent vowed not to let this stand of trees go the way almost all the others had gone along the California coast. In Gifford Pinchot, and ultimately Roosevelt, he found allies.

During our visit I made a point of stopping to pay homage at the Pinchot tree. Environmentalists have a complicated relationship with Gifford Pinchot, and, standing in front of the redwood with the plaque out front bearing Pinchot's name, I knew all the reasons to criticize him and all the reasons to praise him. That day I was in a praising mood. Thank you, I thought. There were things you didn't and couldn't understand in your time. But you did understand the importance of preserving these particular giants. And they are still here now.

With Pinchot brokering the deal, William Kent sold his land to the federal government, knowing they would save it. This sort of transaction was the first of its kind. All previous national monuments had been created not from land the government purchased but from land we already owned. This, which remains the norm, is important to remember. There is no *grabbing* of land when we declare national monuments. In most cases, what occurs is a re-designation. In the case of Bears Ears, our most recent national monument, all of the land designated as a national monument was already owned by the federal government and managed by the Bureau of Land Management or the Forest Service. What does change when land is declared a monument is some of the restrictions, usually of the extractive and exploitive variety, but even then the BLM operates in a business-friendly—and particularly cow-friendly— manner. Grazing is still allowed on a great deal of monument land.

Muir Woods, like all other national monuments, was created by presidential decree. If the Forest Service was the right wing of TR's war for the environment, its practical and business-friendly forces led by a practical and business-friendly general named Pinchot, then the other wing, more purely preservationist and inspired by Muir, would be led by Roosevelt himself. Its chief weapon would be a law whose creation many saw as the high tide of early environmental progressivism. It was through the Antiquities Act that Roosevelt found his ultimate expression as a preservationist.

It is a common misconception that Theodore Roosevelt "created" the Antiquities Act. Actually, two of the earliest key players were Representative John Lacey of Iowa and Edgar Hewett, a charismatic, self-trained archaeologist with a gift for twisting congressional arms. In 1902, Hewett brought Lacey west to northern New Mexico to see the remains of the ancient Indigenous civilization he had heard so much about. Lacey fell in love with the sites he visited. He stared up at the thousand-year-old homes of what we now call the Ancestral Puebloans, beautiful stone villages tucked into the walls of sheer red cliffs. He was shown artifacts, bowls, chalices, and knives, and art painted on the walls, all of it preserved in the dry desert. After that trip Hewett took up the cause of protection full-time. Over the next few years several bills meant to protect Native American antiquities came close to passing, but none could get by Western legislators who were fearful of regulations and restrictions. Hewett crafted the one that would finally slip past, creating a carefully worded bill built to not offend.

The timing was good. The progressive attitude of the era was peaking. No one embodied that spirit more than the young and increasingly progressive president, but he wasn't the only one caught up in the dream of changing, and possibly saving, the world. Still, it is a mystery how the bill passed. Lacey is said to have shepherded it through Congress, though there is not much recorded about how he did that. We know Lacy managed to convince Colorado senator Thomas Patterson to sponsor the bill in the Senate. But how? Didn't Patterson see the danger in what he was sponsoring? Western legislators were still stinging from the Forest Reserve Act that passed fifteen years earlier, which they believed had taken millions of acres of land out of their hands. Lacey and Hewett did everything they could to assure them that this new bill, drafted in late December 1905 and now called "An Act for Preservation of American Antiquities" was different. It was not a federal land grab, but rather an effort to protect those ancient Native American sites that scientists had been pleading with them to protect. It was right there in the language, wasn't it? The act was made to preserve "historic landmarks, historic and prehistoric structures," and those sites were to be "confined to the smallest area compatible with proper care and management of the objects to be protected." To congressmen that must have sounded like saving ancient ruins, not the land around them.

Which was exactly Hewett's intent. He had seen enough of these bills fail. It has been suggested that the bill's first section was written to be particularly innocuous, with its focus on dissuading future plunderers by punishing "any person who shall appropriate, excavate, injure or destroy any historic or prehistoric ruin or monument, or any object of antiquity." Who could argue with that? Most Western congressmen were likely already bored and nodding by the time they got to Section 2, though you would think its first sentence would have gotten their attention: "That the President of the United States is hereby authorized, in his discretion, to declare by public proclamation historic landmarks, historic and prehistoric structures, and other objects of historic or scientific interest." The word "President" and "discretion" in the same sentence? And this president *proclaiming*? If there ever were red flags for Western politicians, here they were. And yet miraculously, the bill passed, and "An Act for Preservation of American Antiquities" landed on Theodore Roosevelt's desk on June 8, 1906. If the congressmen missed the bill's subtleties, the president did not. He knew what he had there. It was with haste and no little pleasure that he signed it into law.

If it is a myth that Theodore Roosevelt created the Antiquities Act, he sure knew what to do with it once it was handed to him. He started small, respecting the act's literal wording of preserving "objects of historic or scientific interest" that should be "confined to the smallest area

compatible with proper care and management of the objects to be protected." But this is TR we are talking about; his ambition could never stay
small for long. The bill passed in June 1906, and by September he had
declared his first monument, Devils Tower (1,194 acres) in Wyoming.
Three months later, he preserved two more monuments, El Morro (160
acres) in New Mexico and Montezuma Castle (161 acres) in Arizona.
He started picking up steam with Arizona's Petrified Forest, a new favorite spot of John Muir's, which came in at 60,776 acres. That was it for
1906. He started up again in March 1907 with Chaco Canyon (10,643
acres) and then added California's Cinder Cone (5,120 acres) and Lassen Peak (1,280) in May. In November of that same year, he declared
as monuments the Gila Cliff Dwellings in New Mexico (160 acres) and
Tonto in Arizona (640 acres), and he rang in the new year with the Muir
Woods in California (295 acres).

It was a pace that wouldn't slacken right up to his last day as president.

*　　*　　*

During my initial scouting mission west in January, when I visited Bears
Ears and interviewed activists like Regina Lopez-Whiteskunk, I also
made a side trip to the Grand Canyon. I figured I had better not waste
any time getting to the place where Roosevelt had made his "Leave It As
It Is" speech.

My route led me through Monument Valley in the corner of southeast Utah and northeast Arizona. As I drove, I considered the usual
Western paradox: a unique and stunning landscape that is also a vast
and beautiful Superfund. I could see the mesas and buttes that John
Ford used in his films; I could also see the tailings of the failed uranium
mines below the sandstone walls. The route I took was the same one that
trucks use to transport uranium to the White Mesa Mill north of Bluff,
Utah, the only working mill of its kind in the United States. It never pays
to forget that what for some is a hiker's paradise and for others a vast
reservoir of cultural and religious significance, remains for others, first
and foremost, a resource colony.

After Monument Valley I passed few other cars. Fifty miles later I pulled over near Black Mesa, Arizona, home of both a notorious coal mine and the Navajo National Monument, the first monument declared by someone other than Theodore Roosevelt. William Howard Taft, TR's successor, wasted no time creating this, his first monument, in March 1909, at the end of the same month that TR, on his way out, designated Mount Olympus in Washington state as a national monument. You could argue that Taft's first declaration was a more perfectly apt use of the Antiquities Act than Roosevelt's last. While Roosevelt preserved more than 295,000 acres of coastal forest, Taft chose as his first monument the relatively tight 360 acres that surround some of the most stunning ancient dwellings in the Southwest.

In fact "perfectly apt" might describe the way that Keet Seel, the ancient village I was soon staring down at, fit into the rounded canyon above it. Keet means "broke pottery scattered around" in Navajo, and the whole village, which might have at one time, a thousand or so years ago, been home to 150 people, has the look of a work of art. My former professor and friend Reg Saner, who spent decades exploring the ruins of the Four Corners, described Keet Seel as "the best preserved *large* Anasazi site in all our Southwest," a place that looks like "human existence condensed to a village." Here the orange-red of sandstone walls and rooms, dilapidated but still clearly recognizable in their function, seem the very definition of antiquity. These are the homes of the Ancestral Puebloans, an ancient people that until recently were called the Anasazi, who inhabited this corner of the world from roughly 200 BC to AD 1500.

It is a place where the past is present, but where you also experience, in Saner's words, "how many seasons lay between" then and now. On that cold winter morning with ice on the ground I had the place to myself. While Yellowstone might have four million visitors a year, national monuments as a rule are less of a draw, the previous year's total here amounting to sixty-five thousand or so visitors. Still a lot of human beings, but, as I say, it remains possible to find yourself alone.

Reluctantly, I hiked back to my car. I wanted to get to the Grand Canyon before dark, and did so, barely. January is the canyon's slow season, and when I called ahead the day before I had no problem renting one of the Bright Angel cabins right on the canyon's rim. When I got there, I threw my backpack on the bed and cracked a beer. It was already growing dark and it would have been idiotic to hike down into the canyon in the dying light, but before I knew it that is just what I was doing. With my beer now disguised in a Styrofoam coffee cup, I paid a quick homage by toasting the cabin next door, that of Roosevelt's friend and fellow Rough Rider Bucky O'Neill, and then headed down the Bright Angel Trail.

This was sacrilege of course: to tramp down the trail as the very last real hikers were emerging while carrying just a black leather-bound journal and a cup of beer, and no food or water. As I approached one earnest couple, decked out in the full regalia of their hiker's tribe, they gave me a disdainful look, irritated by my casual sauntering. You could tell that they wanted to lecture me, to say something like *Can't you see it's getting dark, you idiot? You don't head* down *the canyon with night falling.*

I decided to provoke them further.

"The river's pretty close, right?" I asked.

That did it. They could tell I was a fool right off, and now they knew it for sure. A cautionary lecture burst out of them—they couldn't stop themselves—an overlapping duet of worry: *No one should be on the trail at night and the river is eight miles away and how dare I . . .*

"Thanks," I said cheerily, holding my cup up and saluting them, before continuing down the trail.

The truth is the path was easy enough to follow, even in the gloaming, and I hiked down for a half mile, until I reached a rocky outcropping. This was the same trail that Teddy famously rode down on a mule in 1913. With everyone else soon cleared off the path, I had the place to myself and sat on a rock while watching the last light play on the far canyon wall, its striated and radiant streaks of green, yellow, and orange in sharp contrast to the dark foregrounding hills.

I sat for a while and then climbed back out of the canyon, managing not to fall over the edge and therefore give satisfaction to the pious hikers. My cabin was not fifty feet from the rim, and I slept with the windows open. I woke up at two in the morning and walked outside to take a leak. Stars crammed the sky and great gusts blew up canyon, one after another, like waves, from the east.

* * *

As with everything else about it, the role of the Grand Canyon in the evolution of the Antiquities Act was oversized. Though it wasn't the first monument declared, its declaration, on January 11, 1908, was perhaps the most consequential.

Members of Congress felt blindsided by TR's monument blitz in 1906 and 1907, but Roosevelt was just warming up. If they were frustrated with him, he was furious with them. Furious because of their refusal—their stubborn and idiotic and shortsighted refusal in his eyes—to make the Grand Canyon into a national park. The Grand Canyon! The most monumental and *American* of places, a virtual symbol of our burgeoning greatness and bigness, a place that Europeans envied and that made their cathedrals look puny, and where the true study of geology was practically born, a place where you could see back through eons—*could see time itself.* And these philistines were not protecting it! Meanwhile commercialism was running rampant in the very place that TR had declared should be left as it was. The biggest culprit of all was Ralph Henry Cameron, the Arizona prospector, hotel owner, and, later, senator, who for years had extorted money from canyon visitors by, among other things, setting up a gate at the top of Bright Angel Trail where each visitor had to pay a dollar (while also making them pay to use outhouses along the trail!). In many ways the canyon was starting to look to Roosevelt like another Niagara Falls. In fact, part of the original motivation of creating the national parks was to avoid another tacky tourist disaster like Niagara. How could Congress not see this?

Fed up, Roosevelt did what he always did when frustrated. He acted.

Even for those of us who admire what happened next, it would be hard to argue that the Grand Canyon National Monument, which came in at a whopping 808,120 acres, was "confined to the smallest area compatible with proper care and management of the objects to be protected." The din of protest was loud in Congress, but no one was louder than Ralph Henry Cameron back in Arizona. A bully himself, he refused to be bullied by Teddy. He went after Roosevelt and the Antiquities Act in court, one of several times the act has been challenged. He kept his challenges up even after the Grand Canyon was declared a national park in 1919, and in 1920 his case was heard by the Supreme Court. Their decision, upholding the declaration of the Grand Canyon in *Cameron v. United States*, set the precedent, assuring this and future presidents, in the words of University of Colorado law professor Mark Squillace, "broad discretion to set the size and scope of a monument." The law was not seriously threatened again until 1943, when the state of Wyoming argued against its use in the Jackson Hole case. Wyoming would lose that case, though its legislators would gain a conciliatory amendment to the Antiquities Act itself: no longer could any national monuments be declared in their state.

Another precedent set in the Grand Canyon was the beginning of a pattern of establishing a place as a national monument to save it from immediate threats and then later have declared as a national park. This would become a kind of standard move through the years, especially during the halcyon days of the fledgling National Park Service in the 1920s. In this way the canyon provided a template used later in many places, from the Olympic Peninsula to the Mojave Desert to Utah's Zion and Bryce.

What happened at the Grand Canyon foretold the fights to follow, with the outrage that accompanied its declaration also becoming part of the greater tradition of the Antiquities Act. This has continued right up to the present. For instance, when Barack Obama declared Bears Ears a national monument in December 2016, the howls were deafening. The howling came not just from Utah but from Congress, specifically from conservative congressmen who felt they had been circumvented, and screwed, again. These were echoes not just of the Grand Canyon fight but of the howls that had been heard when FDR declared the 173,065-acre Jackson Hole National Monument in Wyoming and when Jimmy Carter declared fifteen national monuments totaling fifty-six million acres in Alaska and when Bill Clinton declared the 1,880,461-acre Grand Staircase-Escalante National Monument in Utah. If the howling was familiar, providing the underlying music, the lyrics hadn't changed much either, with the same basic themes of "arrogance," "presidential overreach," and the government's "absentee ownership." Trump later struck the same notes when he "undeclared" 85 percent of Bears Ears, his words sounding familiar to anyone who knew the history of the Antiquities Act: "I've come to Utah to take a very historic action, to reverse *federal overreach* and restore the rights of this land to your citizens." Also familiar were his complaints against "egregious abuse of executive power."

While Congress howls, immediate opposition to the declarations of monuments is often most heated at the local level. At least one president has been hung in effigy at the borders of a proposed monument. But historians of the Antiquities Act have pointed out that this sort of outrage rarely lasts. Brigham Young law professor and environmental law expert James R. Rasband writes: "Presidential monument-making under the Antiquities Act has yielded a familiar pattern. Monument proclamations are met by a firestorm of protest in the affected community but the protest is followed by acquiescence and then acceptance." He continues: "Why is it that monument proclamations have so routinely brought criticism, only to see that criticism fade over time? One part of the answer is clear: a vast majority like the results and thus any squeamishness about the means is rather quickly forgotten."

Which brings us back to the present. Donald Trump is not the first president to attempt to reduce land saved by an earlier president. Woodrow Wilson, pressed by logging and mining interests, essentially halved the controversial Mount Olympus National Monument that Roosevelt had created on his way out of office. But that case, which was not brought to court and therefore offers no precedent, is one of the only times a president significantly interfered with the work of a previous president. The reason for this is obvious. Presidents like having the Antiquities Act in their arsenal. The act is one of the few ways that they can legally circumvent Congress almost entirely.

But in this, as in so many other ways, the Trump presidency is unprecedented. Here, as elsewhere, he seems less motivated by policy than by personal grudges. In reducing Bears Ears so dramatically Trump can please his own rural constituency, not to mention Utah senator Orrin Hatch, but best of all he can undo something Obama did. What could be sweeter?

And so on April 26, 2017, Trump signed Executive Order 13792, which directed the secretary of the interior to review certain national monuments designated or expanded under the Antiquities Act. The idea was that Secretary Zinke would conduct an objective review of the recently expanded monuments, but many felt the fix was in from the start. Part of the reason they may have felt this was that when Trump signed the order directing the review he said: "It's time to end these abuses and return the control of the land to the people, the people of Utah." Two weeks later, in mid-May 2017, Zinke launched a five-day "listening tour" of Utah, but many sectors of the population, including the tribes that had helped create the monument proposal, felt unheard.

In "An Open letter to Donald Trump," Utah Dine Bikeyah chairman Willie Grayeyes wrote:

> Let me be honest in terms of what I have seen and heard from Tribes: Secretary Zinke did not meet the requirements laid out in your Executive Order which directed him to meet with state, local, and tribal governments. He did not meet with any tribal presidents or chairmen, nor did he meet with any local tribal officials. Letters of invitation were sent to him from many Utah Navajo Chapter Houses as well as local community groups, inviting him to meet. These letters were ignored. Secretary Zinke

met for just one hour with the Bears Ears Inter-Tribal Coalition in Salt Lake City. . . . The Secretary's words do not match his actions. He chose to meet only with non-tribal leaders and he did not set foot in a single Native community in Utah to learn where our cultural sites are and why they matter to the traditions of our people.

Sure enough the conclusion of the tour was that the monuments needed to be drastically reduced. Despite Zinke's denials, it is now clear that the uranium industry lobbied hard in the reduction of Bears Ears and Grand Staircase-Escalante. Publicly released Interior Department emails also show that the Bears Ears map was redrawn with potential oil and gas reserves in mind, and that a central motivation for the reduction of Grand Staircase-Escalante was the desire to get at coal reserves.

Bears Ears has gotten most of the press when it comes to monument reduction. Less prominent in the news is the other national monument that Trump has attempted to reduce. Declared more than twenty years ago, Grand Staircase-Escalante has evolved well past local outrage, and the surrounding communities have long since not just accepted it but profited from it. "Communities like Kanab bordering the monument have seen increases in population, jobs, personal income, and per capita income that mirror other western counties with national monuments or protected lands," writes the Western author and photographer Stephen Trimble. If there is any outrage left it is on the part not of the locals but of the extractive industries that have been told to keep their hands off. Citizens of Kane County asked to meet with Secretary Zinke during his fact-finding mission, hoping to tell him how their communities had benefited financially from the monument. Just as he had with Native groups, the secretary refused to meet with them.

Grand Staircase-Escalante National Monument contains some of the most remote land left in the contiguous United States. Before the recent attempts at reduction, it spanned 1,880,461 acres, the country's largest monument, dwarfing the 800,000 or so acres that Roosevelt had set aside for the Grand Canyon. This is a place where rock does things you never thought rock could do, from heaped black mountainsides to steep and stunning canyons where waterfalls thunder. It is some of the most amazing and varied scenery in the world, scenery that changed modern geology, and that includes not just the Colorado River, but almost every color, size, and shape of rock in the world, and the last mountain range explored in the Lower 48.

If it is unusual for a president to attempt to alter the monuments of his predecessor, it is more so for a president to go back and attempt to reduce a monument created decades before, one that has seemingly matured into an accepted part of the local community. Why mess with something that has been so successful?

Well, for Trump there is the little matter of the president who originally set aside Grand Staircase-Escalante.

And the fact that that president's last name just happened to be Clinton.

* * *

That night in the Grand Canyon I never did get back to sleep. I kept the cabin windows open and waited for dawn. Eventually, I pulled a couple of my Roosevelt books and my journal out of my backpack. This was still relatively early in my studies of the president, and in my conceiving of a cross-country trip where I would tie Roosevelt to today's environmental fight, and I was having some doubts. Those doubts weren't eased by the environmentalists I had talked to since landing in the West. When I told them about my project, about intertwining the story of the original wielder of the Antiquities Act with the story of Bears Ears National Monument, most were dubious. I saw their point. Why contaminate the purity of the Native monument with the corpse of another dead white guy? There had been this beautiful proposal that grew out of the five tribes, an initiative of Native origin, and now here I was introducing a non-native species. True, the man had been a champion of the act that

they were trying to use to save the land, but wasn't Interior Secretary
Zinke waving Roosevelt's name around like a battle flag?

The tiny town of Bluff, Utah, is at the center of the monument debate,
in part because it is perched on the edge of Bears Ears. On my way to the
Grand Canyon, I had stayed in Bluff, in a trailer behind the home of Zak
and Amanda Podmore. Amanda was the assistant director of Friends of
Cedar Mesa, a local environmental group. Friends of Cedar Mesa was
in fact the only environmental group that Secretary of the Interior Ryan
Zinke deemed fit to meet with on his listening tour, the tour that would
theoretically determine the fate of Bears Ears National Monument. One
morning, over coffee in her living room, Amanda told me the story of
that meeting.

It was a good reminder that, like most parts of the Trump presidency,
there had been not just a racist but also a sexist component to the Bears
Ears reduction.

"The day before I met Zinke I was hiking in Bears Ears with some of
our supporters," she began. "One of them, an older gentleman, told me,
'You know what, you're the most important person in the room tomorrow when you meet him. Because you're the only person in the room
who is not an old, white male.' And that gave me the sort of courage I
needed to face Zinke.

"Sure enough, when we got in the room, he looked at me like *What
are you doing here, small young woman?*

"Still," she continued, "I was hopeful that we would have a truly
adult-to-adult professional engagement. We came prepared with hundreds of pages of the archaeological records and documents from the
public review. We had such a naïve eagerness as we sat down, but Zinke
immediately deflated us. He just sat back in his chair and interrupted
the folks who were introducing us and leaned back in a power pose
with his hands behind his head and said 'Let me tell you how this is
going to be.' He launched into this whole spiel about how he was re-
organizing the Department of the Interior. It was a pure power play,

wasting our time about an unrelated topic for fifteen minutes. So by the time we had a chance to discuss the stewardship work we do in Bears Ears, the archaeological sites we know would be threatened by any action to reduce the boundaries of the monument, we were kind of at a loss for words."

The group from Friends of Cedar Mesa tried to make their argument, but Zinke had effectively taken the steam out of the room. He barely listened. They explained that only about 6 percent of the land in San Juan County had undergone a true class 3 archaeological survey, and that 6 percent had yielded more than thirty-two thousand cultural sites. So, extrapolating, they conservatively estimated that Bears Ears, which is one of the densest cultural areas not just in the county or state but in the world, had one hundred thousand sites.

"We really think it is likely to have two hundred and fifty thousand sites, but we were being conservative," Amanda said. "When we started to tell him this, he interrupted us and said 'No, no, no, no. I'm a *facts* guy. I only go with the facts, I don't go with estimates.'"

This was supremely insulting to a group of people who had dedicated their lives to learning about and protecting those sites.

"I tried to speak up and tell him about the work we had already done to protect the sites, but he was dismissive. It showed he had already made up his mind about Bears Ears. We weren't surprised, but it was still disheartening to hear."

Since Zinke's early environmental track record as a congressman in Montana had not been all bad, Amanda wondered whether he had secret environmentalist leanings. Was he simply drinking the Trump Kool-Aid? Afterward, she concluded: "He is not just drinking the Kool-Aid. He is mixing, making, and stirring it."

Before we finished our coffee, Amanda told me that, on the way home from their meeting, still fuming, she created a cocktail she called the Zinke Screwdriver:

"A lot of vodka mixed with swagger and bravado poured over crushed dreams with a splash of douchebag and a twist of bullshit."

Zinke, intent on reducing wilderness, loved to claim Theodore Roosevelt as his own. An acquaintance of mine, a Sierra Club organizer, had led Zinke on a hike with some army vets in the Organ Mountains–Desert Peaks National Monument down in Las Cruces, New Mexico. He told me something that others had told me before: that Zinke frequently, almost obsessively, referred to Theodore Roosevelt. He did so often during the hike. "If you like Teddy Roosevelt, you're going to love me," he said more than once to the vets. And: "I'm a Roosevelt Republican."

Particularly appalling for me was the way Zinke loved to claim TR as a sort of spiritual godfather. On a primitive level my thought process went something like this: Wait a second, how can he be *yours* when he is *mine*?

This is not unusual. Over the last century or so Roosevelt's own multifaceted personality has sometimes worked against him, allowing him to be twisted into different shapes by those who hold him up. "In the long run, TR belonged to everyone and his legacy proved to be an elastic one," writes the biographer Kathleen Dalton. But what both conservatives who claim him as their own and young liberals who want to take Roosevelt down forget is what Dalton, in her own reconsideration of TR, calls "the leftward years," a lifelong movement that culminated in his last decade. It was here that Roosevelt demonstrated an ability to grow, and his evolution on issues from race to women's rights pointed the way to a future that would not be reached until many decades after his death.

A key moment, according to Dalton, occurred during Roosevelt's tenure as a New York City police commissioner after he returned east from the Badlands. Something happened there, something that in its way would have as lasting an effect on him as his time in the West. Prowling New York, he was discovering a world starkly different than the privileged one he grew up in. His companion was Jacob Riis, whose famous book's title, *How the Other Half Lives*, succinctly describes what Roosevelt was learning. Kathleen Dalton writes:

Riis could guide Roosevelt to opium dens, abandoned children who lived under wharves, Mulberry Bend, which "reeked with incest and murder," commercialized vice of all kinds in the Tenderloin, stripteases in concert halls and "mixed race resorts," painted male prostitutes at American Mabille, and legions of ill-fed families whose dream of opportunity in a new land had proven to be a mirage. The reporter helped the commissioner see what cruel environments the poor inhabited and how the wealthy profited from high rents that overcrowded tenements brought. With Riis as his right-hand man, Roosevelt learned the names and faces of the immigrant families who sewed shirts at home or peddled rags or fruit on the street.

Roosevelt didn't just look. He learned. Learning would lead not just to battling the trusts and corporations, but to legislation that protected the poor, legislation that by the end of his career anticipated and rivaled the social safety net that his famous cousin would put in place after the Depression.

Teddy Roosevelt not only rode the progressive tide, he practically created it. On all the issues that contemporary Republicans despise, this Republican led the way. He became more vehement in his efforts to tame the power of corporations, to provide support for the poor, and to equalize wealth. He broke the ground for many of the programs Franklin Roosevelt enacted during the New Deal. Compassion for those less fortunate than he was became a guiding force. "People came first, property second," Dalton writes of this "traitor to his class." Meanwhile he was castigated for inviting a black man, Booker T. Washington, to the White House, and his views on race continued to grow and expand. Dalton cites an editorial written by the NAACP when Roosevelt died: "That he was our friend proves the justice of our cause. . . . Even in the hot bitterness over the Brownsville affair we knew he believed he was right, and he of all men had to act in accordance with his beliefs."

At the end of her book Dalton suggests that maybe we are looking at the wrong story when we marvel at how Roosevelt "re-made" himself. It wasn't about pumping iron or roping steers. "Perhaps his long struggle to gain a stronger body had helped him in his longer and more heroic struggle to see beyond the bigotry of his own time." We should all be so open-minded, and so determined. Tearing off the blinders of your time is no easy task.

That is what both his detractors and false idolaters manage to ignore and what the Donald Trumps and the Ryan Zinkes of the world don't understand: Teddy was always capable of empathy.

Which brings us back to Donald J. Trump and the wilderness. Roosevelt had little tolerance for bullies and clearly he was not afraid to fight when it came to righting what he perceived as wrongs. In fact, during that sleepless night on the edge of the Grand Canyon, a fantasy began to grow in my head.

Leave it as it is!

I imagined our twenty-sixth president saying those words, sharply and emphatically and confidently, to our forty-fifth. I wanted to see the fight that would ensue if 45 tried to take away the land that 26 had saved.

Though taller and certainly heavier than TR, Mr. Trump would have his hands full with a president who boxed and studied jujitsu while in the White House. But if witnessing a physical confrontation might be fun, a mental and verbal battle would be even better. The great thinker and speaker, the author of all those books, whose mind ranges throughout history and whose photographic memory can conjure up full pages of the books he reads, debating the non-reader, the non-speaker, the non-thinker. The match would be competitive only in terms of raw belligerence and self-confidence, but unequal in all other ways. Particularly since TR was most eloquent when spurred to outrage and since nothing drove him to outrage like the rising tide of commercialism and crassness that was flooding the America he loved. He hated nothing more than "the wealthy criminal class" and "predatory wealth."

Leave it as it is. *Get your hands off.*

No matter your or my issues with Roosevelt's personality or politics, it is hard to deny that what we need is something close to the combination that TR embodied. We need thoughtful, well-read, articulate human beings, of all classes, ages, genders, and races, who care enough about other human beings to throw themselves out into the world and do battle with the waves of ignorance created by those who live without empathy.

Yes, I'd like to see that fight.

*   *   *

After a long almost-sleepless night I was up at dawn and watched as the colors of the canyon emerged like a great bruise. I hiked along the rim as the sun rose, and then went in search of the Canyon Mine. I knew the mine was close. And I knew it was run by a Canadian company creatively named Energy Fuels. This was the same company that rode shotgun with Secretary Zinke while he toured Bears Ears, deciding its fate, and the same company that had whispered in Zinke's ear that it was best to leave three hundred uranium mining claims outside of the newly configured and vastly reduced map of the monument.

If you were with your family driving north to vacation in the Grand Canyon, you would never notice that this uranium mine was here, just fifteen miles south of the canyon. That's because it's hidden down miles of dirt roads in the Kaibab National Forest. I wouldn't have been able to find it myself if a friend who works for the Grand Canyon Trust hadn't told me how to get here.

"Just follow the power lines," he said. Which, metaphorically at least, is all you ever really have to do.

I followed the lines in my rental car along the increasingly bumpy and muddy road. The forest of ponderosa pines and Doug firs was beautiful, and if I hadn't known where it was leading I would have been entranced. At one point a blur of blue pinyon jays flew in front of my windshield, and I got out of the car to watch a couple dozen of the birds work their way through the trees. But the closer I got to the mine, the more nervous I became. I didn't pass a single car or see another human being until the trees parted and a fenced-in area opened up before me. Barbed wire circled the industrial site, with razor wire up top. This was a less pretty part of Gifford Pinchot's, and therefore Roosevelt's, legacy: national forests were to be preserved, yes, but also to be *used*. That is mined, logged, and now also fracked.

For a high-tech operation the Canyon Mine looked surprisingly anachronistic: the head rig was made up of a rickety-looking thing that a high-dive stuntman might leap off at an old-time carnival, and the waterwheel below looked like an equally rickety Ferris wheel. Retention ponds sat uncovered, providing poisoned drinking water for bats and birds and whatever other animals could crawl below or climb or fly over the fences. The U.S. Geological Survey reported back in 2010 that fifteen springs and five wells were contaminated by uranium in the Grand Canyon Region, and members of the Havasupai tribe, who live inside the canyon, worry that Havasu Creek, its one source of drinking water, will be contaminated.

"It's not about energy," Secretary of the Interior Ryan Zinke said repeatedly when he defended the re-drawing of the maps of Bears Ears.

But anyone who lives in what Bernard DeVoto called "the plundered province" of the West knows that to be a lie. Dig deep enough into any of these conflicts and you will be reminded of a single truth: it's almost *always* about energy.

A cynic might say that, even in this new age of Trump, there is nothing new under the Western sun. In fact, it was DeVoto himself who, writing in the 1940s and '50s, created the template for explaining resource exploitation in the West. DeVoto understood that in the West the past is forever repeating itself, often in rapid cycles of boom and bust. Truly settling places has always been a challenge in an arid, disaster-prone country, and the interests of those who wish to settle have always been in conflict "with those who were liquidating the West's resources." DeVoto continues, "Mining is a type-example of Western exploitation," and "Mining is liquidation." This exploitation often occurs on public lands, which can be leased for cheap, and what the leasing companies take advantage of is a kind of socialism in the cowboy clothes of rugged individualism, just like their ranching brethren. At the very moment I was exploring the Canyon Mine, oil, gas, and uranium were playing crucial parts in the re-drawing of the Bears Ears maps, while coal and copper were doing the same in the reduction of Grand Staircase-Escalante. "A few groups of Western interests, so small numerically as to constitute a minute fraction of the West, are hell-bent on destroying the West," wrote DeVoto.

Whatever your feelings about conservation, the practical result of saving land is never an irreversible one. You can always change your mind later and develop it. The resources remain unexhausted. Uranium mining, on the other hand, is hard to back out of. Once the decision has been made to proceed, the results, from a human perspective, are all but final. The land may heal eventually, but when we are talking about an element with a half-life of billions of years, it will not be in any lifetime we can imagine.

Right now mining corporations, eager to take advantage of Trump's attempts to withdraw regulations, are greedily looking at all of the "empty" land of Bears Ears and Grand Staircase as well as the national forest land surrounding the Grand Canyon. These are some of the same companies that have done little to take care of their old messes: hundreds of mines still have not been cleaned up in the Four Corners and many of those Superfund sites are on Native American land.

Staring through the fence at Canyon Mine, a sudden sense of paranoia came over me. It was a similar feeling to the one I had while reporting down in the Gulf of Mexico during the BP oil spill: the one that told me I was clearly in the enemy camp. The extractive industries rely on outposts like this, all over the country, to literally fuel their businesses, and often enough these camps are built on land that belongs to all of us. I climbed back in the car and flew out over those mud roads, almost taking off my rental car muffler on one bump.

From the mine I drove south and east toward Flagstaff and the Grand Canyon Trust, an environmental organization that fights for land in the Four Corners. There Roger Clark, the program director, filled me in on the history of the Canyon Mine. He also suggested that I attend a meeting in downtown Flagstaff later that night about uranium and the Grand Canyon. I didn't want to go, I wanted to get back to Bluff and Bears Ears, but I agreed.

At first I regretted my decision. Meetings are where ideas go to die. And this one was no different: people droned on. The council quarters were modern and sleek and the auditorium was comfortable, and I considered a nap. But then, fairly quickly, the council politely decided to skip ahead to item 12B, a discussion of the city's decision to reaffirm a 2010 edict by President Obama's interior secretary Ken Salazar to remove one million acres of land surrounding the Grand Canyon from uranium mining. I say "politely" because members of the Havasupai tribe, who live in the Grand Canyon, had traveled the 120 miles by car to attend this meeting, and many would be driving back after it was over. That tribe was the one most affected when uranium from the Canyon Mine seeped into the groundwater. Three months before, in October 2017, the Trump administration, through the Forest Service, had attempted to lift the ban on uranium mining. Tonight was about the city reaffirming the need for the ban.

When the resolution opened for public comment, the first speaker at the podium was Ethan Aumack, executive director of the Grand Canyon Trust. He succinctly made the economic case against reopening uranium mining. It was not a difficult argument to make. It was basic economics. He explained that Flagstaff's economy, like most economies in the West, was no longer driven by mining or other extractive businesses but by quality of life, and that people traveled here to hike, raft, fish, and hunt. In fact, the state's $21 billion outdoor recreation industry contributes roughly fifteen times more to the economy than mining, and five hundred times more than uranium mining. Next up was a representative for an Arizona congressman, followed by the Sierra Club's Alison Gitlin, who reported that even with the ban in place, wind and water continue to spread uranium and other trace elements, contaminating the soil. Groundwater is the great unknown. In one experiment dye injected into the groundwater traveled six thousand vertical feet and twenty-six miles in just a month.

I took notes assiduously, the good reporter. But, tired from my travels, I was still not really awake.

It was the next speaker who woke me fully. Over the previous week, having met with environmental and tribal leaders, I had had my doubts about wielding a big stick named Teddy Roosevelt in this new sort of fight. Was it really possible to unite Roosevelt's pugnacious spirit with that of the Native peoples who were driving this effort to preserve? Or was I forcing the issue?

Richard Watahomigie, a councilman for the Havasupai tribe, was not walking up to the podium to provide me with an answer to my question, but as it turned out he might as well have been.

Richard is a husky man. He wore a gray jacket, a camouflage baseball cap, and black fingerless gloves. In a quiet, deep voice he thanked the council and voiced his support for the resolution.

"I just want to say that this is a very important issue not just for the Havasupai tribe but the canyon itself," he said. "What happens upstream ends up downstream. I would like to have seen representatives from the Navajo nation and Hopi nation and Paiute nation here. And people living on the Colorado River, too. I would like for all of us to come together and voice our concerns and bring it in one voice to the president."

He spoke passionately, and I sat up a little higher in my chair and paid closer attention. But I was not ready for what came next. What came next I couldn't have scripted. The words, spoken by an Indigenous man who lived inside the canyon, seemed to reach across a gap of time and culture.

"Let me remind you," he told the crowd. "On May 6, 1903, President Theodore Roosevelt stood on the rim of the Grand Canyon and delivered one of his famous speeches. He said: 'Leave it as it is. You cannot improve on it. The ages have been at work on it and man can only mar it.'"

Leave it as it is.

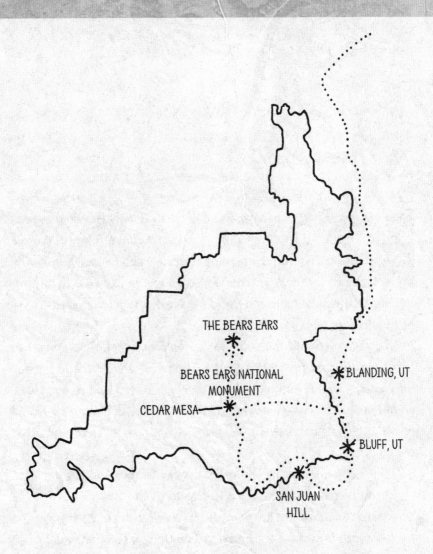

THE BEARS EARS

BEARS EARS NATIONAL
MONUMENT

CEDAR MESA

BLANDING, UT

BLUFF, UT

SAN JUAN
HILL

CHAPTER SIX

Confluence

N oah's part of the road trip was coming to an end. He had now seen California: the ocean, Muir Woods, Yosemite. From California we drove east through Nevada and Utah, and headed to Boulder, Colorado, where I had lived for seven years when I was in my thirties. We recuperated there and then I put Noah on a plane in Denver and he flew back to North Carolina.

He was quiet until the end. There would be no glowing spasms of appreciation from my stoic nephew. Though we had sat side by side for weeks, I was never quite sure what Noah truly made of our cross-country trip. But in the letter he wrote me after he got home, he would prove that what he was seeing had made an impression. He would write:

> The West means crazy animals, dry landscapes and sage. It's a completely different place to live from the East. The West doesn't seem to like to give you ice in your water unless you ask for it. It means you can go to a random gas station and get a lamp that looks like something that would be in a museum in the East. The West is a crazy spurt of insane landscapes such as badlands, arches, and the Rockies. The West has landscapes, animals and people that you could never find in the East. I suppose there are people from every place on earth who would refuse to leave their home, but the West seems to have an allure that is almost magnetic, and I could not imagine someone leaving the West and never looking back.

I was on my own now. I rested for a while longer in Boulder before again pointing my car west. Noah's goal had been to reach the Pacific Ocean. My goal was different. It was time for me to home in on the landscape at the center of the current debates over Western land. Time for me to return to Bears Ears.

* * *

Ever since our meeting back in January, I had been thinking about the words of Regina Lopez-Whiteskunk. In creating Bears Ears, Regina and the rest of the Inter-Tribal Coalition had taken the government's tools and used them in a new way. The density of the ancient sites and artifacts meant that in many ways Bears Ears was a return of the Antiquities Act to its original purpose, the preservation of "historic landmarks, historic and prehistoric structures, and other objects of historic or scientific interest."

But something else was going on, too, something terrifically exciting that hadn't made the headlines. When I listened to Regina describe her coalition's use of one of the country's first environmental laws, I began to see that what had evolved was not just inspiring but *new*. For the first time here was a confluence of the Indigenous ideals of respect and worship for the land, of the land's holiness, with the better motives behind America's "best idea," the ideals that guided the creation of our national parks and monuments.

The coalition didn't put it quite that way, but they worked closely with environmental groups, and it was clear their effort was about pulling people together, not tearing them apart. Once the proposal was hammered out it was time to turn outward. This meant moving beyond the coalition and toward the outer world. Regina found herself thrust into a very public role.

"When I was eighteen my parents gave me a birthday cake and a ride to the county courthouse to vote," she said to me in January. "So I guess I have always felt a pull to civic duty. But I didn't expect what happened next.

"We knew we were speaking for Native Americans but what we didn't anticipate was becoming leaders for the people of Utah beyond the tribes. And then even for people beyond Utah. We suddenly had all these people, and environmental groups, saying we support what you're saying, it's valuable, and asking what can we do. 'Well,' we said, 'you can let us lead the charge, respect our sovereign voices, and know that we as elected leaders can get into doors you can't get into.'"

The next thing Regina knew she was in Washington, D.C. Testifying in front of Congress. Lobbying President Obama to declare Bears Ears as a national monument before he left office. There were times she had to step back and smile at the whole thing. There was something surreal about walking around Washington from meeting to meeting.

"It was such an empowering feeling to know that I myself, as a Native American, could be in Washington, D.C., and feel the movements of my government and participate, and feel like I wasn't threatened or being belittled, or have someone else speaking 'in my best interests.' I was being taken seriously and being part of the conversation and lending my Indigenous knowledge and expertise. That was a very empowering experience for me.

"I learned to be very comfortable in D.C. I could be in a congressman's office and someone in the president's office would call and say 'Can you be here at such and such a time' and I'd say 'Give me forty-five minutes and I'll be there.' I really felt a part of this country. A part of the democratic process."

She paused as if still marveling at what had happened.

"I didn't know I would become such an important person," she said, laughing.

She reached into her desk, searching for something.

"I still have my name cards from the White House. I remember President Obama used to give away little packages of chocolate kisses that said 'The White House' on them. The chocolates are probably crumbling now, but how great is that?"

"It's really great," I said.

When Obama proclaimed Bears Ears a national monument there was a sense of joy among the tribes. A sense of accomplishment and

celebration, and, yes, of healing. Against all odds, the imagined confluence had occurred.

Her smile disappeared.

"Would I go into Washington, D.C., today and feel that way? No. I
don't think so. They are trying to take away everything we built. All that
work, all that healing. And now this."

And now this.

Nothing more needed to be said.

After I said goodbye to Regina, I took a walk through the Ute museum. One exhibit, about treaties between the U.S. government and the
Utes, seemed particularly relevant. It showed photos of talks in Washington between Ute chiefs and the so-called Great White Father, and,
next to these, a fairly startling display of the not-so-gradual reduction of
the Ute land. It was not that the idea of this reduction was news to me,
the screwing over of the Utes and other tribes being common knowledge, but that the presentation, in the form of a series of maps, brought
this concept vividly to life. The display explained that starting in 1849
the Ute leaders traveled to Washington, D.C., by "horseback, stage-
coach, and train," to negotiate treaties with the government. That was
the tradition that Regina had followed. And like her, her forefathers had
adapted to the white man's ways to gain their ends. Their strategy was
smart: they hired lawyers. Or, as Chief Ignacio of the Weeminuche band
put it, "Since we couldn't fight with guns and knives . . . the best thing to
do was to employ men that could fight with their mouths."

But if the approach was sophisticated, the results were the usual
ones. In the museum, four panels illustrate those results. The first of
these panels shows the boundaries of the original treaty, in 1849, and
the yellow blob representing Ute territory covers half of Utah and most
of Colorado, including Denver. By the second panel, the Ute treaty of
1868, the blob has become an upright rectangle covering most of southwest Colorado with only a small splotch left in northeast Utah. Only five
years later a substantial cut has been taken out of the southern section of
the rectangle, leaving a Pac-Man-shaped mouth down by Durango. By

1880 the Utah blob has grown slightly, but the Colorado land has been squashed down into a tiny sliver in the southernmost part of the state.

It is a narrative of rapid and dramatic diminishment. And now here we were again, a century and a half later, back in the same narrative, the government having made another promise about land, a promise it was not going to keep. For a while, there had been a sense of hope, of healing, of the possibility that the people in D.C. would keep their word. Now it looked like that promise, like so many earlier ones, would not be kept.

Just another broken treaty.

*   *   *

After my rest in Colorado, I drove west through the state into Utah and then south to the town of Bluff, the small, southeastern Utah town that was the jumping off point for Bears Ears. If you want to see antiquities of the sort the Antiquities Act was created to protect, you could do worse than traveling to Bluff. Entering town, you will be greeted by this sign:

Est. 650 A.D.
Bluff.

Some of the residents of Bluff, a sleepy town for most of the year, with a population of 258, are ambivalent about their new designation as the "gateway to Bears Ears," but there are few indications that the town is going the over-commercialized way of its northern neighbor, the adventure mecca Moab. Bluff looked pretty much like the place I had gotten to know back during my earlier visits: dry, dusty, quiet. The rise and fall and potential rise again of Bears Ears did not seem to have affected it much, though there was a new hotel being built as you were entering town that would have to be watched like a precancerous mole.

When I visited back in January, I had slept in a trailer behind the house of Amanda and Zak Podmore, the two young environmentalists I had befriended. This time my lodgings were more luxurious: while in Bluff I would be living at a friend of a friend's house that sat below two towering rocks and stared straight into Calf Canyon. The first night I slept out on a lawn chair on the deck as the moon and clouds played a shadow game off the canyon walls.

The next day was, like every day here during the half year that in most places we would call summer, very, very hot. Climate, more than anything or anyone else, more than Teddy Roosevelt or even progressivism, is what allowed for the creation of the thing we call the Antiquities Act. Because without this climate there would be no antiquities. My wife liked to say of our adopted home in southeastern North Carolina that it was "like living inside someone's mouth." The Southwest, in contrast, was like living in a kiln. The kiln bakes this land. And it is the kiln that preserves the pottery and artifacts and ruins of an ancient civilization.

To beat the heat I got up before dawn. It was still dark when I began my hike just outside of town, through a small forest of juniper and sage. I was ushered in by a half-dozen ravens, and dipped down and then up on the sand trail, crunching over a river of last year's cottonwood leaves. I followed a red sand path that led deep into the canyon, until I found myself standing below a spectacular sandstone village backed into the canyon and tucked under a great stone ledge. I looked up at long-abandoned rooms and granaries of the Ancestral Puebloans.

Tall cottonwoods from the valley below had grown up almost to the level of the ledge that held the dwellings. The trees circled a pool that fed them, and that must have been an important water source for the cliff dwellers. Far above the dwellings was a great sluice of rock, where waterfalls flowed during rare summer rains, filling the pool. I imagined sitting in those ancient rooms, tucked in, while a sheet of water cascaded in front of me.

I was wrapped in quiet as ancient as the homes. That was why I was there, what I had hoped for. That is what everyone should have at least once, I thought, or better yet, once in a while. A raven broke the silence and I nodded to it companionably. It felt like there was nobody else around for miles. Happily, I had also left my phone behind.

It is strange the way different sites affect you. For most of us it is subjective. Mesa Verde, which was just across the border in Colorado, has

always left me cold: the crowds, the Disneyland lines, the signs explaining everything. The best sites are the ones that catch you by surprise, as
they sometimes do in the Southwest when you are in the middle of a
hike and then, out of nowhere, you come upon an ancient granary, an
ancient home, maybe an entire ancient village. No signs, no lines, no indication at all of what is to come. Though you know you're not, you may
imagine you are the site's first discoverer. Or, if you are feeling particularly mystical, one of its original inhabitants. It is thrilling. A momentary
connection to the past but also a satisfying over-spilling of the present.

The sight of those stone houses, the most organic of organic archi-
tectures, did something to my insides, something I never experienced
back home. It connected me in an ineffable way to the place and to the
past. Not for any mystical reason but because that dwelling, so integral
to its surroundings it seemed to grow out of the rock, is where my fellow
Homo sapiens had lived more than a thousand years ago.

Later in the day I hiked into an alcove where strange figures with
long hands and birdlike figures adorned the sandstone walls, the lighter
color of the stone, of which the figures were made, shining out against
the darker desert varnish. The central humanoid figure, known as a San
Juan Anthropomorph, floated up above me. "It's shot up pretty good," a
local in a pickup told me when he had pointed me down the dirt road
toward the petroglyphs. When I studied the petroglyphs more closely,
I saw he was right: someone had responded to their beauty by firing at
them. But while pockmarked by bullet holes, the figures had managed to
travel through the centuries with their startling power intact. And there
they were: preserved by our better natures, shot up by our worst.

It occurred to me that for all the technical language of the Antiquities
Act, it had a subtext. Roosevelt knew the subtext well. Yes, it is vital to
preserve historic and scientific artifacts for future generations to study,
and to preserve the land around them for our grandchildren. But we are
also preserving them *selfishly*. For us. For the present. I was there for
opposite reasons: to exult in the physical now and to remind myself that
we are not trapped in this historical moment. I, like many people, was

greedy for these sites and places. Here, linked to the past, I could think of the future.

I am convinced that places like this are exactly what our battered, shallow, exhausted, cynical country needs right now. A place to be reborn, a place to get outside of oneself and one's tired time, a place to make us seem less central to our own story, a place to maybe even feel something like hope.

Which, I think, was the real point of saving land like this in the first place. By saving these places we are helping save ourselves.

Here is the writer David Roberts describing the discovery that changed his life, turning him into an obsessive seeker of ruins: "You cannot, of course, set out to find such a pot. It must burst upon you by accident, when you expect nothing but another corner in the sandstone." Why is surprise, the unexpected, such an important aspect of experiences we deem authentic? I will never be able to shake, or match, the first time I hiked into Cedar Mesa, which was just to the northwest of where I was now hiking, with my friend Rob, and after a couple miles came upon the startling sight of a many-roomed ancient dwelling. I am thankful to Rob for not giving me any warning. This, it seems to me, is what we are missing as we Google and drone our way through every last unexplored corner of earth and knowledge. I am so sick of our culture of self-consciousness, even as I am part of it. What is lost by living like we now do?

Surprise is just one ingredient in this recipe for wonder. We can laugh at the idea of a bunch of Anglo tourists communing with ancient Indians, can call it New Agey, regard it as appropriation or just plain silly if we like. But that doesn't matter much when no one else is around and you are looking at these homes and kivas where people cooked, slept, lived, and loved many centuries ago, and you are feeling what you feel, which in my case is drawn into a place that seems the very definition of organic architecture, the homes clinging to the cliffs like those swallows' caves. I understand that I will never have the direct connection with this place that Indigenous people have. But is it really silly to feel a kind of connection to this art, any sillier than being moved by the work of a long-dead

Dutch painter? Why erect barriers to wonder, rules for delight? As Reg Saner once wrote: "To the extent that humankind is one family, they were my ancestors, too, though in relation more metaphoric than actual."

*　*　*

If the Antiquities Act owes its existence to one man, that man is not Theodore Roosevelt. Nor does that honor go to Representative John F. Lacey of Iowa, who helped guide the bill through Congress, or even Edgar L. Hewett, a Westerner and archaeologist, who not only lobbied hard for the bill, but actually wrote it. No, the Antiquities Act grew out of a sense of threat to the prehistoric objects that required protection, and the man who embodied that threat, and who was the prototype of the kind of man it was meant to stop, was Richard Wetherill.

Few men have had as fluctuating and volatile a reputation as Wetherill. Read one book he's a hero. Read another he's a crook. Seen from this angle he is an archetypal Western hero, explorer, cowboy scientist, a kind of Western Indiana Jones. Seen from that, he is a thief, a plunderer, a stealer of heritage, an appropriator. A pot hunter. To the Eastern intellectual elite of his day, and those who were laying claim to the burgeoning field of archaeology and anthropology, he was a looter, stealing and stomping on the very things they hoped to study. But that didn't stop his critics from benefiting from his work. In fact, contrary to their accusations, he took great pride and care in his excavation of ancient sites, and many today believe his methods were ahead of his time. Through his obsessive work he turned himself into the scientist and discoverer he had dreamed of being ever since his first great find.

That great find, the discovery that changed his life and is the reason we still know his name, occurred in 1887 when his brother Al went looking for lost cattle that had strayed from their ranch in Mancos, Colorado, and stumbled upon the ancient village that would later be known as Cliff Palace, the most dazzling of the Mesa Verde ruins. However we may judge Wetherill now, what can't be denied is that this discovery thrilled and obsessed him. If these ancient cliff dwellings can still excite us, when we know they are out there, imagine the electric thrill that Wetherill and his brother experienced when they stumbled upon what they called their "lost civilization." In Willa Cather's 1925 novel *The Professor's House*, a young Tom Outland, clearly based on Wetherill, describes a similar discovery of what he would call "Cliff City":

> Far above me, a thousand feet or so, set in a great cavern in the face of a cliff, I saw a little city of stone, asleep. It was as still as sculpture—and something like that. It all hung together, seemed to have a kind of composition: pale little houses of stone nestling close to one another, perched on top of each other, with flat roofs, narrow windows, straight walls, and in the middle of the group, a round tower.... I can't describe it. It was more like sculpture than anything else. I knew at once that I had come upon a city of some extinct civilization, hidden away in this inaccessible mesa for centuries, preserved in the dry air and perpetual sunlight like a fly in amber, guarded by the cliffs and the river and the desert.

For Wetherill this was just the beginning. He would uncover other sites all over the Southwest, most famously at Chaco Canyon and not incidentally at Cave 7 in Bears Ears, a groundbreaking find that led to the understanding that rather than one ancient people, what he was unearthing was a series of peoples layered on top of one another. Respected scientists would come to rely on Wetherill, and his knowledge, but the scientific world at large, which of course meant the *Eastern* scientific world, was suspicious of this untrained Westerner. These same scientists held the twin, and hypocritical, beliefs that the sites should not be disturbed by amateurs but that it was fine to ship the contents of the finds back east to American museums. It was the threat of these American artifacts being shipped overseas that brought true outrage. In 1893 that outrage focused on Gustav Nordenskiöld, a Swedish collector and archaeologist, who excavated more ruins in Mesa Verde, with

Wetherill's help, and shipped them out of the country and back home. A significant number of East Coast scientists and politicians began to call for legislation that would protect these sites from plunder, or at least from the kind of plunder they frowned on and deemed unofficial.

There was a subtext to this conflict, one that won't sound at all unfamiliar to anyone living in the West today. The late Hal Rothman wrote perceptively of the Western fear of Easterners trying to control Western land and of Eastern insensitivity to Western needs:

> To many southwestern settlers, the land containing prehistoric ruins had more immediate uses; in that arid region, settlers coveted land with water, and the majority of prehistoric sites were located near sources of water. The survival of homesteads and ranches depended upon access to water, and giving up their livelihood to reassure anxious antiquarians made little sense to people struggling for subsistence. With no obvious economic advantages in the age before mass tourism, preservation meant little to settlers, many of whom had recently battled what they incorrectly thought were the descendants of the cliff dwellers. Some westerners argued with disdain that these relics of an ancient civilization were only houses, and abandoned ones at that. As eastern society began to mythologize its past, the practical perspective of westerners put them at odds with emerging public sentiment.

This was the clash that served as the backdrop for the creation of the Antiquities Act, and that to some extent remains the backdrop today. The early efforts to translate the sentiment for preservation into law began in 1900, but those early efforts were blocked by Western congressmen who fought back against what they saw as unnecessary interference in their backyards. While the resistance was strong, momentum for some sort of protection kept building. The market for authentic Indian artifacts was booming, and the sites were being cleaned out. Vandalism and looting were common, though not all of the damage was malicious. Some of it was as much cultural as criminal: tourists and other curio-seekers would simply pick up pots they found at sites and wander off with them.

It would be nice if we could relegate this sort of behavior to the past, and to say we have evolved past it.

It would also be untrue.

*　*　*

The rattlesnake didn't rattle so much as make a watery seething noise. It paused for me a moment, and I sashayed past it down the trail. Vaughn, who was ten yards in front of me when the snake came out from under the rock, ran back to study it before it retreated into the shady hole.

"Eight or nine years old, I would guess."

I was glad to know its age, gladder not to be bitten.

Vaughn Hadenfeldt and I were hiking down not up, dropping into the canyons to explore ancient ruins in the heart of Cedar Mesa, which had briefly been Bears Ears National Monument land. Vaughn was something of a town legend in Bluff, an adventure guide and archaeologist who had been featured in more than a few books and TV shows. I had first met him in January when I was having dinner with an old friend, Greg Lameman, at the Twin Rocks Café in Bluff. Greg was a Navajo who had lived in the area his whole life and who had become a river guide at Wild River Expeditions. That night Vaughn stopped by our table and said to Greg: "You paddle for a living. I walk."

Vaughn looked the part of the professional hiking guide, still whip thin in his sixties, with long gray hair and goatee, and a prominent beak of a nose. He was the board president of Friends of Cedar Mesa, the environmental group that Amanda Podmore worked for and that Ryan Zinke had met with. On my second day in Bluff, on my way back to Calf Canyon, I had pulled over when I saw him out by his truck in front of his garage. He invited me in for a beer and before long was telling me how he'd ended up in Bluff.

Vaughn had grown up in Nebraska but moved to Colorado early on and always considered himself a mountain person. But a friend kept insisting he had to see the ruins in the Southwest.

"That was 1980," he explained. "My sense of place was certainly in the mountains. But I came here basically to stop my buddy from harassing me about coming down into these canyons. I was always into archaeology, but I was into these high-altitude macho people living in the mountains, and I always looked at these ancient Southwest folks as a bunch of farmers, and that didn't really intrigue me much.

"But my friend dragged me down onto Cedar Mesa. We spent a week backpacking the canyon. In those days you didn't hardly ever see anybody. And I was hooked. The preservation of things in the desert Southwest is just outrageous. In the high mountains you find a lot of tools made out of stone and that's basically about all you ever find. It is different here. All of a sudden I was looking at rock art from a thousand years ago, and I was looking at structures and cliffs, kivas with intact roofs and then at a ladder going into the kiva, ceramics, all the perishable things.

"So yeah, my worldview did a radical switch and I weaned myself off of the whole mountain guiding, hanging out in the mountains, and started driving three hundred miles from where I was living to get to these canyons. I eventually sold out of my mountaineering store business in Colorado and moved here to Bluff. This is definitely my last stand and my place till the bitter end."

Before we said goodbye, Vaughn agreed to lead me on a hike up into Cedar Mesa, to land that had been cut out of the monument but that was, he told me, some of the most archaeologically rich not just in the state but in the world. A couple days later he picked me up before dawn, and just as the light was breaking we headed up the Moki Dugway, the ridiculously steep dirt road that leads to the plateau below the Ears. A former fireman, Vaughn had rescued more than one person from this road, including a woman who had gotten halfway up when, terrified, she refused to drive any farther. She got out to walk back down, and when Vaughn hiked up to drive her car back he found physical proof of her terror when he sat in her wet seat.

We had met the rattlesnake in the first ten minutes of our hike and it, along with the black coffee we had been drinking, kept us wide awake. After that encounter we dropped down out of the stunted juniper forest and followed the canyon creek bed. Though mostly waterless, it was filled with shellacked red mud from recent rains. Our first stop was at a sandstone boulder that sat at the confluence of our creek with another. Its open face was dark with desert varnish, and on that face danced dozens of figures and forms. Pictographs of bighorn sheep jumped and ran and a rubbery-armed figure appeared to be jumping rope. Most impressive of all were two dancing twins with squiggling arms and synchronized swimming legs.

"This rock art seems to run through a lot of time," Vaughn said. "And maybe when you start running through time your arms squiggle."

From the boulder we climbed up to find an almost intact dwelling below the cliff edge. One of the rooms was a perfect example of wattle-and-daub architecture, sticks and hardened clay forming a wall that, again, made me think of the nest of a cliff swallow. We stood in the shade of a home where others stood a thousand years before.

He pointed out a painting of two red bighorns on the wall.

"Kind of faint," Vaughn said. "The sun has about wiped them out."

"Well it's survived longer than most art," I said. "You would have to do pretty well to outlast this stuff. Shakespeare's less than five hundred years old, so by these standards he hasn't really passed the test of time yet."

Though he has traveled all around the world, Vaughn has found nowhere as archaeologically rich as his own backyard. And he has not just walked amid these ancient ruins for decades, but has guided hundreds of others to these sites. His is a strange and perhaps soon-to-be-obsolete profession; he acts as a tour guide not just to out-of-the-way places but to the experience of wonder, essentially re-creating that wild and thrilling experience he had all those years ago.

"I don't know who came up with this term," he said. "It's been around for a long time. It's 'planned romance.' So, as a guide, a lot of times, I'm kind of out here . . . I know what's already here, but you try and let people kind of lead themselves into seeing something cool. It could be a ruin, rock art, or whatever."

In other words, while the canyon was all new to me, he knew what was around every corner. When he showed me the shards of some ancient pottery in a cave, he reached under a rock and pulled out a small, perfect, red, rust-colored pot with a fine design of black circles. Maybe he had done this a hundred times before. It didn't matter to me at the moment. It might have been more authentic to come across the pot on my own, but it would also have been next to impossible after more than a century of looting. So this was the next best thing: to see the pot where it was actually used as a pot, and only a few feet from where Vaughn had first found it.

With all the looting it was a miracle any pots could still be found. It was looting that led not just to the creation of the Antiquities Act, but less directly to the creation of Bears Ears National Monument itself. In 2009, the FBI charged twenty-four citizens of Blanding with stealing, selling, and trading ancient Indian artifacts. In Blanding these charges were greeted with anger at the federal government, particularly after one of the men involved, a prominent citizen named Dr. James Redd, killed himself two days after being charged. But it wasn't the charges against citizens of Blanding, but the actual looting, which included more than two thousand intact ceramic vessels, that outraged the Dine Bikeyah and many other Native Americans. It was the beginning of the push to create some sort of protection for this oft-robbed landscape.

Vaughn had nothing but disdain for looters. But he was also aware that his own profession of archaeological tour guide might not be around for long.

"The problem is that there are now a lot of us out here," he told me. "And a lot of people want to experience these places and these moments. How are we going to protect particularly fragile archaeological sites? It's one thing to have a really beautiful landscape, which this is, but then to put cultural resources on top of that, makes it a challenge. And how do we preserve these things as long as possible?"

When you are hiking around Cedar Mesa, without seeing another human being all day long, it is hard to imagine that these places are over-used. But Vaughn was right. While I valued solitary moments of wonder more than almost any other moments of my life, could a place like this, could any place these days, support me and so many others wandering through it?

"Up here everybody's pretty free to go wherever they want at the moment," Vaughn said. "There are some restrictions now, but it proba-bly has to be really tightened up. I hate the thought of it, but I'm seeing the resources really taking a hit—not from malicious vandals necessar-ily though we have some of that and some looting, but the majority of problems we're seeing are just over-visitation. And uneducated people over-visiting.

"It's going to be a challenge. We've got to move forward, and we have to come up with clever ways of managing these places to try and keep them in as good a shape as possible. There won't be any perfect answers and we're going to continue to lose resources in so many ways, which has been occurring in places forever. But I'm hoping that if I were to have grandkids, that there's still that opportunity to hike in a canyon and see a ceramic vessel that was left here a thousand years ago in situ. It's still an incredible outdoor museum at this point, and you don't head to a museum and break the glass and grab the stuff."

"But museums have guards," I said.

"Yes, they do. But we have to come up with new thought processes of these as outdoor museums, and they deserve just as much respect and protection."

"Right," I agreed. "They do. But you are dealing with human nature, also."

"You are. And people like to collect things."

"And touch things."

"Yes. And some things are okay to touch. That's a human trait, to touch things. When I first came to these canyons, what's the first thing you want to do when you come to a rock art panel? You wanted to put your hand on the rock art, particularly if it's a handprint that's been painted on a rock wall. We all need to get over those things, or the collecting of arrowheads and stuff like that. I grew up as a kid on ranches collecting arrowheads. Where do they end up typically? Most people put them in a cigar box, and years later, their kids open the box and go, 'Where'd this crap come from?,' and it gets tossed in the trash.

"Most of those things that we collect lose their magic as soon as we collect them. They're better off left in place so other people get the same opportunity to experience that thrill of discovery and enjoyment of the fact that they're still there. I prefer to consider these places outdoor museums and leave things where they are, and hopefully the next person leaves them, too."

But management of the sites brings its own issues. It isn't just collecting that deadens the mystery. Every time a gate or sign is erected, some magic disappears.

The enemy, more than maliciousness, is our own acquisitive nature, and not just for things but for experiences. We want to know everything, but sometimes our knowledge deadens the mystery. With the rise of GPS the old uncharted places are there for all to find. Our phones guide us. Vaughn doesn't reveal the locations of his best places, but secrets are no longer so easily kept. He now warns his clients not to post pictures of ruins on Facebook. If they do, pot hunters can determine where the site is by the time on the photo and the position of the sun or by the GPS stamps automatically placed into the metadata of photos by some phones and cameras.

"I took a party up to one of my favorite sites recently," he said. "I'd brought lunch along and thought we would stay there for a while. But as soon as we got there it was like they had checked it off their list. One guy said 'If we hurry we can bag another ruin.'"

Vaughn shook his head slowly.

"*Bag* another ruin," he repeated.

In modern academic circles, Vaughn might be accused of the sin of appropriation, that is of messing around in someone else's culture. But while his skin color might not qualify Vaughn for a millennium's worth of connection to the land, he was generally considered to know Cedar Mesa like almost no one else. Over the years he has been respectful in his pursuit and studious in his approach. In Friends of Cedar Mesa he is the head of an organization that has fought hard for both preservation and Native American comanagement of the monument. One of the people he has guided through this land was Obama's interior secretary Sally Jewell, with whom Vaughn climbed to the top of Comb Ridge.

Jewell was in town for the Bears Ears hearings, which drew fifteen hundred people into the tiny town of Bluff.

"I took her out hiking that morning," Vaughn told me. "She's fit. Most of the other people in the news media were struggling. We got to Procession Panel and that pretty much wiped out a lot of those folks. And then I said to Sally, 'So do you wanna go to the real top?' Which is another kind of push. And she's like, oh yeah, and so we're cruising up there and we get to the top and I look back at Bluff."

It was at that point that she made a promise to Vaughn. One of his biggest concerns was that the monument boundaries wouldn't reach Bluff. Jewell, looking down at the town, promised him they would.

His experience with Zinke had been slightly less exhilarating.

"We put together a dossier for Sally Jewell of hundreds of pages of photographs of archaeological sites within the Bears Ears monument. But at the meeting with Zinke he didn't want to hear about the possibility of a hundred thousand archaeological sites in the Bears Ears. Even though you wouldn't find any competent archaeologist who would disagree with that. He was only interested in counting the sites that had already been recorded. As someone who's worked in the field of archaeology, recording a site is different than knowing a site exists.

"If you were to look at all those pictures of the ruins and the rock art and all those things, just a small percentage of them have actually been recorded. It takes time, money, people on the ground to do those things. We've only recorded maybe thirty thousand sites in the original Bears Ears boundary. But we've only surveyed eight to ten percent of the landmass. For him to dismiss anything beyond thirty thousand sites was a horror to anyone working in the field of archaeology."

Of course even thirty thousand sites make this potentially the richest area in the entire country.

We spent the next three hours visiting a half-dozen sites, dazzling in their beauty and variety, most of them now excluded from the monument. One was an outlying Chacoan community of multi-room houses and a great kiva, a thousand years old or so, not built into a cliff but atop the plateau, one of the far-reaching outposts of the ancient road system extending from Chaco Canyon. It too was no longer part of the monument. Another group of homes were tucked up high in the side of a canyon wall, seemingly impossible to enter, stunningly intact.

Not far from this last site, in the heart of Bears Ears, was Cave 7, which is where Richard Wetherill made his historic discovery. Vaughn believes that time has vindicated Wetherill, and that he was far from the looter some have made him out to be.

"His methods for their time were as good as it got," he said. "They tried to do it right. Many now consider him the father of Southwestern archaeology."

If that is so, it is due in large part to what he found in Bears Ears. It was here that he dug through layers of dirt and understood before others did that these were not the homes and tools of one "ancient people" that were being uncovered. Evidence of multiple cultures was evident at different levels in the soil, and he hypothesized that what they were seeing was an earlier "basket people" culture (now called "Basketmakers") overlaid with a more recent culture that created the pots and more advanced masonry. Though these two peoples are now considered to be different epochs of the same basic culture, the breakthrough was an enormous one and led directly to the various classifications that we continue to use today.

"So you see Bears Ears isn't just archaeology," Vaughn said. "But archaeological history."

"Kind of fits the definition of 'objects of historic or scientific interest,'" I suggested.

He laughed out loud.

"If this place doesn't deserve to qualify as antiquities then pretty much no place should qualify," he said. "This is the living embodiment of the Antiquities Act. What people don't understand is that as far as cultural resources go this is the big enchilada."

The day of hiking had been, like so many days here, very hot. Back in Vaughn's air-conditioned truck we cracked beers and cooled off. On the drive home he pointed to a rock outcropping jutting upward on Comb Ridge and told me that this formation had different names in different languages.

"The local Mormons called those rocks the Highland Lady," he said. "I guess the rocks below are supposed to represent her skirts. But the Navajo and Ute name is slightly different and more descriptive. They call them the mountain sheep's testicles."

I nodded.

Looking closer, I could see it both ways.

*　　*　　*

It would be hard to find a place as rich in anthropology, archaeology, and geology as Bears Ears. But it isn't too shabby in the paleontology department, either. Three weeks after Trump's attempt to shrink the monument became official, paleontologist Rob Gay announced that he had discovered what could be "one of the world's richest caches of Triassic period fossils" inside the monument's original boundaries. The headliner for the find was the ancient crocodile, the intact remains of a creature named phytosaurs, that lived in the late Triassic, somewhere between 251 million to 199 million years ago. "It is extremely rare to find intact fossil skulls of specimens from this period," Gay said, calling the sixty-nine-yard site the "densest area of Triassic-period fossils in the nation, maybe the world."

As it turns out, one of the paleontologists working beside Dr. Gay in Bears Ears was Wallace Stegner's granddaughter, Allison Stegner. By the time I learned this, Allison had moved on to a postdoc at University of

Wisconsin–Madison, but when I called she filled me in on a detail about the crocodile find that I had not heard.

"The field season was ending when Rob found a phytosaur with a missing snout," she told me. "The piece had clearly been stolen—you could see the plaster on the specimen. Rob texted the BLM paleontologist to explain the issue. And as it turns out, she had just seen a talk by the people who had the missing piece of the snout. It is kind of incredible. The piece had been looted thirty or forty years ago by an amateur preparator, and he kept it in his garage for decades. He finally gave it to a museum and the people at the museum studied it, knew it was from southeast Utah but didn't know where, and had no hope of relocating the site. It is sheer luck that the BLM paleontologist happened to hear them give a talk and then get the text from Rob not long after, and that the snout and body were reunited. And, of course, the fact that it was looted in the first place is a prime example of why protecting the objects in the monument is so important."

She mentioned that the Society of Vertebrate Paleontology, of which she was a member, was one of the plaintiffs in the suit against the Trump administration over Bears Ears. Excitement filled her voice as she talked about the paleontological possibilities in Bears Ears.

"The rock strata in Bears Ears is incredibly important to understanding the evolution of life. There are fossils everywhere, complete skeletons, things that have never been seen before, and they cover two mass extinctions. The oldest rocks in Bears Ears are Pennsylvanian, which is right before the Permian, which was the largest extinction that we have experienced. Permian is when we had the 'fins to limbs' transition, when things were coming out of the water onto land, so of course that is a major, major event in evolution. And the younger rocks tell the story of the time of the dinosaurs."

True to the family name, Allison grew up interested in conservation. She always had a knack for science and was drawn to paleontology or paleoecology because she felt that the perspective of time was important for figuring out how to preserve biodiversity.

More simply, she just liked being outdoors.

"I pretty much always wanted to be outside and camping and look-ing at plants and rocks," she said.

The first time I met Allison had been in Vermont a decade before when I was working on a biography of her famous grandfather. She showed me a book of pressed ferns that her grandmother had made for her with their common and Latin names written below. That early learning stuck.

Though it wasn't part of a master plan, over time she has grown even fonder of her chosen field because of the way it allows her to connect people, including kids, to science. As it happens people of all ages and all political persuasions like dinosaurs.

She admits to empathizing with those who worry about a monu-ment designation bringing more people.

"Before the monument was designated nobody really knew about the place. And it was great to *not* see it in the news. I think the people in the area are worried that it will become a national park and then you won't be able to do anything. I've spent many months camping out there and I see people all the time collecting firewood, hunting. It's an area that's really used by locals in a way that I respect. And I think that it would be a shame if it were sealed off."

This is a worry shared not just by many of those against the monu-ment but many of those for it. They want it to be successful but not *too* successful. They want to protect it from extractive industries and new roads but fear that very protection could lead to another sort of exploita-tion. It would be hard to say this is not a legitimate worry. How to keep a place authentic, a place where humans come to interact with, not merely gawk at, nature.

I told her that I had been thinking about her grandfather's "Wilder-ness Letter," of its continued relevance in the twenty-first century.

"Well, I agree with Grandpa on almost all fronts but I've always felt a little squeamish about the national parks being America's *best* idea," Allison said. "I mentioned that to a friend once and she said, 'Well, it wasn't America's *worst* idea.' National parks in some ways have become our sacrificial lambs. The parks like Canyonlands that are huge and undeveloped have it better than the more popular ones. When I think about where I want to camp I look for a national park and then try to find forest service land nearby."

Before we said goodbye I told her that we could at least be thankful that her grandfather never had to experience Trump.

"Oh my god. I can't imagine."

* * *

Ever since I had gotten to this corner of southeast Utah, and learned that the area had its very own San Juan Hill, I knew I was going to climb it. There was no way a Roosevelt-obsessed writer wasn't going to head up a hill with that name. Years ago I had visited Teddy's San Juan Hill in Cuba and had enjoyed walking up the sloping grass toward the battlements. With that as comparison, I can tell you that Utah's San Juan Hill, which is not a hill but part of a crazy, upward-thrusting, 120-mile-long crest called Comb Ridge, a great spine of rock that local Utahans say you can see from space, is much, much steeper. I'm not sure Teddy or his Rough Riders would have had as much success if they had had to climb this.

As I slogged my way up, I thought about how climbing—ascension— had been a persistent theme in Roosevelt's life, from youthful climbs of the Matterhorn and Katahdin, to his fame-gaining charge up Kettle and San Juan Hills, to his metaphoric climb to the country's highest office. Hills give birth to stories, and Utah's San Juan Hill, like Cuba's, has its very own set of myths that have built up around it. It was almost the end of the line for the God-fearing, God-driven pioneer Mormons who climbed it. Of all their crazy feats on their crazy journey starting back in 1879, along what would become known as the Hole-in-the-Rock Trail, climbing San Juan Hill might have been the craziest. The mission they had signed up for was to explore and settle what was the least known corner of this region, and as it turns out Bluff was the end point of that mission. Along the way men, women, and children riding in—and sometimes pushing or lowering by pulleys—their covered wagons, traveled straight up and down sandstone walls, crossed the Colorado, and weathered blizzards and blazing heat, all the while seeming to play out a giant version of the game Roosevelt so loved back on Rock Creek: his "point-to-point walks" *over, under, through,* but never *around*. When you actually look at a map of their route, you begin to question the navigation gene in the Mormon clan. Their ineptitude, or madness, or divine inspiration or whatever you want to call it all culminated here, on San Juan Hill, during the first three days of April in 1898, when they drove their covered wagons and their poor, starving, dying animals up this steep rock wall to the top of Comb Ridge. It was not surprising that one of the oxen died in its yoke and that the bloodied horses fell to their knees. You can still see the scrapes from the wagon wheels and the pockmarked steps they cut into the stone. And you can see the words that one of them had the energy left to chisel into that stone: "We Thank Thee Oh God."

At the time Mormons were under fire from the federal government for what their people somewhat euphemistically called "plural marriage." Things were also a bit touchy with the human beings who had lived on the land before they got there, though they themselves saw this as a mission of peace, not conquest. In *A Guide to Southern Utah's Hole-in-the-Rock Trail,* Stewart Aitchison writes:

> One of the objectives of the San Juan Mission was to cultivate better relations with the Indians. Brigham Young had always believed that it was "cheaper to feed them than fight them." Additionally, church doctrine taught that the Indians were descendants of the House of Israel who had strayed from the righteous life but would eventually embrace the gospel and become a "white and delightsome" people.

"Those pioneers were crazy," Louis told me as we hiked, and I, barely able to drag myself to the top, let alone drag oxen and wagons, grunted in agreement.

Louis was my guide, and a friend of my friend Greg Lameman's, and he also worked for Wild River Expeditions. Louis was voluble, funny, outgoing, and smart. We had just spent an enjoyable couple of hours rafting down the San Juan River, a tributary of the Colorado River. Along the way we stopped to bushwhack up to some ruins he had never explored before, before pulling over here, near the River House site at the base of San Juan Hill. The original plan had been to come by truck to San Juan Hill, but when the storms washed out the roads the only way to get here was by boat.

Louis had a slightly more cynical take on American presidents than I did. Earlier, as our boat approached this confluence of the San Juan and Butler Wash, he told me the story of his visit to Mount Rushmore.

"I walked up below the statues and gave them the middle finger," he said.

Then, almost apologetically, as if Teddy Roosevelt were my relative, he added, "But it was mostly aimed at Lincoln."

Louis explained that he was Navajo but also part Sioux.

"And Lincoln presided over the biggest public execution of the Sioux people. He had over thirty Dakota Sioux hung on one day, after an uprising. But the uprising happened because the U.S. government took land they had promised the Sioux."

"Maybe we should have a Bears Ears uprising," I suggested.

"Without the hangings, though, okay?"

"Right. No hangings."

Now, as we ascended the stegosaurus spine of Comb Ridge, we had a view of the whole world below, including the red valley and the green line of the river. Louis is tall and lean and seemed to be barely breathing hard, while I was huffing and puffing as I climbed farther up the ridge.

"You've got to elevate," Louis said encouragingly. "Like the San Juan anthropomorphs."

He was referring to the pictographs of seemingly floating people painted by the ancient ones, like those I had seen on the rock walls near Bluff.

Far below, the brown wash ran. Even though we were hundreds of feet up, you could hear the river in an otherwise silent world. We had seen bighorn sheep on the river, but the only animals we saw now were turkey vultures lifting on the thermals.

A sense of exhilaration came over me when we at last reached the ridge. I knew that this feeling was tied to the sweat and effort it had taken to get up there. "The pleasures of the difficult" is what my former professor Reg Saner called it. Quieter minds might be able to achieve the happy calm I felt upon reaching the top without beating the crap out of themselves first. But for most of us effort and ease are inextricably tied, and ease, strangely, has to be earned. Certainly this was true for Roosevelt. The effort before the ease accomplishes several things: it assures the always carping superego that this is a hard, and therefore worthwhile, pursuit; it circumvents the brain and its habitual worrying; and, when we are lucky, it allows us to quietly see what is.

What I saw was a great arcing half moon of rock and a purling brown creek that joined a green river where their colors mingled. As I stared down at the water, I noticed two tiny vehicles crossing the brown creek, ATVs or "Razors" (spelled RZRs) as Louis called them. Around here one person's fun is the other's hell, and recreational choices are sometimes like choosing arms for a duel. Hiking boots or an ATV? At the moment I didn't begrudge those down below their pleasure as they splashed across the water I had thought unpassable. If we had different perceptions of what constituted wildness and freedom, so be it.

Back in the Badlands I had found myself thinking that the ridge above Medora, which the Maah Daah Hey trail ran along, was a handy metaphor for the path that Roosevelt walked between idealism on the one hand and pragmatism on the other. If anything, Comb Ridge, which stretches all along the Bears Ears eastern border, was handier.

Throughout his presidency Roosevelt traversed just this sort of ridge. He wrote of how we must hold high ideals and then work through practical methods to achieve those ideals. Or, to put it another way, we must decide what the right thing to do is, but realize that this is only the first step. The next is getting others to do that thing in a form as close to the original conception as possible. He disliked those he regarded as rigid and impractical reformers who would never budge from their pre-determined platforms even though, as his politics continued to move leftward, he found himself allied with just these kinds of characters. He was wary of extremism, though when he returned to run as the Bull Moose third party candidate, he became, for others, a symbol of just the sort of single-minded fervency he criticized. They saw a glint of madness shining in his eyes.

But the target of that fervency redeems it, at least for me. His environmental prescience was almost matched by his keen insight into the rotting effect of wealth, of making money for money's sake, on our national politics. He reviled "the elite criminal class" and claimed to hate "the scoundrel who succeeds" more than the "scoundrel who fails."

He fought the fight many of us do today, but the enemy has grown more cunning. They were cruder then, less self-aware. The owners of coal mines, for instance, believed that it was their God-given right to rule and care for their workers. One of those owners, George F. Baer, said: "The rights and interests of the laboring man will be protected and cared for—not by the labor agitators but by the Christian men to whom God in his infinite wisdom has given the control of the property interests of this country."

The current plutocracy might feel the same way, deep down, but they have managed to tell a different story, a story that seems to have pried the votes of the middle and lower classes away from what would seem to be their own best interests. They have become experts at this division, shucking minds like mussels. Out here in southeast Utah that means a story that says that the federal government wants to take away not just your guns but your land. It is a story that divides a town like Blanding, though one can't help but think that the attitudes and needs of the local Indigenous people are not so different than the attitudes and needs of the local Mormons. Certainly, both groups have a long and well-earned history of wariness toward the federal government and its claims to the land. What is different, at the moment, is that for the first time Native Americans have found a way of using the rules of the legal game, rules that were historically so often used against them, to get something they want. In this instance what they want is a national monument that they have a say in running. Those who oppose the monument do so fearing that something will be taken away. Meanwhile, those who advocate for corporate interests see that there is much to be gained by playing to the latter attitude. They tell people the land belongs to them, knowing that this could lead to changes that would allow the land to belong to their companies.

Trump recently sang the same song during his stop in Salt Lake City to un-declare the monument. "Some people think that the natural re-sources of Utah should be controlled by a small handful of very distant bureaucrats located in Washington," he said. "And guess what? They're wrong."

It is now a timeworn story. And an effective strategy that achieves its result: division. It creates a narrative that one side clings to while the other rails against it. And increasingly, people are willing to defend their stories with not just vehemence but violence.

*   *   *

"Appropriation" is an in-vogue word these days, but it is too gentle a term for what has happened to the Native people in the Southwest. Here the culture and cultural items have been vandalized. Stolen. Looted.

You could argue that this was the very thing the Antiquities Act was created to counter. Parts of the act are written as if in a direct address, and a scolding address at that, to Richard Wetherill and his breed. It is right there in the first sentence, the threat of a ninety-day jail term and a five-hundred-dollar fine for "any person who shall *appropriate*, excavate, injure, or destroy any historic or prehistoric ruin or monument, or any object of antiquity."

But if that line sounds wise to the point of prescient, over the next few paragraphs the Antiquities Act begins to sound sketchier. One of the troubling aspects of the act, one of the aspects that the creation of Bears Ears was meant to both subvert and repurpose, is the language in the last section that grants the government the right to decide who will be permitted to examine and excavate the sites and gather and collect the artifacts. These studies were to be conducted, according to Section 3, by institutions that the government "may deem properly qualified to conduct such examinations, excavations, or gatherings . . . for the benefit of reputable museums, universities, colleges or other recognized scientific or educational institutions, with a view to increasing the knowledge of such objects, and that the gathering shall be made for permanent preservation in public museums."

This was enlightened language for the time. But it left the descendants of the ancient cultures out of the conversation. There were many Native peoples who thought of the soon-to-be monuments as sacred ground, not as archaeological sites. If Americans had been outraged when Gustav Nordenskiöld had taken their relics back to Stockholm, imagine how it felt for Native people to see their culture shipped back to Eastern museums.

What Bears Ears proposes is no less than a way to reclaim and re-imagine the Antiquities Act. For starters, these sites and artifacts need to be afforded the respect and dignity we grant the museums they were once shipped back to. As Vaughn pointed out, they are outdoor museums. At the same time remember that these places are actually *not* museums. While these lands must be respected, they can also be used. Used how? Not by collecting and displaying. Not by appropriating. But in traditional ways. For the gathering of herbs and plants. And for the gatherings of people. For ceremony.

This may be the most radical thing about the Obama Bears Ears proclamation. It articulates the idea that while we need to treat these sites with the respect we do a museum and that they are in a way living museums, the concept is different from a traditional museum or park. Museums are places for passive viewing, for spectating. Bears Ears is a place for ritual, a place not to merely view the past but to interact with it in the present.

Of course the implication, if not the outright intent, is that this type of interaction is meant for Indigenous people. I get it: no one wants a bunch of New Age Whitey would-be shamans sprinkling seeds and dancing at the doorstep of the ruins. But, as described by Native leaders, this isn't exclusive, and they have spoken eloquently of how we can all learn from their connections. Even if Anglos were excluded entirely, which they won't be, the idea is still thrilling. The idea that nature is a place for interacting, for living inside of, that nature can give us something that museums, and TV shows or podcasts about nature, can't. I love the fact that this place, so famous for a climate that mummifies and preserves, offers us possibilities in the present and for the future.

It will take imagination and smarts to make this ideal plausible. And it will take the large-scale equivalent of zoning, with different areas being set aside for different uses. Some sites might have to be sacrificed and Disneyfied—that is, to almost become dioramas of their original selves. This is already true in many parks: I can't imagine anyone meaningfully interacting with nature at the visitor center across from Tower Falls at Yellowstone, and maybe Bears Ears will have its equivalent. I nominate the only site that Secretary Zinke visited for this Disneyfication, since it is an easy one mile walk in and right off the road. There are many amazing sites within Bears Ears, but the dwelling called House on Fire isn't, to my eye, one of them. (Greg Lameman and I were unimpressed when we visited it and took to calling it "House *Somewhat* on Fire.") By all means put up signs and sacrifice this particular site in the name of tourism. But keep other places private. Leave them as they are. Require a permit and make getting that permit take a little work. Let them remain sign-less and even trail-less. Let them be like the hidden chalice in Robert Frost's poem "Directive," places that exist "under a spell so the wrong ones can't find it." This is more practical than it seems. There is an advantage to being a national monument, not a national park. Sure, there will be plenty of traffic, but the less sexy designation of "monument" makes it a less sexy destination. And the fact that much of the land within Bears Ears is not as obviously spectacular, not as filled with waterfalls and mountains as the most famous national parks, also protects it to some degree. You can be standing a hundred feet from where a canyon suddenly drops down and have no idea what it drops into or even that the drop-off is there. These are reasons for hope.

In other words: let the Antiquities Act do what it was meant to do, but also let it do more. In the early twentieth century the act expanded to fit the times, protecting the land around the ancient sites as well as the sites themselves. And now it must expand again. In a warming world the act must protect the wilderness that another Republican president, this one named Richard Nixon, called "the breathing room of the nation." But it also must help us protect the architecture and art found there in new and creative ways, ways that reach back to traditional uses for the land just as they reach forward imaginatively toward new ways of perceiving parks and monuments. That's asking a lot of a little act that barely squeaked through Congress.

We ignore the past and future of the Antiquities Act at our own peril. We needed it then. We need it now. We can't lose it. A Supreme Court without an understanding of the act's history, and what it has meant to this country, could casually overturn our heritage of preservation and open these lands to corporate plunder. Which is why, if we care at all about the future of public lands in this country, the Antiquities Act must be protected as fiercely as the land itself.

★   ★   ★

Barack Obama didn't declare Bears Ears a national monument until December 28, 2016, just a little more than three weeks before he left office. When he did so, he was working within a long tradition of last-minute presidential proclamations. The clock had almost run out on Theodore Roosevelt's presidency when he designated the Mount Olympus National Monument on March 2, 1909, one of his last acts as he was packing up and leaving the White House, just two days before William Howard Taft's inauguration.

Though the spectacular landscape of the Olympic Peninsula speaks for itself, there was an added bonus to TR's final act of presidential preservation: the new monument was the habitat of a breed of elk that the soon to be ex-president was particularly fond of. As always with this man, his motives were complicated, his righteousness (one of his favorite words) softened with a true love of the natural world but also spiced with ego. Roosevelt admired the huge mammals for their size, grace, and beauty, but their name didn't hurt either. The American biologist C. Hart Merriam was the first to identify them as a subspecies, the largest remaining elk in North America, and he named the animal in honor of the accomplished naturalist who was then not quite yet president. And so in saving 639,200 acres of the Olympic Peninsula, Roosevelt also saved the last remaining herds of *Cervus canadensis roosevelti*. Or, as it is more commonly known, the Roosevelt elk.

The Mount Olympus National Monument was the last name in an impressive litany of monuments named by TR. Here it is:

Devils Tower	Muir Woods
El Morro	Grand Canyon
Montezuma Castle	Pinnacles
Petrified Forest	Jewel Cave
Chaco Canyon	Natural Bridges
Cinder Cone	Lewis and Clark Caverns
Lassen Peak	Tumacacori
Gila Cliff Dwellings	Wheeler
Tonto	Mount Olympus

The first national monument proclaimed in this country was Devils Tower. The most recent, as of our trip, was Bears Ears National Monument. But there is an important difference between the ideas that propelled the creation of that first monument and the creation of the last. Devils Tower in Wyoming, proclaimed by TR in 1906, an almost nine-hundred-foot-tall granite monolith made famous in *Close Encounters of the Third Kind*, had long been called Bears Lodge by the Plains Indians, and was considered sacred by many tribes. Which means that in "saving" it, the United States government also claimed it. This usurpation of sacred ground would be repeated again and again in the creation of parks and monuments: lands that were places of ceremony and cultural import were claimed in the name of recreation, conservation, and science.

Over the years there has been some grudging, incremental movement toward tribes becoming more actively involved in the workings of national monuments and parks. A precedent for the creation of Bears Ears occurred in 1951 with tribal participation in the creation of Grand Portage National Monument in northern Minnesota, where the Grand Portage Band of Minnesota Chippewa and Minnesota Chippewa Tribe asked for tribal land to be recognized as a national monument. More recently, there have been attempts to have the South Unit of Badlands National Park, the park where Noah and I stayed, become fully managed by the Oglala Sioux, the tribe that currently coadministers that section of the park. Not far from Bears Ears, Canyon de Chelly National Monument is effectively comanaged by the National Park Service and the Navajo Nation, who own the rights to the Navajo Tribal Trust land that the park is on. While the park service takes care of park and visitor services, the Navajo Nation manages the land and resources, including the mineral rights. But studies have characterized the relationship between the Nation and the park service as historically "turbulent."

The Bears Ears proclamation takes what was best about the park and monument ideals—setting land aside from development and protecting wildlife—and melds it with something better. To read the document proclaiming Bears Ears a national monument is to feel hope. It contains the idea that we can still be more than tourists, more than spectators. That not all our romance has to be planned. It is an idea that I have bet my life on: that with the right amount of discipline and restraint, we can become wilder. That we can become our own tour guides, develop our own rituals, and still find our place in the living wild world. That we can learn to know our places.

The document is somewhat of an anomaly, but only somewhat. To look back at these monument proclamations over the years is to see that we have been moving in a more expansive and inclusive direction, and that we are already well underway in our revision of Roosevelt's story. Originally the proclamations were direct and concise, much like the Antiquities Act itself. This started to change with the Carter administration, but really changed under Clinton. The proclamation for the Grand Staircase-Escalante National Monument grew out of the work of several Clinton aides and Utah scientists, including soil scientist Jayne Belnap, but was written by University of Colorado law professor and public lands expert Charles Wilkinson. "The Grand Staircase-Escalante National Monument's vast and austere landscape embraces a spectacular array of scientific and historic resources," the proclamation begins. "This high, rugged, and remote region, where bold plateaus and multi-hued cliffs run for distances that defy human perspective, was the last place in the continental United States to be mapped."

The Grand Staircase-Escalante proclamation paints a complete picture of the landscape, its geology, paleontology, archaeology, flora, and fauna, but it is also the first time that a proclamation approaches the level of literature. It makes the point repeatedly that "the rugged canyon country of the upper Paria Canyon system, major components of the White and Vermilion Cliffs and associated benches, and the Kaiparowits Plateau" are scientifically and historically vital for the United States, and therefore fit the criteria laid out by the Antiquities Act. But it also tells a good story.

The Bears Ears proclamation outdoes it. Drawing heavily on the original proposal written by the Inter-Tribal Coalition, and then tweaked and refined by Interior Secretary Sally Jewell, and the acting chair of Obama's Council on Environmental Quality, Christy Goldfuss, it describes the land thoroughly and at times even poetically. How many government documents contain sentences like these? "From earth to sky, the region is unsurpassed in wonders. The star-filled nights and natural quiet of the Bears Ears area transport visitors to an earlier eon. Against an absolutely black night sky, our galaxy and others more distant leap into view. As one of the most intact and least roaded areas in the contiguous United States, Bears Ears has that rare and arresting quality of deafening silence."

The proclamation tells the story of the area down to the black-tailed jackrabbits and sacred datura plants and alcove columbines. It is an American story of place that includes the first Americans, along with the archaeology, anthropology, natural history, and even the phenology of the place. In it we learn that "numerous seeps provide year-round water and support delicate hanging gardens, moisture-loving plants, and relict species such as Douglas fir." It also tells of the human beings who inhabited the place, beginning with the Clovis people who "hunted among the cliffs and canyons of Cedar Mesa as early as 13,000 years ago, leaving behind tools and projectile points in places like Lime Ridge Clovis site, one of the oldest known archaeological sites in Utah," and moving through the Ancestral Puebloans who built their rock homes as early as twenty-five hundred years ago to the Native farmers and the Navajos who came later. "The landscape is a milieu of the accessible and observable together with the inaccessible and hidden," the document/prose poem continues. "The area's petroglyphs and pictographs capture the imagination with images dating back at least 5,000 years and spanning a range of styles and traditions. From life-size ghostlike figures that defy categorization, to the more literal depictions of bighorn sheep, birds, and lizards, these drawings enable us to feel the humanity of these ancient artists."

A key concluding sentence effectively connects Native knowledge of the place to the prime directive of the Antiquities Act: "The traditional ecological knowledge amassed by the Native Americans whose ancestors inhabited this region, passed down from generation to generation, offers critical insight into the *historic* and *scientific* significance of the area." Western values of science and study, values that led to the creation of the Antiquities Act, are not ignored, but a different way of knowing is also put on the same plane, the same level. This is radical. This is new. This is a possible confluence. And then one final nice touch. This traditional way of understanding the land is not just a way of knowing. It, too, is something that the act must defend. "Such knowledge is, itself, a resource to be protected and used in understanding and managing this landscape sustainably for generations to come."

The document also brings the natural and human history into the present. "The area's cultural importance to Native American tribes continues to this day. As they have for generations, these tribes and their members come here for ceremonies and to visit sacred sites. Throughout the region, many landscape features, such as Comb Ridge, the San Juan River, and Cedar Mesa, are closely tied to native stories of creation, danger, protection, and healing."

And yet for all the promise of the proclamation, it falls short of what many of the advocates of the monument had hoped for: true comanagement of Bears Ears by the tribes and the government. It almost gets there but not quite. The poetry turns practical near the document's closing, where it states that the Secretary of Agriculture and the Secretary of the Interior will manage the monument through the U.S. Forest Service and the Bureau of Land Management, while a Bears Ears Commission, made up of a member from each of the five tribes who brought forth the original proposal, will "provide guidance and recommendations." The commission will "effectively partner with the Federal agencies by making continuing contributions to inform decisions regarding the management of the monument." Guidance and partnering are fine. Actual authority and comanagement would have been much better.

* * *

Theodore Roosevelt was a great man. I believe that. If I didn't, I wouldn't be writing this book. I am not out to cut him down to size. But while I want to be generous and to extend historical empathy, I also want to see him clearly. He was a leader of a country that, touting its national virtues, broke promise after promise to the Native people, driving them onto smaller and smaller parcels of land. This, bluntly put, is a history of lying, of promising something and then breaking the promise, of giving something and taking it back.

The slaughter and extirpation of North America's Indigenous population is our *original* sin, our sin of origin. Anyone who cares to think deeply about the idea of America must contend with it, stare it in the face. We killed those who were here. Not just the animals, but the human beings.

Yes, yes, this was happening all over the globe. And no I am not trying to dredge this up so that we can all shrivel into a blubbering ball of liberal guilt. I'm just asking you, dear reader, to really think about this for a few minutes and let it sink in. And then, once it has sunk in, to consider Bears Ears.

Leave it as it is. If "as it is" never was, it certainly complicates Roosevelt's famous statement. And it has obvious and direct relevance to where we are right now. There have been attempts to allow Indigenous people to re-inhabit those "empty" places where they once lived, and even attempts in some cases to consult about park management with those whose ancestors lived in these places for hundreds of generations. But nothing nearly as ambitious as what was proposed at Bears Ears. Bears Ears points to nothing less than a way of reimagining our so-called best idea. Forty years ago the Pulitzer Prize–winning poet Gary Snyder wrote that we needed to "re-inhabit" this country. His words were an inspiring call to wedge down into our places, to learn about the land where we live. But as profound as that was, it was about a *metaphoric re-inhabiting*. What Bears Ears proposes is an *actual re-inhabitation* by the ancestors of those who once lived there.

I am not deluded enough to think we can go back in time and have a genocide do-over, making up for what our ancestors did. But we can learn. And we can try to see clearly what was once gauzy and imprecise. We can strip "wilderness" of some of its romanticism and still keep its beauty, wildness, and power.

What I am saying is that Bears Ears offered and still offers a possibility. That by doing this *right*, and doing it now, we have a chance not just to save some land but to put forward no less than a new wilderness ideal. It is an ideal that imagines both a large wilderness and an inclusive one. An ideal of the land not separate from people. Nature not as an island or zoo or setting for a reality show, but as a place *for* humans, not apart from them.

And if those humans happen to be Indigenous people, all the better.

* * *

"*Nahodishgish*," Greg Lameman said, as he observed the land below us.

"What?" I asked.

We were sitting at the base of the western butte, that is the western ear, of Bears Ears. The ground was covered with snow and red rock jutted up through the white.

"*Nahodishgish*," he said. "In Navajo it means 'places that should be left alone.'"

I nodded. *Nahodishgish*. TR couldn't have said it better himself.

This was back during my January scouting mission. While part of the idea had been to make a pilgrimage to Bears Ears, it had taken me until my last full day in Utah to finally get to the twin buttes that gave the newest national monument its name. Early on that last morning I headed south from Bluff to the reservation land where my friend Greg, the Navajo river guide, lived.

He had given me directions to his place the night before, but I still got lost. I pulled up to the wrong trailer, one that I soon learned belonged to Greg's grandmother, and was surrounded by a dozen dogs and several old goats.

"All the goats are over the age of twelve," Greg told me when I reached the right trailer and he got in the car. "And all the dogs are ones people left on the edge of the highway. My grandmother takes them all in."

I hadn't seen Greg, a stout, strong man in his mid-thirties, for a couple of years, and I was a little nervous about spending a whole day together. But it turned out there was no reason to worry: I quickly remembered how gregarious and easy to talk to he was, and soon we were recounting past adventures.

"I finally brought my sister on a backpacking trip," Greg told me. "She said: 'Is this what people do for fun, walk in the heat with heavy shit on their backs?'"

Another thing I was anxious about that morning was driving up the Moki Dugway in winter. The dangerousroads.org website, which I'd nervously read the night before, called the Dugway a "staggering, graded dirt switchback road carved into the face of the cliff edge of Cedar Mesa" that consists "of 3 miles of steep, unpaved, but well-graded switchbacks (11% grade), which wind 1,200 feet from Cedar Mesa to the valley floor near Valley of the Gods." I'd driven up that ridiculously steep dirt road before, and it was with more than a little trepidation that I began the vertigo-inducing climb. After taking one blind turn, I told Greg: "They beep at these type of turns in the Alps."

"Well, we don't beep here," he said.

He had little sympathy, having made the same drive dozens of times in a van with a trailer full of boats behind it.

Soon after we got to the top, we saw them. They were such a striking and obvious feature of the landscape that I actually started to ask "What are those?" but then caught myself, laughing.

Hoon'Naqvut, Shash Jaá, Kwiyagatu Nukavachi, Ansh An Lashokdiwe. The words are different for each of the tribes, but the meaning is the same. Bears Ears. And they really did look like ears. The two distinctive orange buttes, spotted with snow, that gave this place its name. They grew larger and larger as we drove close. We pulled off at an overlook for Natural Bridges, a national monument that Theodore Roosevelt created in 1908, and I climbed out on an elephant-backed bluff that jutted out like a boat's bow over the land below. I was struck by the silence and clear air.

We got back in the car and headed up a snowy dirt road, closer and closer to the Bears Ears. We passed not a single individual or car. We parked below the western butte and began a snowy, treacherous climb to the base.

My heart was thundering in my chest and my bad knee was aching, and Greg didn't seem to be moving much faster than I was. But we worked our way up, slipping and sliding, our boots clumped with red dirt and snow. It wasn't until we were at the base, in the shade of the western butte, that we realized that this was the first time in an hour that we didn't have a view of both ears.

We settled in. Greg rolled a cigarette and I pulled two beers from my pack. We toasted, celebrating our ascension.

"Is this sacrilege?" I asked him, nodding toward the beer.

"Possibly," he answered.

But if Greg was aware of the sacredness of this place, he was also on familiar terms with the profane.

"My grandfather worked not far from here in a uranium mine," he told me.

"In Bears Ears?" I asked.

"Yup. Right in Bears Ears."

We leaned back against the butte's hard base and took it all in.

Below us the landmarks of the Four Corners were laid before us like a map, and Greg pointed them out to me. There was Navajo Mountain and there was Monument Valley and there was where Grand Gulch started as a shallow wash. It was stunningly beautiful country and easy enough to forget that it was also ground that was coveted for what was below it. This was mid-January, just two weeks before the monument maps would be redrawn, and when it came to that redrawing, a Canadian uranium company would have more influence with our "America First" government than a coalition of five tribes of America's first people.

If one were to consider the misdeeds of the man who is currently president and rank them in a tournament of malfeasance, few would give the reduction of Bears Ears a top seed. With children being separated from their parents, coercion of foreign governments for personal gain, and seeming support for white supremacist groups, and all the rest of the coarseness that goes with the daily Trump show, it might not seem that saving some arid land in Utah should get people too excited. But I would contend that this is because most of us do not understand that Bears Ears is not just about the potential destruction of the land, but about the destruction of an ideal. Or rather, the destruction of a new confluence of ideals.

If the newspaper headlines were any indication, this place was the center of the world, but it sure felt empty. Later Greg and I would hike in and explore just the sort of ancient sites that the Antiquities Act was created to protect, and ones that, thankfully, would remain within the redrawn maps. But for the moment we were content to sit and stare out at the vastness.

Maybe it was the beer or the exertion, but for the moment I was focused less on the politics of the fight than on the sheer quiet beauty of the place. It would be hard to call this a hopeful time in our national history. But I believed, and still believe, that wild, beautiful land is the greatest thing about our country. It is the single best reason for hope. Not small and quibbling human plans and contretemps but the land. A physical statement of our belief in the future.

With so many other pressing issues, it might seem that fighting for an empty place in the middle of nowhere does not qualify as a burning priority. But it does for Greg Lameman, for Regina Lopez-Whiteskunk, and for many of us. For the five tribes that formed the Bears Ears Inter-Tribal Coalition, and came up with the plan for the monument, this is a place of origin, of stories, of history, of culture. For many others, Anglos like me included, it is a place of beauty, a place to connect to the natural world. But it is also more than that, I thought as I sat in the shadow of one butte and stared at the other. It is about a dream of the confluence of ideals, a flowing together of Native respect for the land with the ideals, however sometimes flawed in practice, that created the national parks and national monuments, and preserved other public lands. It is about belief itself, the notion that there are still things worth fighting for, large and great and hard-to-express things in a world grown crass and petty and small.

Theodore Descends

The eagle feathers and animal skins flutter on the cord atop the ladder. His nature is not a cautious one—he is a plunger-inner—but as he descends through the hole in the sacred kiva's roof, he experiences an odd sensation. Is it fear? He grips the wooden rungs a little tighter. He feels the trickling of sweat on his neck and arms. He has trained himself to be brave from an early age: to keep his hand steady on the trigger when charged by elephants or grizzlies, to embrace the passion of battle, to speak in front of enormous crowds as comfortably as you or I speak to an old friend.

And yet the sheer strangeness of this place does something to him. As his eyes adjust to the dark, he takes in the sights in this dry, dusty fifteen-by-twenty-five-foot-long room. Back on the slightly raised dais behind him are more than thirty slithering rattlesnakes, interlinked in a ball but some writhing free. Not far away smaller snakes—striped ribbon snakes—squirm in the ceramic pot that holds them captive. His hosts, ten or so Hopi priests wearing nothing more than loincloths, greet him with what he will later call "grave courtesy." He returns the same, bowing. They gesture toward the blanket they have laid down on the dais, where the former great chief from Washington should sit. Which puts his back to the rattlers. He nods and takes his seat, acting as nonchalant as possible. He will not flinch of course. He would rather be bitten. With a naturalist's eye, he glances back and makes note of the beautiful yellowish stripes that run down the body of the slender ribbon snakes. One of the priests shepherds the snakes on the dais with a kind of fan made of three eagle feathers. Roosevelt stares over at the altar on the other side of the room where a drawing is scrawled. A coyote surrounded by paintings of squirming snakes.

The year is 1913, which means that Theodore Roosevelt is fifty-four years old and has been out of office for almost a full five years. But of all the vivid and strange experiences he has lived through, from eating a lion's heart during his safari in Africa, to discussing military strategy with Kaiser Wilhelm on horseback, to being charged by a grizzly in Montana, these next months will provide among the strangest and most vivid. For weeks now he has been traversing the canyons, mountains, and deserts of the American Southwest, mostly on horseback but sometimes on foot, with his teenaged sons Archie and Quentin and their twenty-year-old cousin, Nicholas Roosevelt. They have hunted cougar on the rim of the Grand Canyon, crossed the Colorado and ascended up into the cool of Buckskin Mountain, and then, in Roosevelt's words, dropped down "from the land of pine and spruce and of old, clear springs, into the grim desolation of the desert." They have camped in cowboy fashion along the way, using just their "slickers and horse blankets," and have marveled at the beauty and stillness, and the ancient ruins they have come across. Of one such site Roosevelt later wrote: "The lower rock masses were orange-hued, and above them rose battlements of cliff; where the former broke into sheer sides there were old houses of the cliff-dwellers, carved in the living rock. The half-moon hung high overhead; the scene was wild and lovely, when we strolled away from the camp-fire among the scattered cedars and pinyons through the cool, still night."

A highlight of the trip was sleeping below Rainbow Bridge back when few white visitors had seen it, long before that stunning landmark could be reached by a boat ride and hike. "It was difficult to grasp the size of it until we came beneath it," Nicholas Roosevelt scribbled in his diary upon first viewing the massive sandstone arch. "Then TR, Archie, Quentin and I lay down on our backs and looked up at it as the sun was going down behind the cliff walls. In this manner we could see the enormous beam of the arch, as high above us as the vault of a cathedral." Soon Roosevelt was swimming in the fern-laced pool at the bridge's base. As the sun died, they built a fire, and the fire's flame, along with the rising full moon, played a game of light and shadow on the arch's underside. They all slept well that night. "Only those who live and sleep in the open fully realize the beauty of dawn and moonlight and starlight," the ex-president would write.

That he is writing up the event as he is living it, almost immediately on the heels of experience, is a given. It is habit by now to live a sort of double life: to be in the midst of experiencing something while recording it, memorizing it, noting it for the narrative to come. There are those who think there is a little too much Roosevelt in his work. But there is something beyond self-mythologizing, beyond the self, that Roosevelt has glimpsed. The goal is not to become a mirror, but a window. To look outside of yourself and see the world and not just a reflection of your inner mythos. Of course none of us is pure, and these two ways of seeing often work in concert. Clearly this is true for Roosevelt. His early scientific training, his birding, and even his hunting help him see the world outside himself, often in great and stunning detail. He sees that world with a scientific eye, an artistic eye, a literary eye.

The last is the one that probably gets him into the most trouble. Roosevelt's self is a large one to leave behind and what makes it even harder is that part of his job description as a writer is telling stories about himself.

He has never stopped writing, through all the adventures. Which means that throughout his life when he isn't busy being a family man, a diplomat, the field naturalist he dreamed of being as a boy, and, oh yes, president of the United States, he always remains a writer and a storyteller. Even in the midst of his hyperactive presidency, he managed to devour books each night and never stopped writing. "Theodore's habit, in moments of joy or sorrow, had always been to reach for a pen, as others might reach for a rosary or a bottle," his biographer Edmund Morris will write. As president he published three books, four if you include the five chapters he contributed to a natural history text called *The Deer Family*. In this decade he is in now, between leaving office and his death, he will write nineteen more books, including his wonderfully readable autobiography.

In short, he is a pro and has been for years—"a corpulent middle-aged literary man," he once called himself—and this trip to the American Southwest will yield three extremely readable articles that will appear in a popular magazine called *The Outlook*. By the time they are published, he will have pushed off on his next adventure, to a place whose drenched humid climate couldn't be more different than the dry dusty Southwest. But even deep in the Amazon, and even wracked by fever and heart trouble, he will keep to this engrained habit of recording his adventures as he lives them. Experiencing is not enough; communicating that experience is necessary. By the next winter he will be descending the River of Doubt in central Brazil, taking morning baths with piranhas and paddling the river while battling exhaustion and disease, barely making it out alive.

His future biographer Kathleen Dalton will write that in first coming west Theodore Roosevelt entered the hero land of his imagination, and certainly mythmaking is easier in a mythic landscape. Down in the kiva it is like being right inside a myth, or a dream. As the snakes slither, the humans also go about their business. In the article about the experience, "The Hopi Snake Dance," Roosevelt writes:

> Some of the priests were smoking—for pleasure, not ceremonially—and they were working at parts of the ceremonial dress. One had cast a rattlesnake skin which he was chewing, to limber it up, just as the Sioux squaws used to chew buckskin. All were scantily clad, in breech-clouts or short kilts or loin flaps; their naked copper-red bodies, lithe and sinewy, shone, and each had been splashed in two or three places with a blotch or streak

of white paint. One spoke English and translated freely; I was careful not to betray too much curiosity or touch on any matter which they might be reluctant to discuss.

In Roosevelt's eyes, these men have the advantage of not only being priests but also being one of the former president's favorite things: Americans. In fact, during the month which he has traversed the lands near the Grand Canyon, including the vast Navajo Reservation lands and now the First Mesa of the Hopi, he has also undertaken a mental journey, one quite characteristic of him. Seeing the land and its people with his own eyes, he has been thinking hard about the plight of the Navajo and other peoples of the Southwest. As he works through that plight in his mind, and on the page, he might sound to our ears wrongheaded, but one thing he can't be faulted for is apathy. From our safe temporal distance, we can watch as he struggles forward.

"Ultimately, I hope the Indian will be absorbed into the white population, on a full equality," he will write, "as was true, for instance, of the Indians who served in my own regiment, the Rough Riders."

His thinking will never quite escape that of his own time and prejudices, and he is almost by definition patriarchal. His attitude toward Native people will remain stunted; he will never come close to describing what occurred in his beloved America as genocide. And he will never quite shake the belief that assimilation into the larger American culture should be the ultimate goal. But it isn't that simple. Elliott West will write: "In a part of our history that makes us uncomfortable, there were prominent and respectable figures espousing racial theories of Aryan supremacy that were disconcertingly suggestive of others with hideous consequences a few decades later." Two of those figures are Madison Grant and Henry Fairfield Osborn, long acquaintances of Roosevelt. But while Roosevelt will continue to correspond with Madison Grant, a proponent of racial superiority in books like *The Passing of the Great Race*, there are also signs that he is evolving far beyond him. In *The Strenuous Life*, Kathleen Dalton will write: "Roosevelt called that man 'an addlepated ass.' He insisted to Grant that race and ethnicity did not matter because 'men of foreign parentage across the nation fought well, including Jews.'"

When Osborn wrote him criticizing Indians, Roosevelt wrote back that there had been fifty men of Indian blood in his regiment in Cuba and that they "behaved exactly like the whites, and their careers since have been exactly like the white men."

The language of the early twentieth century will not travel well into the future: even the sentences combating racism sound racist. But language of our time may not travel well into the future either. What is going on inside Roosevelt is a kind of wrestling match between old ideas and new. Importantly he, unlike many, is not for ditching the culture the modern tribes grew out of. More and more he sees Indigenous culture, including its poetry, music, and rituals, as part of "our national cultural development" and wants others to see this, that is to elevate these aspects of their cultures in the national psyche. On this trip he will talk to everyone, Natives and non, and his sponge-like mind will soak up Navajo and Hopi culture. Back at Rainbow Bridge his guides had been John and Louisa Wetherill, who ran the trading post in Kayenta. (John was Richard Wetherill's brother.) Theodore had particularly intense conversations with Louisa, who spoke Navajo fluently, was friends with many members of the nearby tribe, and studied Navajo art and myths. Theodore and Louisa, according to Nicholas, "spent interested hours in discussing Indian mythology and the problem of how to educate Navajo children for more active participation in American life without undercutting their cultural heritage."

And now it is as if he is living inside those myths. In a short period of time he has, in his usual fashion, gobbled up as much information about Native culture as he can. Since he is of his time, much of that learning has come from white people, including Natalie Curtis, who has made it her mission to preserve Native poetry and lyrics, and Geoffrey O'Hara, who works for the Department of the Interior and studies music and has said: "If the Navajo can bring with them into civilization the ability to preserve this striking and bewildering rhythm, he will have done in music what (Jim) Thorpe, the Olympic champion, did in athletics." In Roosevelt's words, "Miss Curtis and Mr. O'Hara represent the effort to perpetuate Indian art in the life of the Indian today, not only for his sake, but for our own. This side of Indian life is entirely unrevealed to most white men: and there is an urgent need from the standpoint of the white man himself of a proper appreciation of Native art. Such appreciation may mean much toward helping the development of an original American art for our whole people." He continues: "A great art must be living, must spring from the soul of its people." Nor was he for throwing out the older rituals. The snake ceremony itself represents "a mystic symbolism which has in it elements that are ennobling and not debasing." And: "Nothing that tells for the joy of life, in any community, should be lightly touched."

So while assimilation into the larger prevailing culture remains his stated goal, and while that goal is often stated in cringe-worthy sentences about the "progress" of Native people toward civilization and how "Indians can be just as good as whites," a counter impulse, toward preservation, is beginning to rise. His thinking will never quite get there, even relative to his progressive contemporaries, but it is moving. And that movement has practical consequences. In the articles he is writing about his trip a familiar emotion has begun to well up in his chest. Righteous indignation has been a lifelong friend, and he now experiences it when thinking about the movement, led by the railroad barons and rich ranchers, and agitated for in Congress, to break up the large Navajo Nation lands into smaller sections. It is an outrage, he tells his readers, and we should not stand for it.

He is never short on outrage. The same articles reveal that a similar feeling is stirred by those who rail against federal lands, national parks, and forests. He saw then the roots of the public land "rebels" and "rebellions" we see today. He writes:

> Among the real settlers, the home-makers of sense and far-
> sightedness, there is a growing belief in the wisdom of the

policy of the preservation of the national resources by the National Government. On small, permanent farms, the owner, if
reasonably intelligent, will himself preserve his own patrimony;
but everywhere the uncontrolled use in common of the public domain has meant reckless, and usually wanton, destruction. . . . Continued efforts are made by demagogues and by
unscrupulous agitators to excite hostility to the forest policy of
the government, and needy men who are short-sighted and unscrupulous join the cry, and play into the hands of the corrupt
politicians who do the bidding of the big and selfish exploiters
of the public domain.

*   *   *

There is a moment when one snake gets too close. Brave as he might be,
even Theodore Roosevelt grows nervous when a rattler slides within three
feet. He gestures subtly toward the watcher of the snakes, and the watcher
uses the eagle feather to shepherd the wanderer, by stroking and pushing
its head, back toward the rest. The ex-president nods in appreciation.

Smoke and dust fill the kiva, as do the guttural chants of the priests.
The snakes move sluggishly, and the translator tells Roosevelt that they
have been "given medicine." This may help explain why "every move was
made without hurry and with quiet unconcern; neither snake nor man,
at any time, showed a trace of worry or anger; all, human beings and
reptiles, were in an atmosphere of quiet peacefulness." This calm will
be even more striking the next day, when he will descend again into the
kiva to find the snakes have greatly multiplied in number. He will watch
in astonishment as the priests chant and pick up handfuls of rattlesnakes
"in tranquil, matter of fact fashion" and plunge them into a "great bowl
of water, a writhing tangle of snakes and hands." The snakes will then be
thrown across the room to the floor of the altar. The same casual han-
dling will mark the snake dance itself, later that day, though during the
dance the priests will hold the writhing snakes not just in their hands
but in their mouths.

Theodore Roosevelt rises bulkily, unbitten. It is time to leave the mythic world behind. From his reading and conversations over the last month he must know that kivas symbolize emergence, birth. He thanks his hosts, and some of them come over to shake his hand. Then, with an air of great composure, he walks over to the wooden ladder and, bidding goodbye to both men and snakes, climbs back toward the outer world.

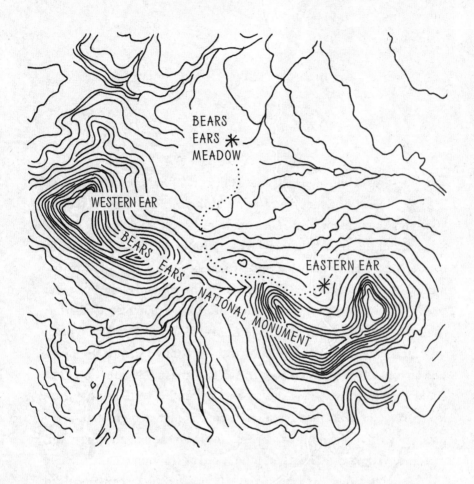

CHAPTER SEVEN

Under Siege

My trip culminated high above the world, this time up on the eastern ear, or rather the eastern earlobe, of Bears Ears. In January Greg Lameman and I had made it to the base of the western ear, but this time I climbed higher. From where I was I could look back on the meadow far below and two miles north where a 120-by-60-foot white tent marked the social center for the reunion of the five tribes during the weekend's fourth annual Bears Ears Summer Gathering. After two months on the road I was tired—*fried* really—ready to point my car east and go home and reunite with my family. But then the invitation arrived, through a friend of a friend, to come to this gathering. How could I say no? Two miles away a couple hundred Native Americans from many different tribes, along with environmental organizers, and a dozen or so of my fellow media people, made up the first meeting of this sort since Trump and Zinke had announced the monument's reduction.

Our public lands have been referred to as our national commons. But the ancestral land below me had been a commons since long before Europeans landed on this continent. Ute traditional territory encompasses Bears Ears, while the Ancestral Puebloan people, including the ancestors of the Hopi and Zuni, have left the elegant evidence of their lives throughout these canyons. The Navajos, who came later, knew this as the birthplace of one of their greatest chiefs and a place of trade. The meadow where the tent was had once served as a gathering place where tribes met, ate, danced, and traded each summer. And for the next few days it would be this again.

The theme of the gathering was "Bears Ears Is Healing," and the morning's speakers stressed that Bears Ears has traditionally been a place of peace, not conflict. But not everyone had gotten the message. Though this celebration was taking place legally on public land—land that was still, despite the reduction of a million acres around it, a national monument—the event hadn't exactly been greeted with open arms by the local ranchers. In fact, as one young Navajo man put it, "It feels like we are under siege."

All day long we had been harassed.

"You look like an environmentalist. Get back in your truck!"

This was the greeting one of my fellow celebrants got when he stepped out of his car on the road to check how deep his back tire had sunk in the muck. The local rancher who yelled it at him had been tailgating the driver on the narrow, bumpy dirt roads.

Amanda Podmore had picked me up in Bluff at dawn and given me a lift here in her truck, and we were among the first arrivals. We found that the signs pointing toward the celebration had been torn down, and that the ribbon that marked the pull-off for the entry road had been stolen. Some of the signs for the event had not simply been torn down but moved so that not just attendees, but also the porta potties, ended up in the wrong place. To fight back, Amanda and a few other volunteers stood out at key points on the roads to point the way and make sure guests weren't being misled. But the hassling continued. Not long before my hike a private plane had buzzed low over our campsite.

"This has happened in past years, too," Dine Bikeyah chairman Willie Grayeyes told me not long after I arrived. "We just ignored them and reestablished our path and kept going forward. That's the only way to do it. These are public lands, federal public lands. It's open to everybody. And they are welcome to put forward a proposal to the United States government. Just as we did."

"You can tell how special a place is by how many people try to keep you away from it," Navajo elder Jonah Yellowman said.

I had seen what he meant during my hike up to the Bears Ears. After a lunch of mutton stew, the matching buttes on the horizon beckoned, and since we were on monument land I assumed I could walk directly toward them. But barbed wire fences and grazing cows cut off most of the access, siphoning me to a point where my only choice was to open a gate, the kind with the barbed wire latch, then scramble up a gully to the public road, and finally arrive at the base of the eastern butte. From there I climbed higher, up the rocks themselves, but still the barriers followed me. In a strange marriage of red rock and barbed wire, of public and private, the fence continued right to where the rock turned vertical, a place no cow could climb to.

It felt odd to be fenced in on land that even Trump and Zinke admitted was still part of the monument. Public lands are said to belong to all of us, but as I climbed I experienced the anxiety of the intruder. Fencing goes where cows go, and nothing says *private* and *stay off* like a fence. Millions of acres of barbed wire and other fencing weaves throughout our public lands, halting the movements of wild animals, many of whom must migrate to survive. The function of the fences is to keep cows in, but they also amount to a giant "UNWELCOME" sign to other human beings, including those humans who are American citizens and therefore the true shareholders and owners of this land.

From where I sat, in a fought-over spot in a fought-over landscape in a fought-over country, I could look out at hundreds of miles of land and a half-full moon in a still-blue sky, all through an opening in a barbed wire fence. Maybe, I thought, maybe this place in the middle of nowhere embodies our world right now. All the battles between red and blue, future and past, are being fought right here, at the point where red rock meets barbed wire and where Native people celebrate while ranchers resentfully prowl the outskirts. This is the battlefield upon which the fate of our public lands is being decided.

San Juan County, which includes Bears Ears, is America, though America seen in a funhouse mirror. The land below me was a place where the local politics seemed so strange as to be otherworldly, but at the same time the issues reflected what has been happening in this country over the last few years. They are like us, only more so.

After I climbed down from the eastern peak, I cut up the public road and then back down the gulley toward the meadow. Just a week before, the trial of environmental activist Rose Chilcoat and her husband Mark Franklin had begun in a case some of us were choosing to call Gate-gate. Chilcoat was a former director of the environmental group Great Old Broads for Wilderness (GOBs), and she and her husband were accused of purposefully closing a gate on state land that denied a rancher's cows access to a watering hole. I took note and since I didn't feel like getting arrested or shot for trying to reach a national monument, I was very careful to follow ranching etiquette and reattach the wire loop that secured the gate that led back to the meadow. Bears Ears might be healing, but good old San Juan County remained a war zone.

In fact at the moment I was hiking down from Bears Ears, San Juan County was involved in several more controversies that might seem exclusively local but had implications that reached far beyond its borders. More importantly, for me, they had implications for how we will treat public lands in this country. Gate-gate wasn't even the strangest of the controversies. The strangest was another local battle that focused on the question of where a candidate's umbilical cord was buried.

Really. The umbilical cord belonged to Willie Grayeyes, whom I had talked to that morning and who was running for county commissioner. Grayeyes had recently stated that the cord in question was buried in Utah, tying him to the land according to Navajo tradition, and that, not incidentally, he had lived for many years in the state. He made his statement in response to a lawsuit brought by an Anglo Blanding resident who claimed that Grayeyes actually lived in Arizona and therefore couldn't become a San Juan County commissioner. Of course Grayeyes also released a thirty-point affidavit proving his Utah residency, but the umbilical cord got most of the attention.

Here the battles never seemed to stop raging between environmentalists and those who resent federal intrusion, and between Native peoples and locals. But who were the real locals? More than 50 percent of the residents of San Juan County were Native American, and by the end of the year two out of the three San Juan County commissioner seats

would go to Navajos. Meanwhile one of the "local" neighboring ranchers and one of the most vociferous opponents of Bears Ears was actually a Colorado resident who leased Utah land, including the Bears Ears
meadows, from the government. As for the land I was walking through,
it was once the childhood romping grounds of the great Navajo chief
Manuelito, who used Bears Ears in the 1860s to hide out from the U.S.
Army but then gave himself up to join his people, and care for the children and elderly, during the Long Walk, the tragic forced eviction and
march of Navajos to Fort Sumner in New Mexico.

"Chief Manuelito wanted peace but he was ready to fight," Kenneth Maryboy, a Navajo who was the Democratic nominee for one of
the three county commissioner seats, had told the crowd over the mic
that morning as a large group of us worked together to set up the huge
tent. Perhaps Maryboy was in a fighting mood, having just won the primary for a commissioner seat over Rebecca Benally, the Native woman
who stood next to Trump when he announced the Bears Ears reduction. Whatever the reason, his talk was the one aggressive note in an
otherwise placid stream of speeches. And while it might not have been
in keeping with the healing theme, it was my favorite.

Maryboy ended his talk by quoting Chief Manuelito, who remained
defiant in the face of the invasion of his homeland by federal troops:
"There is a day when my enemy is going to kill me. But I'm not going to
go quietly. Trees and rocks will be ripped up around me. I will take many
with me before I go."

These words suggested a different, more aggressive route toward
healing.

*   *   *

As I had for much of the trip, I wondered what good an injection of Theodore Roosevelt would do to this strange place. The divisions in southeast Utah, like the divisions in the West and throughout the United
States, are sharp and deep. There are no instant bridges to be built, and
it would be naïve to think that a modern-day TR could come to Bears

Ears and sweep all the anger away. Even during the peak of his popularity he had many haters. But the public as a whole, including the Western public, didn't seem to mind his decidedly environmental bent: the conservationist president would win every Western state when he ran for reelection in 1904. One can't help but wonder if even today a rough-and-tumble Westerner, a hunter maybe, or at least an outdoorsman of the sort Interior Secretary Zinke claimed to be, could make environmentalism seem less precious and crunchy.

The divide then has become a massive chasm now. But does either side really want the land, our great legacy, to be owned just by corporations or the super-rich? "Cows not condos" has become a Western rallying cry, and if those were the only choices most would take cows. While I believe that public lands belong to all Americans, I am not foolish enough to doubt that locals, having lived here for generations, have a much deeper connection to these places. In fact the land, and a love for it, may be the one bond that holds together the warring factions that are currently fighting over this place. The groups may tell different stories, but this is their common ground. If our public lands are battlefields, they also remain what they have always been: the great American commons.

We need to remember that it was Republicans, beginning with Lincoln and culminating with Roosevelt, who ushered in conservation as a national issue, and for more than a century the effort to protect our land, air, and sea was a bipartisan effort. Theodore's distant cousin Franklin, the prototypical Democrat, saved millions of acres. The Wilderness Act, which preserved nine million acres while officially defining wilderness for the first time as "an area where the earth and its community of life are untrammeled by man, where man himself is a visitor who does not remain," was signed into law by Lyndon Johnson. But it was none other than Richard Nixon who presided over the largest and perhaps most important passage of environmental laws in the country's history, laws that included the Endangered Species Act, the Clean Air Act, and the creation of the Environmental Protection Agency. For a long time it made sense that the word "conserve" was contained in the word conservative, since the wealthy, who had a whole lot invested in keeping things as they were, had been among the front guard of conservationists.

Perhaps the most fateful day for public lands in recent times, and the day that has had the greatest effect on lands like those I had looked down at from the Bears Ears peak, was December 12, 2000, the day that the Supreme Court decided that George Bush, rather than Al Gore, would be the next president. There are other dates you could choose, but for the Bureau of Land Management and the hundreds of millions of acres it manages, this would prove a turning point. The BLM, newly anointed as the manager of Grand Staircase-Escalante National Monument by Bill Clinton's interior secretary Bruce Babbitt, had finally begun to think of itself as the protector of its vast domain, not just the administrator of more than twenty thousand oil, gas, and coal leases, on top of its leases to ranchers, under the doctrine of "multiple use." But that brief renaissance ended with Bush's election, the agency stripped of funds and stocked with pro-ranching and often Mormon administrators, and barely improved under Obama.

Since then there have still been occasional spasms of morality and vision, like the BLM's "Treasured Landscapes" initiative. You might consider my ideas about taking the land back from the ranchers and the cows, and restoring habitat on public lands while linking those lands as migratory paths, to be pie in the sky. But that was exactly the vision that the BLM, that most conservative and time-rutted of government land organizations, came up with in 2010. This included connecting the parks, in part by creating a Theodore Roosevelt Wildlife Conservation Area that would link the North Rim of the Grand Canyon with Utah's Vermillion Cliffs. But that flame, like the others, began flickering almost immediately and with Trump it was snuffed entirely. The words "conservative" and "conservation" have now been formally divorced. During his campaign Trump called the Environmental Protection Agency "a disgrace," and when asked who was going to protect the environment if not that organization, he said: "We'll be fine with the environment. We can leave a little bit, but you can't destroy businesses."

There was always a practical side to Theodore Roosevelt, sharing space with his inner radical. He knew that by preserving public land he was preserving natural resources and that while those resources were to be used wisely, the idea was that they were eventually going to be *used.* But he also believed this: "There is nothing more practical than the preservation of beauty."

A country as surely grows out of its physical features as human beings grow out of their physiology, and the existence of so-called wild places has always been part of this country's DNA. I am not claiming that Americans are the only people on earth to have a deep relationship with their place. That would be absurd and jingoistic. Cultures all over the world have grown out of the land on which they live, and have beautifully expressed their love for those lands. But while Americans are not unique, it is not absurd to say that we, too, have developed a certain sort of language, and a kind of spiritualism, in our attitude toward the land. It is reflected in our literature and our art. I remember speaking to a book club in Colorado made up of people you would otherwise mostly regard as nonreligious, and hearing their tone shift to one of reverence when I asked them about nature. I don't think it is an exaggeration to say that for more than a small percentage of Americans, nature *is* their religion.

Now imagine a people who have lived in this same landscape for not hundreds but thousands of years, and who—for most of those people and most of that time—regarded the land itself as sacred. Let's follow Regina Lopez-Whiteskunks's lead and leave aside for the moment the story of how much of that land was ripped away from them, dwelling instead on the simple fact of the relationship between humans and the land. We know it did exist for millennia. Does it still exist? Can it still exist? Does a Hopi performing a ceremony in the shadow of Bears Ears have a similar experience to an Ancestral Puebloan? Or is it closer to a hiker on the trail up to Half Dome? Is the Native and Anglo experience by definition dissimilar, or does having the land in common give us other things in common, too?

If we still believe in the land in this cynical, self-conscious, virtual, divided time, then the experiment called Bears Ears is vitally important, not just for itself but for our larger thinking about public lands. This is not mere romanticism. I am well aware that most Native Americans, even those who live nearby, know little about the debate over the national monument. I understand that not every Indigenous person who enters this landscape feels a deep spiritual connection. No more than most Anglos do. Not everybody who walks into church has their thoughts turn to God either. Which doesn't mean churches are worthless.

The most radical idea at the center of the creation of Bears Ears is that for *some* people, perhaps for only a few, this land can continue to serve the purpose it has for thousands of years. It can be protected, yes, the way other parks and monuments are protected, and parts of it put aside from any human use. But it will also be not just a place of hiking trails and trailhead signs, but also a conscious and active place for ceremony, for the collecting of plants and herbs as well as wood, for social gatherings and storytelling. For seeing religion, something sacred, in the land. And what could be more American than that?

*   *   *

Like Chief Manuelito, TR was never going to go quietly. Everyone knew that. He was blessed with a moral certainty that we might envy, or possibly, fear. He was not afraid of being called a hypocrite. He could kill animals and fight for them in one breath. He would attack his enemies with a relentless fury but then surprise them with his magnanimity and kindness. A lover of birds, he was a strange one.

Leave it as it is. The truth is that while it was a nice phrase, in his personal life Roosevelt was never so great at leaving things as they were. For all his claims of *dee*-lighting in the moment, he always seemed ready to rush off to the next thing. He lived inside a busyness that many of us have come to accept as the only way of being, but since this is Roosevelt we are talking about, his busyness was much busier than yours or mine. On top of everything else, he was a compulsive letter writer, and one imagines that if he lived today he would have shot off thousands of emails a week.

His days as president, when he wasn't romping on the White House lawn with his still-young children or boxing (which he wouldn't quit until a blow led to blindness in his left eye), became, more and more, a crusade against those he called the "malefactors of great wealth." Those same malefactors, in joining together, had formed massive corporations that seemed to serve no interest but their own profit, and they began to regard this rambunctious new president as dangerous and radical. In battling the trusts, Roosevelt saw his mission as a moral one. He railed against "predatory wealth" and "purchased politicians." He, in his own words, "strove manfully for righteousness." We can laugh at the "manfully," but we sure could use the "righteousness." Roosevelt had his flaws, but he was always good in a fight, demonstrating the advantages of pugnacity. Not the current brand. But fighting for good. Or, since "good" is so subjective, at least for something beyond one's self and one's profits. Particularly when that meant fighting for individual humans, or groups of humans, aligned against corporations.

He said: "The Constitution guarantees protection to property and we must make that proposition good. But it does not give the right of suffrage to any corporation. The true friend of property, *the true conservative*, is he who insists that that property shall be the servant and not the master of the commonwealth. Who insists that the creature of man's making shall be the servant and not the master of the man who made it. The citizens of the United States must effectively control the mighty commercial forces which they have themselves called into being."

Edmund Morris tells us that Roosevelt believed there could be "no check to the growth of special interests so long as channels of collusion flowed back and forth between secretive boardrooms and secretive halls of government." As Roosevelt wrote: "Of all the forms of tyranny the least attractive and most vulgar is the tyranny of mere wealth."

This belief came through in his early battles with J. P. Morgan and the railroad trusts, and, more subtly, during the first great crisis of his presidency, the coal strike of 1902. Though he sympathized with the strikers and the charismatic union man who was their leader, John Mitchell, and though he threatened executive action against the owners, what really characterized his leadership during the negotiations between the two sides was restraint. Unexpectedly for this famous rattler of sabers and wielder of big sticks, this same quality would come through in his foreign policy as well. TR was a peacetime president: during his seven years in power he managed not to start a war, and for his role in negotiating the Russo-Japanese peace settlement he became the first American to win the Nobel Peace Prize. Which is not to say he had laid to rest the strain of aggressive imperialism that all but defined him for some. Though he tried dearly, there is really no way to rationalize his seizing of the Panamanian Isthmus, other than to say: he wanted it and so took it. His navy, which he built into a "great white fleet" that steamed around the world, flags waving, gave cover to Panama as they revolted against Colombia, and in return Panama gave TR what he so wanted: a canal that linked the two great seas.

In the end, Roosevelt's presidency was a study in contradictions—the child of wealth was a great friend to labor and foe of corporate malfeasance; the bellicose man started no wars; and a final contradiction was that a man who so loved power gave it up so easily. Peremptorily, on the very night he won a landslide victory in November 1904, he decided, and later announced, that he would not run for reelection in 1908, though he had not yet served two full terms. It was a decision that he and many others would come to regret. Certainly those of us who love wilderness still regret it, as he would have no doubt consolidated and then added to the land he saved.

His handpicked successor, William Howard Taft, disappointed him. Probably anyone he picked, that is anyone other than himself, would have disappointed him. Taft's firing of Gifford Pinchot would prove the last straw, but what Roosevelt claimed to object to was Taft's resistance to the progressive movement of the Republican Party that TR had initiated. What he really objected to of course was not being president.

Meanwhile the progressive wing of the party had grown larger and louder, and after a period of equivocation, an inevitable marriage occurred. The Progressive Party, or Bull Moose Party as it would be nicknamed, emerged and their nominee was Theodore Roosevelt.

The progressive platform was stunning in its modernity: a social insurance system for the elderly, unemployed, and disabled; strict campaign finance restrictions; women's suffrage; an eight-hour workday; a minimum wage for women; an inheritance tax; worker's compensation for injuries in the workplace; and a vow to "destroy this invisible Government, to dissolve the unholy alliance between corrupt business and corrupt politics." And, since TR was in charge, this declaration: "There can be no greater issue than that of conservation in this country." Critics accused him of being a socialist, a communist, and indeed one of his most famous backers, Thomas Edison, boasted that Roosevelt was for the "equalization of wealth." The increasingly radical party, and its increasingly radical leader, affected a split in the Republican Party that shook it to its core. "Has the Republican Party ever recovered the liberal wing which abandoned it to follow TR in 1912?" asked Louis Auchincloss in his short biography of Roosevelt in 2001. The answer, obvious enough then, seems irrefutable now.

The comeback version of 1912 was a different Roosevelt, the one with the glint in his eye and a rising megalomania, "radiant with righteousness" in the words Edmund Morris used to describe TR's fellow progressives. He no longer seemed as interested in walking the ridgeline between the practical and the progressive. If his presidency was relatively pacifistic, his comeback tour had an intensity that rivaled the Crusades. There could not have been a more fitting soundtrack than "Onward, Christian Soldiers," the song the Bull Moose Party played at their convention in 1912. Roosevelt declared his candidacy by coining a phrase: "My hat is in the ring!" But it was another phrase, less colloquial and more like the pronouncement of a true believer, that he yelled out to the adoring crowd after accepting the nomination at the convention: "We Stand at Armageddon, and we battle for the Lord!"

The most memorable moment of the campaign that followed was also one of the strangest in the history of American politics. That occurred when Roosevelt, stepping out of his car and doffing his hat to a crowd of supporters, was shot in the chest from close range by a would-be assassin named John F. Schrank.

It was Roosevelt's words that saved him. Not anything he said to his attacker, but his speech, folded neatly in his breast pocket, which along with his metal spectacles case might have slowed the bullet enough to save his life. As was characteristic with TR, it was a very long, and therefore very thick, speech, fifty pages long and a hundred folded. "I've been pinked," Roosevelt is reported to have said when he reached below his overcoat and found blood. All those around him urged him to get to the hospital, and anyone but Roosevelt would have done so. But he had a speech to give, and as I mentioned above, it was not a short speech. He asked the crowd to be quiet, explaining he had been shot, but assuring them that "it takes more than that to kill a bull moose." He spoke for forty-five minutes, paused, then went on for another half an hour. Only then did he consent and allow himself to be brought to the hospital.

If it wasn't Armageddon, it was close. It would have been fitting for Roosevelt's campaign, with its zealous feel of a mission, to have ended in martyrdom. But Roosevelt recovered, though he was forced to sit out the rest of the campaign at Sagamore Hill. Most think the assassination attempt actually helped his chances by swelling the sympathy vote. It wasn't enough, though he made a good showing in the end, beating Taft by more than a half million votes but effectively handing the election to the Democrats and Woodrow Wilson, whom he would soon enough grow to despise.

While the Bull Moose charge fell short, the ideas that grew out of that campaign became part of the national dialogue. Roosevelt hadn't succeeded at this only because he willed it to be so, no matter how much the mythmakers, himself included, would like us to believe. He succeeded in part because of who he was, a force of nature, but also because his timing was very, very good.

"Perhaps once in a generation," Roosevelt wrote in "The Purpose of the Progressive Party," "perhaps not so often, there comes a chance for the people to play their part wisely and fearlessly in some great battle for the age-long warfare for human rights."

The progressive window opened at just the right moment for Roosevelt to launch some new ideas through it. As despairing and desperate as the current times might seem, it may be worth noting that there *are* openings. One of the tragedies of Bears Ears is that it seemed, for a brief moment, to be just that sort of opening. A moment of redress, yes, but also of joy. As with all such moments there was a double-take aspect to it. *Wait, really? This might actually happen?* The extraordinary thing is not that cynicism usually wins out, but that sometimes it doesn't.

*   *   *

Driving into the town of Bluff means seeing the sign saying that it was founded in AD 650, but in the town of Blanding, just to the north, you will see different sorts of signs, many of them with the message "RESCIND BEARS EARS." Both towns lie just to the east of Bears Ears and both towns were founded, in their modern incarnations at least, by Mormons. Less than thirty miles separate them, but they are worlds apart. Blanding, with a population of 3,373 at last count, is still primarily a Mormon town, though plenty of Native Americans, some also Mormon, live there. Bluff has a motley, almost hippie-enviro feel, though it has its share of Mormons, too. The two towns mirror the national scene.

Many of the local controversies swirl around the County Commission, which for years has been dominated by Anglos and Republicans. When Trump claimed he had "local support" for shrinking the Bears Ears monument, he meant, in part, that the commissioners had supported him. But that was changing: during my first week in Bluff a federal judge ruled that the county districts had long been gerrymandered, gerrymandering that worked against the county's Indigenous citizens, and the court had ordered that the maps for the next election be redrawn. Which meant that it looked like two Navajo candidates, one of them being Willie Grayeyes if he could prove he lived in Utah, could have a majority on the commission. Which, of course, would also mean a majority of the local government would be supporting Bears Ears.

If it is hard for outsiders to comprehend the strangeness of local politics here, in this corner of southeast Utah, it is even harder to understand the pervasiveness of Mormonism in San Juan County. A couple of days before heading to the Bears Ears celebration, I had driven up from Bluff to stop in at the accounting offices of Phil Lyman, a county commissioner in favor of the Bears Ears reductions, on Main Street in Blanding. When I told the receptionist I was a reporter there to see Mr. Lyman, she looked wary, as did Lyman himself when he invited me into his sparse office in the back of the building.

He was right to be wary of course, since I was an environmentalist and he was a known enemy of my kind, infamous not just for his stand against Bears Ears but for many years of similar stands, including a staged all-terrain vehicle protest with Ryan Bundy, son of the famous Oregon Malheur Refuge "rebel" Cliven Bundy, that landed Lyman in jail for ten days. It was Lyman's seat that Willie Grayeyes was trying to win, and Lyman in turn, realizing he had little chance in his newly un-gerrymandered district, was running for the Utah House of Representatives.

Lyman was younger than I'd expected, and calmer. Could this clean-shaven baby-faced man really be the bogeyman of environmentalists' nightmares? This was a kinder, gentler sort of Bundy, and what caught me off guard was how soft-spoken and reasonable he was. In a manner that would be familiar to those who have heard Mormons preach, he spoke in a quiet, inoffensive, almost feminine-sounding voice. He sat behind his desk and politely offered me a seat, though he worried out loud about being smeared by yet another liberal reporter.

"I'd actually like to see the Navajo have a greater presence in the government, in the city government, on the councils, and the school board, all those things," he said. "And I look forward to that, not because I think it's racially politically correct, but because I'm familiar with their culture, and it's amazing. It's got a lot to offer our society, and we are living below our privileges if we don't take advantage of that opportunity to develop relationships."

How could I argue with that? I couldn't. Though it contradicted everything I'd read about him, he was saying it now and saying it in a soothing, believable way.

"It's not a Native American versus a non-Native fight to us," he continued. "It's very much a neighbor versus neighbor, friends versus friends. A lot of the Navajos in San Juan County are very opposed to the monument, and a lot of whites in San Juan County are very in favor of the monument. So this idea that it somehow divides along skin color is, I think it's offensive on the face of it at the premise."

"Why do you think Navajos might oppose the monument?" I asked.

"I think the biggest fear that we had was that a national monument would bring unwanted attention and visitation to something that we all agree is sacred. And it has done that. The traffic is way, way up. Tourism is way, way up. Just because something is appealing to a lot of people doesn't mean you should sell it. And a national monument feels like it is selling Bears Ears to the rest of the world."

This, too, was not unreasonable. Though so far I hadn't run into a single Navajo who actually opposed the monument, some environmentalists in Bluff expressed the exact same worry, that if their town became the "gateway to Bears Ears," Bluff could become another Moab. In this part of the world "Another Moab" is shorthand for the garish commercialization that can come when the adventure and tourist biz overruns a town.

If you wanted to play devil's advocate, you could argue that it is the people in Blanding who want to "leave it as it is" or at least as it has been for the last century or so. What it has been is their backyard, a place where cows graze, a place where people go for firewood, a place with few tourists, a place you head up to in your truck to hunt and camp unbothered. While people might have different ways of describing what it is that they get from places like Bears Ears, "freedom" is a word used in Blanding and Bluff by Anglos and Native people and environmentalists alike. If they could all keep it like it is, minus the looting, and barring any extractive industries muscling in, they all might be happy enough. But that "as is" is no longer possible. The usual problem—too many humans—combined with GPSs that can track down previously unknown ancient sites, have made that impossible. Also mining and energy companies, emboldened by the new administration, are eyeing the empty spaces on the maps. Which means that while the debate is over where to go next, going backward isn't an option.

At first what Lyman said made sense to me, and I was partly won over by his manner. It was only when he started to talk about my sort, his *enemies*, that cracks began to show in his reasonableness. It started slowly.

"My observation is that the environmentalists, the liberals, are the first ones to sell out," he said. "Someone waves a little money, and they are ready. And they do it while wrapping themselves in the flag of environmentalism and protecting the earth, and they sell right out. Conservatives aren't as likely to do that. They say, you know, 'I'm happy with being poor and being free. I'm not interested in selling out to anybody for any price.'"

He had particular ire for Patagonia, the sportswear and mountaineering company that, along with many environmental groups, had supported the Bears Ears cause.

"That's what's so ironic about a company like Patagonia coming in and criticizing local county commissioners, like myself. It's like, 'Wait a second, you're the one that's in the industrialized tourism business. Listen, the reason you're a heavyweight with politicians is because you throw around so much money.' And then they come out here and act like they're trying to save this area with a national monument, which has brought exactly the thing that's going to, as Wallace Stegner or Edward Abbey would say, bring industrial tourism, that's a bigger threat to the environment than a few non-Native people trying to make their mortgage payment each month."

My jaw didn't drop, but I was truly surprised that this Republican anti-monument rebel was quoting Abbey and Stegner to me. And talking about "industrial tourism." It was quite brilliant really: he was speaking my language. Moreover, he was taking the words of his opponents and using those words against them. I was impressed.

Gradually, however, a deeper sense of victimization crept into his monologue. When he told me the story of how the national monument came to be, after attempts to negotiate between the San Juan County commissioners, the state, and the Dine Bikeyah and environmental groups, that sense became more pronounced.

"The biggest misconception of San Juan County is that we are really engaged in this fight. We are certainly concerned. But we have so little to say over what happens on public lands. If you take San Juan County south of Monticello only one percent is private property. So you are talking about people who live on little islands of private property in an ocean of public land. We are used to not having control of what happens on that land. We were used to being treated kindly and fairly, up until about twenty years ago, and since then we have been treated like trespassers on our own land. Process is more important than product. And the process that they've used to do this is really an offensive process."

"What is offensive about the process?" I asked.

"I don't want to drift into anything with any kind of crude connotation, but in our society we place a high value on consensual engagement rather than nonconsensual engagement. So when they come to a community and say 'Hey, we'd like to do a monument or other designation here, will you work with us?,' we say 'Yes, we'll work with you on that,' and then they get to a certain point and they say 'Screw this, we're doing what we want to do and you can just bend over and take it. Because we've got the power to do that.' And then they do that."

Suddenly he was sounding a lot less like a Mormon preacher.

"In a one-on-one relationship that sort of thing creates some really hard feelings. People never get back that kind of trust. And yet we're supposed to just overlook that and say 'Oh well, it's what we were going to do anyway.' So the fact that they just took it without our consent I guess we are supposed to just say it's okay."

"And who is the 'they'?" I asked.

"Obama. President Obama."

And there it was. Phil Lyman knew the West much better than I did, had lived there his whole life, but I would argue with his contention that local people in his position thought they were being treated fairly and kindly "up until about twenty years ago." Rather I would say that his stance toward those in Washington who control federal lands is no different than how his great-grandparents felt when Teddy was doing the designating. Local versus federal. The song remained the same.

In Lyman's retelling of the monument creation myth he was not just the victim but the hero. In this story he, far from opposing Dine Bikeyah, helped create the Navajo organization, and then supported the idea of setting apart more than six hundred thousand acres of Cedar Mesa as a national conservation area, an area that was to be called *Nahodishgish*. (A word that Lyman interestingly defined differently than Greg Lameman, as "broken-up land," not land that should be left alone, showing how the local fight extended even to the definition of words.) Then, in Lyman's retelling, the bad guys stepped in and caused trouble. Those bad guys were the environmental groups that misled the poor Indians.

Still, when the conservation area was proposed, Lyman had agreed that if the land was sacred to some members of the community it was sacred to all members. But next Dine Bikeyah, now headed by an Anglo environmentalist not a Navajo, demanded even more land. To which Lyman claimed to have said: "Now it feels like you are trying to take advantage of this and you won't take yes for an answer. I know the Delphi method of argument. You are trying to blow things up. You are trying to make the county the villain and we are not the villain."

In Lyman's story the environmental groups had hijacked a legitimate grassroots effort. And also portrayed Lyman and his allies as white and racist.

"Again that same rapist mentality," he said. "*I would rather force this on you than have you go along with it.* It's not a situation where two people can't get along. It is one where one is constantly forcing their will nonconsensually on the other and the other is pleading, looking for somebody in the media or politics to actually tell the truth about this."

After the interview I walked out into the streets of Blanding with my head spinning. This was a different story. No wonder the two sides couldn't agree: their narratives were completely at odds. At least, unlike some politicians, Lyman told a coherent story. A little heavy on the rape analogies but relatively coherent. I had no doubt that he loved the land. And I knew, for instance, that the story of his own ATV rebellion had been mischaracterized by the media. When he said he did not actually trespass during the ATV rebellion, he was telling the truth. It was the young Ryan Bundy, son of Cliven, who actually stirred things up and rode his ATV up among the ruins of Recapture Canyon. Lyman had stayed back at the trailhead, but he was the local politician and so he took the fall and went to jail.

It is not as if I was completely buying what Lyman was selling. While his voice was soft, his tones at the very least mimicking the reasonable, what he was saying contradicted most of what I had read and most of what the people I had talked to had said. The smooth voice overlayed an almost Nixonian sense of victimization.

Yet it was good to hear a different story. If all we are ever going to do is yell our own stories at each other, without even attempting to empathize with the other side, how can we get anywhere? I question coming into a place or to an issue with your mind made up. If I see everything just as an advocate, I will not see what is in front of me. But how do we both open our minds and fight for what we believe?

Is it possible to both empathize with the other side and take a stand? The current president has given fighting a bad name, but can't we advocate intelligently, without descending to name-calling and pettiness? Our twenty-sixth president had a little of the forty-fifth in him, and when he attacked he attacked like a street fighter. But at least he thought first. At least he listened. At least he read. At least he could consider opposing points of view. He could keep an open mind, but once that mind was made up, watch out.

* * *

Gradually the outside anger at the Bears Ears gathering died down and was almost forgotten. The weekend continued peacefully, including prayer, medicinal plant walks, programs for kids, traditional Ute music, and the dedication of the Bear Totem Pole that was carved and brought as a gift of goodwill and support from the Lummi tribe of Washington State.

I liked the routines we found ourselves getting into up in that cool mountain air below the Bears Ears. This was the most social camping I'd ever done, dozens of tents and trailers dotting the meadow, and before dawn many of us emerged from our tents, mumbled hello to one another, and then went off like zombies in search of coffee in the kitchen tent area. There was even a militaristic aspect to our rituals. Each morning a color guard made up of Native veterans raised the American flag. After the day was done, we all would wander out to greet the sunset near the Bear Totem Pole.

The weather was perfect, and violet morning light played off of the ramparts of the Bears Ears, with their rich, almost edible, red-orange colors shining from below the green of pines and firs. Mountain bluebirds and swallows shot from tree to tree. You could see why this was a natural place to meet and trade over the centuries, for gatherings between tribes in a field that looked up at the great green arching cradle between the two ears. It smelled good up in the pines and felt good, too, after weeks of baking. You could almost fantasize that members of the tribes and ranchers could meet in the same meadow and talk out their differences. Almost.

Up in the meadow I heard different stories from the one Phil Lyman told me. I spoke with Tommy Rock, who had recently earned his doctorate in earth science and environmental sustainability at Northern Arizona University and was working as a postdoctorate research associate at the Rocky Mountain Center for Occupational and Environmental Health. Tommy grew up on Navajo Nation lands in Monument Valley where the unemployment rate was almost 50 percent. He had taken a job in the tourist industry but at one point decided that he had had enough: he was going to go to college. With no clear path toward that goal he stuck out his thumb and hitchhiked south to Arizona and somehow managed to enroll at Yavapai College. That was the beginning of an intellectual journey that would lead to grad school and ultimately wind back to the reservation.

Tommy Rock was soft-spoken and bespectacled but intense. He grew up among the uranium tailings from abandoned mines and watched his grandfather die of cancer after working in the uranium mines. His dissertation was on uranium exposure in sheep. Sheep are a staple of the Navajo diet, and uranium from abandoned mines bioaccumulates in the animals.

"Uranium mines have been an issue in the Four Corners for a very long time," he told me. "There are about five hundred and twenty-three abandoned uranium mines in the region and a history of companies not cleaning those mines up."

Tommy's interest in science came first, but then in 2016, as part of his research, he discovered that the drinking water in the mostly Navajo town of Sanders, Arizona, was contaminated with uranium. The water company did not alert the citizens to the problem, but media coverage of Rock's findings did. Schools and homes started shipping in water, and the contract with the original water provider was terminated. For the first time Tommy Rock had a clear sense of how science combined with advocacy could help the people in his community.

Another highlight of the celebration was speaking with Mark Maryboy, Kenneth's brother, who in 1986 became Utah's first Native American county commissioner. That wasn't his *first* first: ten years before he had graduated from the University of Utah after being, along with his brother, the first two reservation kids to attend and graduate from public school in San Juan County. That school was in Blanding.

"I would say that this is a continuing struggle between Native Americans and non-Native Americans, specifically in this area since 1879, when the Mormons arrived," he told me.

We have all watched the impact that born-again Christians have had on our country's politics, but most Easterners remain unaware of how great an impact Mormonism has had on our public lands. A persecuted people, and a people who saw themselves as chosen, it is undeniable that they had a genius for cultivating land that many thought uncultivatable. They also had a gift for community, for understanding that it was just the opposite of rugged individualism that was needed to settle a vast and arid place like the West. But they also labored under the conviction that the land was theirs, God-given, and that what God wanted was for that land to be cultivated by *them*. Which left little room for others or other traditions of land use. It wasn't just Cliven Bundy and his sons, and their more extreme followers, who were Mormon. In Utah, Mormons had long controlled local and state government, and the religion colored the politics of other Western states as well. A recent report by the Religious Congregations and Membership Study concluded that Mormonism was the fastest growing religion in twenty-six states in the U.S., with two million new adherents over the last decade.

"The ranchers up here are upset that we are encroaching on their land," Maryboy told me. "But where we're sitting right now is where Navajos used to live. Where the first chief, the leader of the Navajo Nation, was born. This is a ceremonial place, a very sacred land, a homeland."

He shook his head slowly.

"Since the day the Mormons came, there's been nothing but conflict. And that continues today. The only difference is that in the past Native Americans as a whole have never attempted to designate a monument that would protect their homeland. We never thought we had to—we thought of it as *our* land. But it's the looting and the threat of industrial activity that has caused Native Americans to act. Drilling for oil. Mining for uranium. Leaving toxic material in the ground. It had huge impact on the health of Native American people."

I knew the issue wasn't as clear-cut as either side made it out to be. I had been told by both Navajo and Anglo friends that some Indigenous people who use Bears Ears for wood-cutting, far from being engaged in sacred ceremonies, often leave behind a trail of Bud Light and diapers. And I knew that in the local battle of ignorance, between Mormons and Native people, many of the Native people are at the very least competitive. Maryboy, shaking his head, told me what one of his own people had said to him while explaining why they didn't believe they had the right to the land: "I thought the white people were here first." *I thought the white people were here first.*

But Maryboy put the lie to one of the stereotypes being perpetuated by those who opposed the original map of Bears Ears and supported the current reduction. The stereotype is that the decision to create Bears Ears as a monument was rash, fast, thoughtless. It is obvious to anyone who takes more than a few minutes to look into the issue that long study was a crucial aspect of the monument's creation. But what Mark Maryboy made clear to me is that Bears Ears has been a Native American priority for much longer than that. He told a story of being a kid in the sixties on the reservation and having his parents say 'Mark, you have to come hear this man speak tonight.' The man was Bobby Kennedy, who was running for president, and who was visiting the reservation. That night Kennedy asked the elders on the reservation what their priorities were and how the federal government could help. And Mark remembers what the elders said to Bobby Kennedy: "You need to protect the Bears Ears."

Another stereotype is that people say the tribes couldn't have possibly conceived of this idea, and had to be put up to it by white environmentalists. This proposes that Native people are being used as unknowing props to achieve liberal environmental ends. In fact, the union between the two groups seems, to my eye, happily reciprocal, a sense I first got from talking to Regina Lopez-Whiteskunk, who was thankful for the help from non-Indigenous groups as long as they let Indigenous groups lead the way.

*   *   *

On Saturday, Regina joined the gathering below the Bears Ears. Throughout the weekend she was everywhere: giving a talk under the big white tent, playing with her grandchildren and drumming with her father, joining in the 5K on the last morning.

Maybe Regina Lopez-Whiteskunk and Teddy Roosevelt were unlikely costars in my summer's drama, but maybe not. They both held agendas and ideas wrapped in great energy and personal charm. They both committed themselves to a fight, but not at the expense of the rest of life and its pleasures. They both spilled over with personality. And, importantly, they both seemed to have a lot of fun.

I didn't get a chance to sit down one-on-one with Regina during the gathering, but a week before I'd driven to see her at the reservation visitor center near her home in Towaoc, Colorado, not far from Mesa Verde. Outside the center, we sat and talked inside her Dodge Challenger.

"Our history is written on the land," she said. "It is written on the rock walls. You let them destroy that and you're ripping out my textbook, my history, and my history is my grandchildren's history."

I mentioned how Bears Ears seemed to contain almost every aspect of the public lands debate.

"I think so," she said. "I think this is the one example that is going to lead us into the bigger conversation about public lands throughout the country. This is setting the tone. This is going to set those precedents that others will follow and use. And to see and to know that the original designation was a request of Native Americans saying, 'This is a tool that's always been used against us. In the best interests of Native people, we're making a decision.' Well, we asked and we requested for the tool to be used in our best interest. So, there's a certain amount of empowerment and responsibility, duty and obligation, that we're joining in efforts together with environmental groups, with the federal government. To be able to have joined all of that together, and say, 'We want this as a larger group of people. Use the tool the way it was set up to be used. That was to preserve and protect Native American antiquities.'

"Seeing Bears Ears reduced by eighty-five percent, to two small pieces of land, leaves us with a memory that we've already gone through,"

Regina continued. "The only difference about this time is it's not my people specifically, the Ute Mountain Ute or any one tribe, that feel that reduction in the pain of feeling like something was taken, but it's the American people. The American people now, as a whole, because it was a public land area, we all feel the pain of having something taken away from us. And so now, it's not just a tribal people. It's all the United States citizens whom all public lands belong to. We all have a say in that. And so, the pain is shared."

It is a time of crisis, of seeming regression, but Regina for one hasn't given up.

"I need to let people know where we've gone, what we've been through, where we are today. This is a call to action. A time to set the tone for future land debates and set the tone of the Indigenous voices in those debates."

It was good for me to hear her voice again. Despite all the anger and the divisiveness, I still cling to the belief in a possible confluence of the ideals that drove us to preserve parks and an older relationship with the land. I am not suggesting that it is likely that such a confluence can occur, and it is even less likely that it will manifest itself in government action. A confluence, by definition, is a coming together, and we are told again and again that we have never been so far apart, so divided, in this country. But if spending all this time with Theodore Roosevelt has taught me anything, it is that ideas matter.

One thing I know: the old myths of preservation, with their secret underbellies of plunder and violation, must die. That means that we will need new myths. Myths that will help us fight together, not against one another, for the greater preservation of the land. Myths that don't just allow us to save and protect land, but that help us reenvision and reintroduce ourselves to the still-vast wilderness that has been handed down to us.

Roosevelt started the story for us, but it is our job to finish it. Bears Ears, it turns out, is not a bad place to look for new myths, myths that have grown out of an older time, to help us when we need them most. Bears Ears shows how we can take a good idea and make it better.

Preserving the land is a fine impulse, but it can be married to something even finer. Here, on lands sacred, ancestral, and, yes, public, you can find pretty much every issue affecting the debate over the future of our lands, and almost all the characters who play parts in that drama. Bears Ears is not just the home of cows and cowboys and Native people and ancestral sites, it is also a land that reaches down to the Arizona border, where it connects and creates a path from the lands north of the Grand Canyon. The dream of a great migratory pathway through the canyon and deserts and up the spine of the Rockies, the visionary dream of forward thinkers like Harvey Locke and Dave Foreman and the father of conservation biology, Michael Soulé, is not as far-fetched as some think. Just look at a map. If you do, you will see just how connectable these land islands are, how Teddy and others have given us a potential escape route we can offer to the species stranded by the changing climates that our industries have wrought. And more than that their work suggests a new, and deeper, relationship with the land.

*　　*　　*

On Saturday night, the last night of the gathering, I decided to pack it in early after a delicious dinner of bison and beans. Too tired to conduct any more interviews, I stumbled back to my tent. I was sitting in my camp chair back in the pines when a mule deer walked right up to me and stared with big black eyes and long delicate eyelashes. I didn't take it as a sign; maybe it was, but if so I didn't know of what. When the sun went down, I read with my flashlight, but didn't make much headway.

It occurred to me that I'd been working within two traditions this summer, oral and written. I had collected hundreds of hours of tapes of people talking, and I'd learned a lot from them. But I'd also been reading with a voraciousness that was unusual for me. Maybe Roosevelt was contagious: with his nightly addiction to reading—"Reading is like a disease to me"—he understood that books were a way to commune with the past, to talk to those who'd gone before.

It seems to me that this sort of resurrective activity, that of deep reading, is increasingly unpopular.

"I don't read," an Anglo biologist had said smugly while in line for breakfast that morning.

I was stunned by how proud of herself she seemed. When I followed up, she answered curtly: "I'm a scientist." As if that explained it.

In contrast, Mark Maryboy is justifiably proud of being the first college graduate in his family and thinks he knows one of the keys to why he has been able to lead his people so effectively.

"Reading is how I have grown," he told me. "I have always been hungry for books. I worry about our young people. Without education, without reading, we can't go forward."

Revering the tribal elders is a theme of this weekend, and Maryboy is one of those elders. As are Jonah Yellowman and Willie Grayeyes. Regina may not be old enough to qualify, but she certainly has begun to gain an elder's wisdom and respect.

Books, too, I think, act as our elders. I like when they are taken off their shelves, dusted off, and integrated into our lives. There is something almost radical about still believing books can affect our behavior and that we can talk and listen to them the way we do with those we most respect. "I don't read" is an all too common refrain these days. As is bragging about how busy we are. Add these two ideas together and they suggest that no one could possibly find the time to read. But one of the real pleasures of learning about Teddy Roosevelt is to see how he, even in the midst of a life so bursting with enough effort, energy, and events to make the busiest of us look like slackers, still found time every day to lose himself in his books. And "found time" is wrong. He raced to them, found solace in them, called his time alone with books his favorite part of the day. Nor did he find any contradiction between his life of action and his life of reading, claiming that "the love of books and the love of outdoors, in their highest expressions, have usually gone hand in hand." Picture him in the back of the boat on the Little Missouri, wrapped in

buffalo robes with a rifle pointing at the boat thieves, but also managing
to devour *Anna Karenina*. Or see him in the Amazon, cutting through
brush on his way to the River of Doubt but not forgetting to bring along
a small leather-bound library. I love how *unabstract* books were to him.
How a part of him. He argued with these books, let them roil around in
his brain, and often enough let them guide him.

Biographies, I have found, are particularly good guides. The great biographer, and my former professor, Walter Jackson Bate wrote of how
his lifelong subject, Samuel Johnson, gradually began to see "the special
ways in which biography—permitting as it does the comparison between
life and life, between one person's total experience and our own—can as-
sist us by supporting, encouraging, perhaps clarifying, or at the very least
extending the experience of living." Biography, more than most writing,
can be "put to use" and help in answering that ever-pressing question:
"how to live." For me biographies have been many things, but one thing
they have always been is a tunnel out of my own time. On the most obvious level they teach us that there were times other than these, times
when things felt just as fraught. But they also offer us possibilities, ways
of being, ways that may not at first seem viable in our own time, but that
can ultimately prove not just viable but vital.

There is of course the risk of hero worship. But that seems a risk
worth taking in a time when we are daily reminded that there are no
more heroes. Tearing people down has become our national addiction
and daily habit. I think it is important to resist this. To resist slamming
the door on the past even if what we find there seems flawed to our eyes.
The flaws are part of the value. Look under a hero's hood and you will no
doubt find sloppiness and contradiction, and that, in its way, is hopeful,
too. What we rarely find is consistency, which is what we lately seem to
demand of others (if not ourselves). This is not all bad: our attempts to
take down the worst of the old order and to right old wrongs have done a
world of good. But we have also devolved into a world of bickering, pettiness, and the pulling down of heroes that is the opposite of that larger
spirit. Dogma is the enemy. We have forgotten the discipline and rigor,

and forgiveness, required to talk to ghosts. You can't throw out whole traditions due to laziness and easy generalization.

Since it's a cultural confluence I'm after, I am willing to be critical of those who came before, and to be open to new interpretations of our past. But I do not want to give up the best that the tradition of so-called Western thought has to offer. I will continue to read books that have been read for centuries, to listen to great minds, to talk to ghosts. I also understand that this tradition needs to be opened up to the point of being blasted open. Historically, the texts that have been preserved and the voices that were heard were limited and unvaried. It does not have to be that way going forward. Environmentalism can also become broader. One of the tragedies of Bears Ears, one of the reasons its reduction is so painful, is that here was a glimpse of a new environmentalism, a glimpse of something better. Which of course meant it had to be quashed by the rigid and shallow representatives of the old.

We are changing. The culture is changing. Or rather the cultures. It is my dream that, despite recent evidence and recent politics, we will change into something more creative, more open, more fluid; something larger, more magnanimous, more inclusive, and ultimately more exciting. I know this might not happen. I know that it is more likely that the world will continue to grow more overheated, more overcrowded, more violent and tribally divided. But since I was dreaming and since I was in a tent in a meadow where people had dreamed for millennia, I let myself dream of something great, openhearted, and contradictory. Something flawed, but something that abhors both mere "success" and dogmatic "goodness." Something big and rowdy like a desert creek after the monsoon rains, kicking a hundred different ways, roiling back on itself, multifarious, churning forward.

I closed my books. I'd slept pretty well in my tent, thanks to the cool air, but now I tossed and turned on my pad. When I had finally almost settled down, I began to hear music drifting over from the big tent. And then a voice over the microphone. The voice belonged to Regina.

Regina's was the very first voice I had heard tell the Bears Ears story, back in January, before the reduction, so it seemed fitting that hers would be the last. While I could hear her voice over the PA system, I couldn't quite make out the words. I needed my sleep: the next morning, after I decamped, I would begin the long journey back east. But soon I was giving up on my plans for an early night and climbing out of my sleeping bag and heading back to the big white tent. There Regina, dressed in traditional Ute garb, was dancing to music played by her father and other family members. Her granddaughters, also in traditional dress, sat on the stage behind her, whispering and giggling with each other. I sat in a folding chair and watched with about sixty other people. Then, for what she announced would be the final dance, Regina invited us all to join her.

Some people joined right away, while the rest of us stood up reluctantly. But all of us eventually joined in, and soon enough, in the middle of a tent, we formed a huge circle, holding hands. With Regina leading us and her father banging on the drums and chanting, we began to circle around the perimeter of the tent. Then, gradually, the great snaking circle turned inward on itself and tightened. We circled tighter and tighter until we were one great knotted ball. The dance ended in laughter and applause. We no longer felt like we were under siege.

After the dancing, Regina talked to the crowd. The ranchers, she said, were like emissaries from Trump's Washington, trying to tell us we didn't belong here on this land. Regina told us otherwise. She spoke to all of us. But she also spoke specifically to the Native people in the crowd, of their history and how that history could be put to use now.

"This is not new for us," she said calmly. "We are used to this. We have fought this fight before. We will adapt."

She reminded us of what had already been accomplished.

"We did it. We created the monument. Yes, they are trying to take it away. But we did it. The reductions are not valid or legal. Remember that."

Her voice soothed. A perfect way to end my time, our time, in Bears Ears.

But, walking back to the tent under a sky full of stars, I remembered Kenneth Maryboy's sterner message. I remembered him saying that Chief Manuelito would fight until the end. Taken together the two messages sounded something like this:

We talk, we plan, we teach, we learn, we celebrate, we dance. We tell stories. We try to heal.

But, if necessary, we fight. And, like Manuelito, we will fight with fury, and trees and rocks will be ripped up around us.

We won't go quietly.

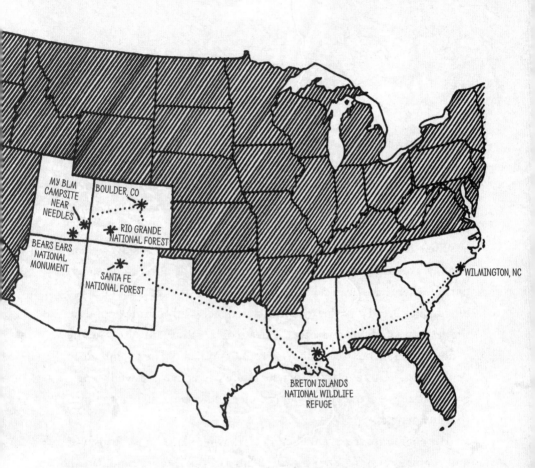

MY BLM
CAMPSITE
NEAR
NEEDLES

BOULDER, CO

RIO GRANDE
NATIONAL FOREST

BEARS EARS
NATIONAL
MONUMENT

SANTA FE
NATIONAL FOREST

WILMINGTON, NC

BRETON ISLANDS
NATIONAL WILDLIFE
REFUGE

* * * CHAPTER EIGHT * * *

Fight and Flight

Things did not end well for Teddy. His inner warrior seemed to take over his personality as the country edged toward the First World War. The decade after he was president was not easy for him, in part because he was no longer president. He liked being in charge it turned out.

There is a price we pay for fighting so hard. Some consider the energy he expended, the many careers he pursued at once, to be superhuman. There have been claims that TR was bipolar, though none of the biographies I read give this idea much credence. Only during periods at the very end of his life and after the death of his father, and also after the almost simultaneous death of his wife and mother, did he fall into deep depressions. That he was temperamentally overactive and wildly energetic was a given, and certainly his coffee addiction didn't tamp down these tendencies.

His engine revved even when there was no place to go. Roosevelt quit running for office after his failed bid as a Bull Moose candidate in 1912, but he never really quit. It's true that throughout his career Roosevelt romanticized the idea of returning to a quiet life at Sagamore Hill, and often promised Edith he would do just that, but he never could. His was the least retiring of natures, and so even his so-called retirement was not a quiet one, from a yearlong safari in Africa to his death-defying trip down the River of Doubt in the Amazon in 1914, a trip from which he really never recovered. He called this trip his "last chance to be a boy," but its overall effect would be turning him into an old man, at least as far as his health was concerned. Heart woes, an infected leg, and malaria were just a few of the ills he would battle over the last years of his life. Of course over the years he had also been shot in the chest and thrown from a crashing trolley car, and no doubt had more than his share of unreported concussions.

His bellicosity would come back to haunt him. He attacked Woodrow Wilson, on the stump and in print, for not being more aggressive about entering World War I, and he began rattling his saber like never before. He just couldn't stop fighting; it wasn't in his nature. When the United States did enter the war in April 1917 he petitioned the president to create his own regiment, to bring back the glory of the Rough Riders and Cuba, romantically supposing that there was still a place for the cavalry within the bloody machine of modern warfare. He was fifty-eight years old, however, and Wilson would not allow it, after which TR's attacks on the president grew even more bitter. Unable to fight himself, he urged his sons to go, exhorting them to dive into battle and get as close to the front lines as they could. They did, and they all paid for it in different ways, his youngest son Quentin with his life. Quentin had been the sunniest and most delightful of his children, and the loss was devastating. All TR's talk of the glories of war circled back on him. Guilt, that unfamiliar emotion, surfaced. The depression that he had fended off for so long descended. His spirits failed, as did his health.

For all that, he was still seen by the national press and millions of Americans as the coming man, popular again as he hadn't been in years, for his early and consistent support of the war, and he was considered the likely Republican candidate for president in 1920. It wouldn't happen. Back when he was a young man his doctor had told him that his heart was defective and that he should therefore live a sedentary lifestyle. He, of course, did the opposite. He decided instead to cram all he could into his life, filling it to the brim, the fuller the better, imagining that he might have sixty years or so to do this. Which was exactly what he got. He died at home in Sagamore Hill on January 6, 1919, at the age of sixty. The cause of death was officially listed as an embolism of the lung, though the complicating factors included a weakened heart and the fact that the pulmonary clot may have traveled to his brain.

Appropriately, Sagamore Hill is now a national historic site, protected and preserved by the National Park Service.

★ ★ ★

On my last morning in Bears Ears I watched a cross-country race through the landscape where Manuelito once hid and fought. Kids giggled and cheered as Regina walked across the finish line in triumph, arms over her head, despite being far behind the winners. Not long after, I said goodbye to Regina, packed my tent, and headed down the hill back to Bluff with Amanda Podmore.

It was time for me to leave the West. But I had one last stop I needed to make. The land outside of the Needles area of Canyonlands National Park was the first place I'd camped in this part of the world almost thirty years before; it was where I started to fall in love with this land. It was also the first time I camped on Bureau of Land Management land, which means we camped for free. The hundreds of acres nearby made up just a tiny percentage of the more than two million acres the BLM manages. Like the rest of BLM land, this is "multiple use": cows graze, rock climbers climb, ATVs charge by. But during the dozen or so times I'd visited, there had been plenty of space and few people. I had come to think of it as "my" place, though it clearly wasn't exclusively so, and in that feeling, some of the beauty and glory of our public lands is revealed.

Summer is monsoon season in the desert and heavy rains had hit. Water in the desert is always welcome, but it can also signal danger. It is a generally waterless land, but when the water comes it comes rushing. It is a strange fact that this dry, dry place is known for its canyons carved by water. During my stay in Bluff I'd gotten to see some of that carving. One minute it was dry and hot and the next water was roiling down old sluices above town. The rain lashed and the red dirt became mucky red gumbo, and before long a half-dozen falls were gushing down from the steep rock walls that circled Bluff. New creeks appeared, too, red in color. When I finally drove away, the rain had stopped but the falls and creeks were still running. My car slipped in the mud. It was more like skiing than driving. You slid with it and leaned and glided along.

On my last day in Utah I hiked into my old campsite. It was next to a creek that was barely a creek and a stone waterfall that had never been a waterfall during my earlier trips. And I expected no more as I hiked in through the desert silence. Then, after about a mile of hiking, I heard the first rumblings. Then the rippling roar. Brown water poured down Indian Creek. The same color as the road and very much like the road but more alive. No babbling Eastern brook this, but more like forceful, flowing dirt. Dirt with a purpose and drive. It was exciting, thrilling even, to see a place I knew so well so changed by water, and when I finally got to the falls I laughed out loud. I had sat below these falls a dozen times, looked up in wonder at its beautiful carved stone steps, but had never observed it serving the function it was built for and that built it. It had taken me twenty-eight years to see it as a true waterfall, and now I did. The great churning surge of water through the desert funneled in and dropped down the steps that earlier rains and floods had created. A muddy rush, a flow of brown life-giving sludge. It dropped three feet to one pool, then circled around as if nervous before making the big drop twelve feet down a chute of purple-blue marbled rock to the next, larger pool. The sight and sound of it had the power to shock: a roaring in the silence, water in the dryness.

It is hard to explain to Easterners who have never visited the West the role that water plays here. When you arrive in the West your nose and tongue know it before your brain does. No one has written more eloquently about the region than Wallace Stegner, who believed that "aridity, more than anything else, gives the western landscape its character." It is aridity that has given the light its clarity, the air its nap, the raw earth its color, and that "erodes the earth in cliffs and badlands rather than in softened and vegetated slopes." Stegner wrote that "the primary unity of the West is a shortage of water," the impact of dryness on the region's people being just as great as on its land and air. Aridity is of course a challenge, a challenge to survival and settling, and one of the great answers given in response to aridity's question is community. Pulling together, contrary to the myths of Western individualism, proves essential in a dry land.

I wanted to simply delight in the waterfall but my brain wouldn't let me. Thinking about water led me to think again about the Canyon Mine near the Grand Canyon and the creek that flowed down to the Havasupai people. When water is your most precious commodity, does it make any sense to mine for uranium? Does it make sense to frack? To log the trees that help keep the water clean, and to allow grazing and shitting cows to turn that water into an E. coli bath? I shook my head. What had always been shortsighted was now closer to actual blindness in a world getting hotter and drier. It felt like an angry insistence that what was wasn't.

As I stared at the born-again waterfall, I gradually stopped thinking about uranium and stopped thinking about aridity and, eventually, stopped thinking about everything except the movement of water. Water. Flowing water. I would say it was like looking at a great painting, but it was too active for that—maybe more like music or watching a thrilling but wordless movie. I pulled myself away and hiked up the dune-like hill that led past the ancient granary and toward the great stone portal that you must pass through to enter a mythic landscape of rock, following the dirt road that led north and west to building-sized stone needles sprouting up in the desert. For all the boom of population in the West it remains a place where it is possible to feel entirely alone, and that was what I felt out on that silent road below the rocks. While it was true that the sheer novelty of this red rock landscape had worn off for me, and that this place did not have the Martian impact it did during my first hikes here, I still occasionally looked up and gawked at the twisting gorgons and mushrooms of stone.

What we call a place affects how that land is treated. As I said good-bye to my first campsite, I considered its changing identity and worried about its future. When I had known this land as a young man it was called BLM land. Then, briefly, it was part of the greater contiguous Bears Ears National Monument. Now it had a new name.

The original name for Bears Ears was the product of much thought. Back in Bluff I had met with James Adakai, president of the Oljato Chapter of the Navajo Nation and a Bears Ears commissioner. We sat on a bench at a picnic table behind the Recapture Lodge, not far from the San Juan River, and he told me about all the work that went into the creation of the Bears Ears monument proposal and the thinking that went into the name.

He pointed west toward Bears Ears, a landmark that it seems you can see from almost anywhere in the Four Corners.

"Those are sacred ancestral hills," he began. "For thousands of years our ancestors drew strength from them. The minerals, the vegetation, the woods, the birds, all the traditional uses. In Navajo it is a way of life. We want to teach that way to future generations. That's what Bears Ears is all about."

Though the Bears Ears Inter-Tribal Coalition is made up of five tribes, James reiterated what Regina had told me: that it was the Navajos who began the work, through the grassroots group Dine Bikeyah.

"Dine Bikeyah did the cultural mapping of the area. They did the legwork, the foundation, data collection and research, identifying sensitive cultural historical areas in the Bears Ears region. The sacred places, the Anasazi ruins, the burial ground, the vegetation. That was how they formed the maps and decided what should be saved. They also did interviews of eighty elders. The cultural knowledge of the elders, their historical knowledge, was immense, and it wasn't easy to collect. So that contradicts one of the assumptions about the Bears Ears proposal: that it came up overnight. The people think we just suddenly came up with this plan. But it wasn't that way. There was a huge effort put into the research and the planning."

It was after this initial work that Dine Bikeyah reached out.

"While the Dine Bikeyah were putting the plan together, they decided to reach out to other tribes. The Hopi and Zuni because of the rock art and Anasazi ruins. The Ute Mountain Ute, who have historically used the land and still have a piece of land east of Bears Ears. And also of course the Utes who had historical ties. So that formed the Inter-Tribal Coalition."

The original name for the monument was also the product of much thought. Since Dine Bikeyah did most of the early work, the coalition briefly considered using those very words, which mean "people's sacred lands," as the name. But each of the five tribes had names for the twin buttes of Bears Ears, all meaning, roughly, "bears ears." The coalition concluded that the English name was best, to show unity and to avoid conflict between the tribes.

And then along came Trump and Zinke. They not just massively reduced the monument but chopped it into two unconnected sections. Archaeologists who have studied the area agree that there is no scientific or cultural logic to the way that the new borders were created, and that they often cut right through the middle of the archaeological sites of ancient communities. But the administration was not content to slice and dice with no scientific or cultural logic. They decided to rename the two smaller sections as well. They called the southern section, that contains the Bears Ears buttes, by its Navajo name, "*Shash Jaá*." And they called the northern section "Indian Creek."

Zinke claimed to have consulted with the leaders of Dine Bikeyah about the new name. Navajo tribal officers and Navajo Nation lead attorney Ethel Branch have said otherwise: there was no consultation with actual leaders.

The coalition's whole effort was one of healing and unity, and the new names speak to division, disunity. Something historic was created with Bears Ears after much time, work, and thought. And then in no time and with little work it was decided that that thing should be destroyed. Does it really matter whether it was done out of ignorance or with the callous thought of cynicism?

To James Adakai it matters.

"They are trying to split us up," he told me. "Trump is setting tribe against tribe. He is dividing and re-naming the monument in a way that messes with the tribes. Trying to disunite. It is an insult to us."

*   *   *

As I drove back east from Utah into Colorado, I was driving into a land of fire. Forests were burning everywhere; smoke billowing from the hills and mountains. It was the same all over the West, a historic fire season occurring in many places. "Historic" was a phrase that no longer meant much though, as the standards kept changing. Dried by drought to the point of desiccation, trees were going up like torches, with massive fires raging not just in Colorado, but in New Mexico, the Pacific Northwest, and most of the other Western states. In California one hundred million trees had been lost to fires over the previous decade, and 120,000 acres had already burned by July, topping the previous year's number. This was many months before the season-capping Camp Fire that inciner-ated the town of Paradise, the deadliest fire in California history.

The fires that had burned during Roosevelt's lifetime were even larger than the recent ones, but not nearly as deadly and destructive to hu-mans. Massive fires are nothing new to the West; a massive human pop-ulation is. Nowhere in the country have those numbers boomed more than the pot-scented state where I once lived. Consider the fact that all those people moving into Colorado often want to live where they think it is most beautiful, which, as it turns out, is also where it burns. Then add in the fact that almost every year we top records for temperature set the year before. Drought, once cyclical, is now the usual, while the pe-riods of wetter weather are now the punctuators. Shorter winters mean longer fire seasons as well as less of the melting snow that provides the region with its water. This is true for trees as well as humans. Next time you are driving through a Western landscape, observe the cottonwoods that cling to the creeks. Now extrapolate: in such a dry land, where arid-ity is king, everyone and everything wants that same water, while there is less and less of it.

The trees that I saw burning had already been weakened internally.

The spread of billions of bark beetles has led to the coring out of once healthy firs and pines. The various beetle species, including spruce beetles and piñon ips, are given a head start on their annual feasting by the shorter winters. They, like almost every other animal in the West, are on the move thanks to the shifting seasons.

The great die-off of Western trees would be a tragedy on its own. But two other factors make things worse. First, the dry and dead trees are perfect kindling for the giant fires that now rage throughout the region. At the same time the loss of these millions of acres is not just a loss of organic life and beauty and habitat for other species, but a loss of the great storehouses of carbon which are one of our only means of mitigating the great increase of atmospheric CO_2. In other words, their loss means more heat and less snow, more beetles and more dead trees for kindling.

There was a reason that our national forests were once called our forest *reserves*. Remember Senator Charles Fulton of Oregon? He was the man who tried to put a stop to all the foolish saving of forest land that Pinchot and Roosevelt had been doing and also the one who insisted that the national forests no longer be called "reserves"; he hated the connotation of preservation in that word, of *reserving* rather than *using* something.

But while the forests underwent a name change, reserves they remained. True these lands have been logged, fracked, grazed, and drilled for over a century now, but they are reserves still, and what we do with them is up to us, the American people. Is it crazy to suggest, in this age of drought and megafires, that what we ought to do is protect them and their earth-saving ability to store carbon against any interest group other than the greater good, and that rather than sell them off, we should fight to preserve them with all we have? That rather than reduce and diminish, we should expand and protect?

At times it seems as if our public lands are a gift from the past, a prescient gift from an earlier time, a gift that just might be able to save us. Are we really going to look at that gift and think, Hey, no thanks, let's just cash them in?

We may want to throw up our hands and say that this challenge in front of us, one of so many challenges after all, is too daunting. But maybe we can take some relief and encouragement in the fact that the nearly impossible has been done before. The past, which we often seem so scornful of these days, offers guidance. It tells us that rather than "give back" these lands to the states, we should hold on dearly to them. Perhaps we need to leave vast parts of this land alone, as it is, while using the other parts for study and management, particularly the necessary management of climate-threatened species trying to adapt.

We are one of those climate-threatened species by the way. We are threatened in the obvious ways described in my litany above. But in less obvious ways, too. I have already explained how connecting large tracts of land can allow for species adaptability. Adaptability—that is, evolution—is necessary in times of crisis. When we cut off possibilities, we cut off our chances of survival. We cut off the escape route of evolution.

That is why we need to fight for these lands to our last breath. Because if we continue to protect our parks, monuments, and forests, and maybe connect and expand them, something both everyday and miraculous will occur: evolution will keep on working.

*   *   *

In 1907 Theodore Roosevelt took a trip to his rustic presidential retreat near Charlottesville, Virginia, where he personally witnessed, and carefully recorded, what might well have been the very last flock of passenger pigeons in existence. As a dozen or so birds wheeled overhead, he scribbled down detailed field notes. Flocks of up to two million of the same bird had been observed not many years before. The remnant flock that TR saw was the last ever officially recorded.

The story of the passenger pigeon has become a kind of environmental fable, but for TR it was real, just as the diminishment of the wild buffalo, from millions to double digits, was. Roosevelt was also president in 1904, when a seemingly innocuous delivery from a Japanese nursery occurred on the docks in New York City. That would be the beginning of

Chryphonectria parasitica, better known as the chestnut blight, and the end of what was regarded as the great American tree. As Richard Powers writes of the moment the blight began in his beautiful novel, *The Overstory:* "America's perfect tree, backbone of entire rural economies, the limber, durable redwood of the East with three dozen industrial uses— every fourth tree of a forest stretching two hundred million acres from Maine down to the Gulf—is doomed." And that was just the beginning of the plague: fifty years later no one would know the beauty of the forests whose canopies had once shaded most of Appalachia, housing birds in their cavities, providing food and shade, and keeping the waters clean.

Maybe your mind is callused over and you have heard eco-stories like these too many times to be affected. They affected Theodore Roosevelt, however, viscerally and directly, and I like to think that part of the reason they did is the years he had spent perfecting the difficult art of looking beyond one's self. We are all busy these days, but imagine being as busy as Roosevelt, being president after all, and still taking the time to notice, and to *feel,* these great losses. And then to try to do something about it. Despite an action-crammed life, he kept his eyes, and emotions, open to the losses, losses that it is much easier to tolerate when you are not looking outward. To Roosevelt it was personal. Douglas Brinkley writes: "Still, underlying Roosevelt's hostility toward despoilers was his fear of America without a wilderness. Conservation was a way for Roosevelt to grapple with his anxiety."

Maybe that is one thing we all have to learn: to take these losses personally. As I type this, it is being reported that we have almost a third fewer birds in the world than we did in 1970. That means that we have lost 2.9 billion birds, or 29 percent of all birds, over the last fifty years. Take a moment and consider this fact: our birds are disappearing.

I have never hunted a rhino or bagged a lion, but I do share one thing with Roosevelt. That is a lifelong love of birds, and birds have deepened my connection to places. I can close my eyes now and see them: the just-hatched pelicans on a barrier island in North Carolina, the ospreys migrating over the hills where TR fought in Cuba, the snowy owls on the beaches of Cape Cod, the red-tailed hawk I rode shoulder-to-shoulder with down the mountain on my bike in Mendocino, the single great blue heron I watched for days in Colorado, the gyrfalcon I saw dive not far from Roosevelt's house on Long Island, all have left their mark. I am the better for having encountered them, I know that.

Birds also affected the route I decided to take home from the West. I drove first to Boulder, Colorado, where I enjoyed the short break from the road in a friend's house, and both nights I was there, around six, I headed out onto the front deck, a glass of cold India pale ale in hand, and watched the turkey vultures come home from work. These were birds that TR knew well; in a typical example of Rooseveltian multitasking he took breaks from leading the Rough Riders to jot down field notes on vultures while in Cuba. In Boulder I observed the workday of the vultures, which looks somewhat lazy to the human eye, consisting of spiraling upward on thermals each morning and cruising around the tops of mountains where they search, as always, for dead things. When the day's heat finally begins to fade, they glide back down, circling, circling, before landing on their nightly roost, which for a sizable chunk of the local vulture population means the mangy Douglas fir right across from the deck. There they rearrange their wings with a noise that sounds to me, variously, like thick paper rustling or a canvas tent flapping or, sometimes, a wet umbrella closed and then opened to shake off the rain. While the vultures roost, swallows carve the sky in front of them, feasting on the last wave of evening insects. Then comes a subtle shift, a changing of the guard, as the sky darkens and bats replace swallows.

From Colorado I drove south into New Mexico before heading east. The whole way home I encountered land that Theodore Roosevelt had saved. First a detour through the Rio Grande National Forest in Colorado and the Santa Fe National Forest in New Mexico. Then, on the way back I couldn't resist dipping down into Louisiana, another of the places I've learned to feel at home. I had first come to the state during the BP oil spill in the summer of 2010, and, despite the black smears of tarballs that darkened beaches and water, I'd been awed by the enormous

marshes and abundant bird life. I returned a year later to write a grave
report for an environmental magazine on the death and doom of all
things avian in southern Louisiana, but apparently no one had alerted
the birds. Rather than paucity, I found, on a crumbled causeway of a
road below the aptly named town of Venice, at the southernmost point
of the state, a scene of wild abundance as thousands of birds from dozens of species appeared to be swept up in an ecstatic celebration of sunrise. Within a hundred feet of the road anhingas and cormorants and
loons were diving, and an osprey was scaring some turkey vultures out
of a dead cypress while dozens of roosting brown pelicans, a tad slower
to rise, filled the dark silhouetted trees. The rising sun turned a mob of
white ibises pinkish and a roseate spoonbill even pinker, while lighting
up the undersides of the white pelicans that wheeled above the harbor. I
could barely stop laughing at the symphonic craziness of so many birds.
Look one way and there were dozens of black skimmers flying over
Barataria Bay. Look another and you saw a marsh hawk and a merlin;
and over there, in that puddle-like pond, a king rail, an avocet, a black-
necked stilt. . . . The fires of nearby oil refineries flamed into the sky, but
I defy anyone to say there is no wildness left in the world after spending
a morning like that.

Not far from those refineries were the federal bird reservations of
Louisiana, including Breton Island. Bird reservations had not existed
before Roosevelt, and he created the very first reserve in 1903 in an attempt to save the birds of Florida's Pelican Island from poachers. He did
this, as he did so many things, boldly and by proclamation. The government already owned the land and after inquiring as to whether there
was any legal reason he could not designate the island a federal bird reservation, and being told there wasn't, he said, with the confidence that
charmed some and drove others crazy: "I so declare it."

Breton Island captured Roosevelt's imagination during a visit in
1915, four years before he died. There is an easily accessed film of Roosevelt's boat ride and visit to Breton, a barrier island in the Gulf just to
the west of the mouth of the Mississippi. Like most islands in the Gulf,

it is flat, sandy, and treeless, and all but covered in birds: terns, pelicans, egrets, skimmers, gulls. In the film we see a clearly corpulent Roosevelt, maybe even a little roly-poly, exploring the island while wearing rolled-up pants, a white billowing shirt, and a white floppy hat. Anyone who has visited these islands knows how absorbing they are, with their wild ballets of birds in flight. The cameraman follows the ex-president as he sits on the sand and stares, walks shoelessly and stares, lies on the sand and stares, wanders off and stares. What he is staring at is hundreds of terns, nesting and circling above with a sort of aggressive defensiveness (an emotional state that the man watching them knows firsthand), and hundreds more clown-nosed black skimmers, an improbable bird with a candy corn–colored bill, and white pelicans as well as brown ones. Though he always loved attention, you get the sense that at one point TR wished the filmmaker would just put the camera away and allow him to simply get lost in the world of birds.

He wrote up the trip later in *A Book-Lover's Holidays in the Open*. The chapter bears a fairly mundane title, "Bird Reserves at the Mouth of the Mississippi," but ends with one of his most beautiful and rightly famous descriptions:

> Birds should be saved because of utilitarian reasons; and, moreover, they should be saved because of reasons unconnected with any return in dollars and cents. A grove of giant redwoods and sequoias should be kept just as we keep a great and beautiful cathedral. The extermination of the passenger pigeon meant that mankind was just so much poorer; exactly as in the case of the destruction of the cathedral at Rheims. And to lose the chance to see frigate-birds soaring in circles above the storm, or a file of pelicans winging their way homeward across the crimson afterglow of the sunset, or a myriad of terns flashing in the bright light of midday as they hover in a shifting maze above the beach—why, the loss is like the loss of a gallery of the masterpieces of the artists of old time.

Reading this brings to mind Roosevelt's night around the fire with Muir, and by this point, late in TR's life, the two men's languages have thoroughly mixed, intertwining to the point where they are nearly one. Both men understood that by saving nature we are saving ourselves. I have met one of Roosevelt's grandchildren, and have visited his home on Sagamore Hill, but perhaps my most direct and authentic connection to TR is through John Hay. John Hay was a dapper and witty Midwesterner who became Abraham Lincoln's private secretary and was with him when he died, and who, later in life, became Theodore Roosevelt's secretary of state. A century later I became friends with another John Hay, the secretary's grandson, while living near him on Cape Cod. "Strange to have come through the whole century and find that the most interesting thing is the birds," John said to me during our very first walk together. "Or maybe it's just the human mind is more interesting when focusing on something other than itself."

John was in his eighties by then, but his eyes shone with delight when he looked out at gannets diving into the choppy waters of Cape Cod Bay. He was a nature writer who had written sixteen books about the natural world, particularly delighting in the migrations of our local herring and the world-traveling terns, whom he called "the birds of light." He had trained himself to look outward, to look beyond himself, at the world. "The answers to life can't be found by trying to solve things in our brains," he said, "but by stepping out of our brains entirely." He believed that we can expand ourselves only by looking outward toward the source, toward the mystery, and by joining the ritual of the natural year we can join that mystery. It was something I had always vaguely thought but not been able to articulate, but spending the days with him I came to believe it, too.

From Louisiana I made a beeline east and then north. It was in late July that I finally returned to my home in North Carolina. I liked the feeling of settling back in, unaware that in little more than a month the world would unsettle me again.

*   *   *

One of Theodore Roosevelt's great legacies, not as great as the land itself but far from insignificant, was giving us a story to tell ourselves about this country and its land. Not the story of American exceptionalism. That is mere gloss. Not the story of expansion and ownership. Not even the story of stewardship and the wise use of resources. Yes, these all played into how Roosevelt saw the land. But so did something else, something more sustaining. He believed that it was part of us, and we were part of it. It defined us, and our love for it was one of the best things about us. These ideas may now sound like platitudes; to him they were felt truths.

To revise Roosevelt's story for our time we must take what was best about it, discard what doesn't fit, and add the new. Any revision will have to look our changing climate in the eye. Not long after I returned from my trip, and not long before the fires engulfed Paradise in the foothills of the Sierra in California, a powerful hurricane named Florence zeroed in on my home in coastal North Carolina. Those two events, one of water and the other of fire, reinforced the fact that nowhere is safe in the age of climate change. As powerful as Florence proved to be, something bigger is coming, something no reasonable person should remain skeptical about. That something is a change on an almost unimaginable scale.

Most of us can no longer afford to be skeptical. Something else is coming and it is coming to our front doors. Not the scary weather but the scary climate. We need to feel this with the urgency that drives those boarding up their windows before the hurricane or those evacuating along fiery roads. The challenge is that long-term danger has never gripped the human mind the way that short-term crisis does. Hurricanes and fires are like being hung on the fortnight. They concentrate our minds.

We can no longer ignore the fact that the years of record-breaking heat have now become a decade of record-breaking heat. That the larger, fiercer, more slowly moving storms that were predicted are already here, along with the megafires. The increased flooding of coastal cities and the great blazes in the West are not individual events, but part of the greater pattern that must be addressed. Any ecologist, a term that had not been invented in Roosevelt's time, could tell you this. And any naturalist, a term that did, could as well.

Ten days after Florence hit, I returned to see what the storm had done to my home and my town. My neighbor Tony, who had stayed, showed me a picture of the writing shack I'd built behind my house, filled with six feet of water. It had not floated out to sea but had lifted off its moorings and appeared to be popping a wheelie. Two of the walls and doors had blown off and the rest was warped and wet. Over the next few months it would slant ever earthward before collapsing into the ground in early February.

As it turns out, "Leave it as it is" is not a bad way to respond to hurricanes. On the coast this will mean deciding the fate of the beaches and the property that serve as our only buffer as the sea encroaches. This will, as usual, include the difficult problem of private property, especially as houses fall into the sea and homeowners attempt to rebuild in increasingly untenable and dangerous places.

There is little question how TR would have responded to this. The greater good would be obvious to him. Hints of what must happen were already clear in the wake of Hurricane Sandy, when the New York State government bought back plots from some landowners, plots that they would leave undeveloped. The strategy here is one that necessity, and the astronomical costs of insurance and government bailouts after the disasters, will make more accepted as we go, and will be true for Western fires as well as our Eastern floods. Don't rebuild. Leave it as it is. If Roosevelt were in charge, he would act quickly and decisively: the burned foothills in the West would be federally purchased and left alone to regrow, while coastal land would also be federally purchased and left alone for as long as it remained land.

Not everyone believes that mere preservation is still relevant. It's an old story, some say; it's passé, not the right story for our techno time. We should instead be thinking about large-scale world-altering climate-fighting schemes and tending the attenuated garden of Anthropocene earth that is left to us. I get it. Merely preserving land isn't going to reverse climate change. But I do believe that land, undeveloped land, might do more than we think, might hold a secret for future generations just as the land TR saved still holds a secret for us. Think of our parks and monuments and reserves as a great Noah's Ark that will hold some species, though not all, during the coming floods and fires. If we let it, and let it alone, the land can give back more than we think, more than we might ever know.

The West from Above

June 2019

A year has passed since Noah and I drove west. This year, unlike the last and many of the recent years, the snowpack lies heavy and deep in the Western high country. It's a brief sign of hope; it's a tease—take your choice. At the moment I am looking down at all that snow from ten thousand feet as I fly over the jagged peaks of the Bob Marshall Wilderness in northern Montana. Mountain after mountain stretch all the way to Glacier National Park to our north along the Canadian border. Snow runs like the frosting of a cake over a great buttress of gray rock, which as enormous as it is in itself is just one parapet in the great fortress wall of mountains below us. A human being could try not to be exhilarated taking in these sights, but they would really have to work at it. And speaking of human beings, we have not seen one or any human habitation over the last forty-five minutes of flying. If you are a fan of unpopulated places and staggering beauty and varied geography, you could barely pick a better place on earth.

This is day three of an enormous lap I'm taking around the interior West in a prop plane, circling from Colorado to Wyoming to Montana and then back. My pilot, and the only other person on board this single-engine Cessna 210 airplane, is Bruce Gordon, the president and proprietor of EcoFlight, an organization committed to helping environmental organizations get a literal overview of the lands they are trying to save. Bruce isn't doing all this flying for me but for two environmental organizations, the American Prairie Reserve and the Yaak Valley Forest Council, a group dedicated to saving the last grizzlies in a remote patch of northern Montana. He has been kind enough, however, to let me hitch a ride.

My own purpose is to see the land I have been writing about trying to save; I want to picture the potential connectivity that Karsten Heuer and others have described for me; and I want to know if a larger Rooseveltian vision is still possible in these smaller times. So far this trip has been all that I hoped for, and more. Three days ago we took off from the Aspen airport and flew north over Glenwood Canyon and into the Flat Tops Wilderness, Colorado's second-largest wilderness area, made up of two national forests, where the average elevation tops ten thousand feet and more than a hundred lakes dot the landscape. Volcanic peaks jut into the sky, and around one of these peaks curled a lake of green ice like an emerald necklace. It was June, but it could have been the dead of winter. We looked down at thousands and thousands of trees, our great ally in the fight against climate change.

We also looked down at hundreds and hundreds of dead trees. Some dead from fires. Others dead from a bark beetle epidemic in the 1940s, an epidemic that may well have been a precursor of future beetle kills as the climate warms. And this is how the trip has gone so far: I find myself constantly batted back and forth between hope and despair. Hope because the land is so vast and unscarred. Despair because much of it isn't. The most stark example of this came after leaving the Flat Tops, flying through the Red Desert, and then entering Wyoming's Pinedale Anticline, a landscape dotted with hundreds of gas pads and pumps for fracking, and spiderwebbed with roads connecting the pads. Retention ponds and pipelines propagated in the shadows of the magnificent white-peaked Wind River Mountain Range, and in this wet spring the olive-colored Wind River spilled over its banks and flooded the pads. Flying over the Flat Tops it was easy to imagine connecting vast swaths of the West, and to picture animals freely migrating through these lands, but Pinedale told a different story: a great roadblock to migration standing in the way of the ancient migratory route of the pronghorn antelope.

The trip has had all the West in it. The beauty. The exhilaration. The emptiness. The scars. The exploitation. Before I could despair too much about Pinedale, Bruce pointed the plane northwest toward the Grand Tetons, where it had snowed the night before. We flew through an ocean of clouds right up to the mountains, a thousand feet below their peaks, and what we saw was a sharp and cutting sight. Fresh snow over gray jagged rocks, and the peaks themselves so snow-covered and close they shone like sharp chunks of ice.

Soon after we passed the Tetons, Bruce put us on autopilot and started reading the paper. I had set up shop in the two backseats, where I studied maps and scribbled notes down in my journal. We flew north over Yellowstone and refueled in Missoula before landing in Libby, Montana, close to the Canadian border, at an empty airstrip.

I spent the next two nights at the Yaak Valley home of an old acquaintance, the writer and activist Rick Bass. On the first night Rick hosted a meeting/party of the Yaak Valley Forest Council. Since I was the only non–council member at the get-together, and since they had business to discuss, I was chosen to grill our dinner of antelope. The goal of the meeting, and the group at that moment, was to alter the route of a proposed hiking trail that ran across northern Montana directly through grizzly country. For this remnant population of twenty-five grizzlies along the Canadian border anything that increased their encounters with human beings could spell their end. What the Yaak Council was proposing was moving the trail south of grizzly territory, and Bruce Gordon would spend the next two days taking politicians, media people, and environmentalists up in his plane to show them the proposed new route. On the second night of the trip we drove to Libby to listen to a lecture by grizzly expert Dave Mattson. The message was clear and simple: bears die where roads and human paths are. If a bear distribution is long and narrow, it is in danger. The bears need space, lots of it, which it just so happens Montana can still provide them with. *If* we give it to them.

It was actually another environmental group that had planned, pro-posed, and invested in the hiking trail through grizzly country, which made this a kind of civil war. If there is one tribe that I have perhaps been a little too easy on so far it is my own: the hikers, the recreators, who use the West as a vast playground. This is a lesser known new front in the Western eco wars, dealing with the conflicts that recreation can bring. We preach self-restraint to others. But we need to restrain ourselves.

I found myself thinking of the words of David Kroenke, a stranger whom I had struck up a conversation with while he was drinking coffee at a roadside pullout while watching the sunrise over the Valley of the Gods.

"It's not the miners that are the real problem around here but the tourists," Kroenke said. "A hundred years from now we are going to say that it was the tourists who ruined the land. We have to recognize the true enemy. We can't go on fighting twenty-first-century threats with twentieth-century methods. Or, to put it another way, let's fight 2020 environmental problems, not 1950s environmental problems."

The hikers who wanted the trail built through bear country weren't bad people. They wanted to be in the wilderness, to experience *this* wilderness. The problem is that the bears wanted to be in the wilder-ness, too, and didn't have other options. We can talk abstractly about re-wilding, but here it is. This is what we mean by connectivity. We mean occasionally looking beyond the human, and human needs.

It was inspiring to watch a local group fight for their local animals. More than inspiring. It seemed a model of how to fight, a way of taking what was an impossibly large and intractable problem and reducing it to the particular and concrete: twenty-five or so individual bears that would die without their help. Roosevelt had operated on a grand stage. Most of our stages are smaller.

Maybe it is naïve of me to still feel hopeful in the age of climate change and extinction. Maybe it is just my temperament. I understand that the Western landscape is injured, battered, threatened, all of that. There is no sense claiming it isn't. But it is still glorious. It still holds not just hope but possibility. Imagine what would happen if humans simply left it as it was for a year. Imagine if we did it for two years, or five. Imagine the resilience of a place like this, still, even today, if we left it as it is.

The landscape Bruce and I are flying over now is a perfect example of this. "The Bob," as the Bob Marshall Wilderness is called, is just the sort of wild place that we desperately need to hold on to. Down below us no machines (including bicycles) or roads are permitted (for now), which allows for our country's densest grizzly bear population outside of Alaska and thriving populations of moose, lynx, mountain lion, bighorn, and wolves. The land, over a million acres, is made up of national forests designated as roadless areas under the Wilderness Act of 1964, and no mining or logging is allowed. It stands as something of a miracle in these crass and commercial times.

We fly over the snowcapped peaks of the China Wall, a twenty-two-mile-long landform that arcs like a dragon's back, guarding the wilderness, and down into the grasslands of central Montana. Bruce and I land in the town of Lewiston, where we take the courtesy car, the keys left for overnighting pilots like Bruce, over to the Super 8. In the morning we take off with a small group of media people and environmentalists and fly along the Missouri River, over the American Prairie Reserve, a corrugated landscape of hills and grasslands that runs east toward Roosevelt's Badlands. The purpose of the reserve, once again, is to connect, and the first thing that the APR hopes to connect is people to the land. Here, along the Missouri Breaks where Lewis and Clarke paddled, ten million acres of public land is landlocked, hemmed in, by private ranch land, and the goal is to open that landscape up to we, the people. But the other goal is to return all the native animals to the prairie, and thanks to the group's efforts hundreds of buffalo now roam these hilly grasslands. There is another more secret but grander ambition as well: to connect this prairie wilderness to the Bob and to Glacier National Park to the west and north, and to Yellowstone in the southwest, creating a great triangle of connection for wolves, bears, and buffalo. This seems absurdly ambitious, but there is already evidence that it is happening, with wolves, those great roamers, leading the way, and grizzlies tentatively coming down out of the mountains to re-inhabit their ancient homeland on the plains.

Tomorrow we will start our return flight, and I can go back to feeling pessimistic about how human beings have damaged this great world.

Today I will let myself feel we have done something right.

*   *   *

This year, the centennial of Theodore Roosevelt's death, has been a surprisingly busy one for a man who has been dead a hundred years. Just as he was during his lifetime, Roosevelt remains a magnet for media attention. One recent three-week span saw the publication of two books about the man; the death of his greatest biographer, Edmund Morris; and a liberal presidential candidate, Elizabeth Warren, declare that if she could pick any candidate throughout history as her running mate it would be Teddy for his progressive politics, and "because he was brave."

She is not alone. Ask any sitting American president after 1909 who his favorite former president was, and it's a good bet that he would answer "Theodore Roosevelt." There would be a few Lincolns sprinkled in, but the question wasn't who was the *greatest* president, and after some brooding most would come around and admit their fondness for TR. You could even argue that if the game was started a little earlier, in say 1905, the sitting president at the time might have come up with the same answer.

It would matter little whether the president answering the question was conservative or liberal, Republican or Democrat. Republican William Howard Taft, TR's protégé, was so enamored of and intimidated by Roosevelt that long after taking office, and even in private, he continued to call his predecessor "Mr. President." Democrat Franklin Delano Roosevelt grew up hero-worshipping his distant cousin, and modeled his own presidency after him, his New Deal echoing cousin Theodore's Square one. The Kennedys, too, tried to consciously re-create the magic mix of intellectual renaissance and athletic vigor that marked Roosevelt's White House years, while Reagan, ever the actor, drew much of his rough-riding imagery and inspiration from the original cowboy president. Obama recently joined the rest, admitting that Teddy was his favorite. Less powerful presidents no doubt envied the bully in the pulpit: the Bushes were both fond of Teddy. Even Nixon turned to TR during the darkest days of Watergate, quoting him defiantly in his resignation speech right before he walked across the White House lawn to the waiting helicopter.

How has he taken hold of our attention and not let go? How did he live such an extraordinary, memorable life?

Money, genes, luck, skin color, privilege, gender, fate, the historical times in which he lived, the Spanish bullet that hit his friend Bucky O'Neill and not him, the grim fact of assassination that handed him the presidency. The life of Roosevelt depended on so much. But whatever the crazy combination was that allowed TR to achieve what he did, there is no question what *he* thought was the secret to his success. It will sound naïve, and maybe it is, but for him it all came back to *effort*. We might regard someone with a photographic memory, who could recall and quote full pages of the books he read in childhood, who read a book a day and could converse confidently with kings, who knew the Latin names of hundreds of animals and who had debated the great minds of his day, as brilliant. But Roosevelt knew brilliant minds and believed his fell just short of them, and some of those brilliant minds, including both William and Henry James, and Henry Adams, agreed. What he had instead was an irrepressible need to act, a *nearly* brilliant mind, with brilliant areas, that spun thought into action in a way few human beings ever have.

Science now tells us that words like "effort" and "will" and even "decision" are illusionary, mere synaptic flickers in brains that are way, and wordlessly, ahead of us and our notions of volition. Here is what TR had to say about that: he believed that there were "two kinds of success," the first being of those who have "the natural power to do what no one else can do," like "running a hundred yards in nine and three-fifths seconds" or writing "Ode on a Grecian Urn," and these abilities are ones that "no amount of training, no perseverance or will power, will enable any ordinary man to do." It is the second kind of success that is more interesting to Roosevelt, the kind "open to a large number of persons, if only they seriously determine to achieve it" even if they have "no remarkable mental or physical attributes."

"To the average man it is probably more useful to study the second type of success than to study the first," Roosevelt wrote in his autobiography. "From the study of the first he can learn inspiration, he can get uplift and lofty enthusiasm. From the study of the second he can, if he chooses, find out how to win a similar success himself."

This is the open road we can all walk, the one Theodore believed he walked:

> I need hardly say that all the successes I have ever won have been of the second type. I never won anything without hard labor and the exercise of my best judgment and careful planning. Having been a rather sick and awkward boy, I was as a young man both nervous and distrustful of my own prowess. I had to train myself painfully and laboriously not merely as regards my body but as regards my soul and spirit.

The chapter of his autobiography that these passages appear in, by the way, is called "The Vigor of Life." This was the way his speech "The Strenuous Life" had been translated into Italian: *Vigor di Vita*. "I thought this translation a great improvement on the original," TR wrote, "and have always wished that I myself used 'The Vigor of Life' as a heading to indicate what I was trying to preach, instead of the heading I actually did use."

How useful today are Roosevelt's somewhat antiquated notions of will and effort? It depends, perhaps, on the beliefs of the reader, on a kind of self-hypnosis that allows you to believe, as some would put it, or fool yourself, as others would.

I know that I, when I returned home from my trip last summer, felt a kind of bristling contagion as I continued to read everything I could about and by Roosevelt. Was I really working harder than usual or just imagining it? I felt two opposite pulls, one toward seeing a world beyond the human one, and laughing at our self-importance. But the other side pulled just as hard: a very human ambition to make my voice heard in the fight for the more-than-human. I spent most of the late summer and fall typing up the notes from the trip and turning them into these chapters, but while the work was going fairly well, something nagged at me. I gradually pinpointed what that was: I had set out not just to write a book but to attempt an experiment, one in which I would see if I could push my writerly self into becoming a more political animal.

"One brave act is worth a thousand books," wrote Edward Abbey, and after Hurricane Florence flooded my hometown, my efforts picked up a little steam. I emptied the coffers of the Creative Writing Department I worked for by inviting down the controversial coastal geologist Orrin Pilkey, who told a lecture hall full of undergraduates that it was time to abandon the beaches on our barrier islands and let the houses left there fall into the sea. I also rented out a large hall and brought down Bill McKibben, the writer, climate change activist, and founder of the climate change activism group 350.org, to speak to a few hundred survivors of Hurricane Florence.

Bill McKibben was in a pensive mood during his visit. I had known Bill since college, when he had been the editor of the school paper and I was the political cartoonist. He had turned a corner, he told me, and the recent Intergovernmental Panel on Climate Change report, as well as the fires and hurricanes, had confirmed his sense that there was now no way of turning back. He wondered out loud (and on the page in the article he was writing and proofreading in his hotel room) whether it was "now reasonable to ask whether the human game has begun to falter—perhaps even to play itself out." He had recently watched an enormous glacier calve off and into the sea in Greenland. There was no longer a chance that we could avoid the age of climate change. We were in it. "The world is shrinking," he told me, meaning that both rising seas and fires were making less land available, not to mention less breathing room. Meanwhile the president of the United States had called climate change "a total, and very expensive hoax."

Bill had personal reasons to fret as well. He had been receiving death threats because of his activism, and a commentator on a conservative website had given out his home address for anyone who wanted to follow through on those threats.

When he told me about the threats, I thought immediately of TR. "The Vigor of Life," the same chapter that celebrates effort and will, ends with a nod to another quality Roosevelt valued. Roosevelt believed that courage could be learned, that one could train oneself to be brave. That everyone feels fear when confronted with danger, and the best course is to simply act as if you are not afraid, no matter how you feel inside. "There were all kinds of things of which I was afraid at first, ranging from grizzly bears to 'mean' horses to gun-fighters," Roosevelt writes, "but by acting as if I was not afraid I gradually ceased to be afraid."

Courage is required because, as with Teddy fighting the trusts, we are going up against a powerful and extremely wealthy enemy in the fossil fuel industry. Its interest—profit—clashes directly with the majority of ours, and it is fear, mixed with a sense of powerlessness, that keeps many of us from fighting back.

One result of Bill McKibben's visit was that my graduate students formed a local chapter of the climate change group 350.org and, since they were writers, arranged a meeting with local journalists to learn all they could about writing op-eds. I also founded an environmental group that I was calling Writers for the Wild. The idea was to get writers from all over the country to come out in support of protecting and expanding public lands. Our motto would be: Saving the World in an Un-boring Way. We would embrace the ideas that the poet Gary Snyder had articulated on Earth Day in 1990: "We need to stay loose, smart, creative and wild. The wild is imagination—so is community—so is a good time. Let's be tough but good natured ... warriors make cause with wild nature, and have some ferocious fun doing it."

These were my first, tentative efforts. Nothing earth-shaking, nothing Rooseveltian. But the goal was, the goal *is*, to get the news, both good and bad, about public lands out there, and to make people in this country aware that they are the recipients, and owners, of a great gift.

I knew, and know, that public lands will not magically reverse climate change, but it is my hope that we, as Americans, will come to understand our legacy and the power of that legacy, and to protect it from the threats of the avaricious and shortsighted. And while we have to create a new story for this fight, a larger, more inclusive, more connected story, we don't have to come up with a new rallying cry. That has been with us from the fight's beginning.

Leave it as it is.

ACKNOWLEDGMENTS

First, let me thank my traveling companion, my nephew Noah Lanier. In telling a story like this many of the events from the trip end up on the cutting room floor, and one difference between our grand tour and Roosevelt's, one that I don't mention in the text, is that we played a whole lot of ping-pong. We played in my brother-in-law's basement in D.C., outdoors in front of the Science Center at Harvard, and in a barn in Lodi, Wisconsin. On our first day in Big Sky, Noah beat me in the morning at the house where we were staying, but then I beat him that night in a local bar, which with its dark lighting, drunken atmosphere, and wafting smell of popcorn and beer, Noah said was like my "home court." At that point we had played well over a hundred games and were pretty much dead even, something like 57 to 56 (though youth would be served and he would pull away by trip's end). Thanks, No.

Thanks to Stephen Trimble and Kirsten Johanna Allen of Torrey House Press for including this Easterner in the original chapbook distributed to Congress, *Red Rock Testimony: Three Generations of Writers Speak on Behalf of Utah's Public Lands*. Both Stephen and Kirsten would prove vital throughout my work on the book, from pointing me toward people to talk to, challenging my preconceptions, and, in Stephen's case, reading an early draft of the book. Also thanks to all my fellow contributors to *Red Rock Stories*, whom I reached out to for advice on how to proceed, and to SUWA (Southern Utah Wilderness Alliance) superstars Steve Bloch, Ray Bloxham, and Matt Gross, whom I also leaned on early on.

One name kept coming up when I spoke to people: Regina Lopez-Whiteskunk. This was my first interview for the book and perhaps my most important, and I am deeply grateful to Regina both for allowing me to record her story and encouraging me to tell my own. This interview occurred during my initial scouting trip west in January 2018, and thanks to Jason Mark and Katie O'Reilly at *Sierra* magazine for their support, financial and otherwise, during that trip. As usual, while out West I leaned on old friend Rob Bleiberg, a font of knowledge about southeast Utah, who introduced me to Monarch Cave, and, in a larger sense, to this part of the world. Thanks also to David Kroenke, whom Rob and I bumped into while he was trying to get away from people and enjoy some coffee while watching the sunrise over Valley of the Gods. And thanks once again to the intrepid Greg Lameman, who guided me in multiple ways, and who climbed with me to the base of Bears Ears. Thanks to Zak and Amanda Podmore, for letting me camp out in their trailer, and for giving me a crash course on all things Bears Ears; meeting the two of you was a highlight of the trip. And thanks to Ted Gwinn of the Grand Canyon Library and Roger Clark, the program director of Grand Canyon Trust, and to Richard Watahomigie, councilman for the Havasupai tribe, for letting me use your words. Thank you, James Adakai, for the long drive and the good talk behind the Recapture Lodge.

It is traditional to thank one's agent near the end, but I will thank Peter Steinberg of Foundry Media here, since it was during that early scouting trip that Peter sold the book to Simon & Schuster, a deal that he described to me as I was pacing back and forth atop the Glen Canyon Dam. I have had more agents than Spinal Tap had drummers, and Peter is the best.

That first trip ended during a blizzard in Salt Lake City and an inspiring evening in the home of Kirsten Allen and Mark Bailey, where I was pushed to dig deeper into the Bears Ears story by Terri Martin of SUWA. Thank you.

During our summer trip Noah and I were thankful to those who generously let us stay in their homes: Alex de Gramont and Jacqui de Gramont, and their kids Nico and Gabriel in Washington; Jim and Elizabeth Campbell and Willa and Rachel in Wisconsin; Tom and Sue Beattie in Big Sky; and Jeffy Sandler and Karen Bayle in Marin. Thanks to my former classmate, Representative Jamie Raskin, for taking the time to talk to me and making the distinction between "power politicians" and "justice politicians," and for introducing me to John Lewis, who provided an inspirational high point of the trip. At Harvard thanks to the incomparable Nancy Boutilier, who quoted "The Man in the Arena," and to my roommate from many years ago, Tom Ellis, who treated us to the seventh game of the Eastern Conference finals. And to the always generous Sean Palfrey, who took time out from graduation day to talk about his great-grandfather and to point me toward some important contacts in the Badlands: NRA and anti–gun violence advocate Mike Weisser and Valerie Naylor, former superintendent of Theodore Roosevelt National Park. In Medora and Dickinson thanks to Doug Ellison, and to Sharon Kilzer, who was so generous in offering up her time and the resources of the Theodore Roosevelt Center at Dickinson State University.

Back out West, immeasurable thanks go to Alice Fiori and Bill Campbell for their annual generosity of letting us call their home ours. Thanks to Brian Calvert of *High Country News*, and to Adam Petry for leading my counter-life out West, and to Ed Roberson for his now-annual visits to that home and for his passion for TR and his adopted region. Thanks to Harvey Locke and Karsten Heuer for thinking big and staying hopeful, and to Ian Marshall for leading our crew of nature writers up and around Mount Tam. In the competition for most beautiful home in the world department: Bill Hedden and Eleanor Bliss of Castle Valley deepened my sense of the history of protecting Bears Ears, Scott Berry helped me understand the current legal fight, and Kevin Jones and his wife, Barbara, hosted my family and taught me about both the archaeology and archaeological history of Bears Ears. Thanks to Phil Lyman for sitting down with me; to Bill Boyle of the *San Juan Record* for the same.

Thanks to two inspiring guides: Louis Williams who led me up San Juan Hill and Vaughn Hadenfeldt, who let me experience "planned romance" in Cedar Mesa. While in Bluff I was lucky enough to stay in the beautiful home of Peter Walker, and that was thanks to his connection to a former old ultimate player, Timothy "Captain Dog Doo" Rockwood. And thanks to two writers who know the area so much better than I do, whom I have gotten to know a little in person but mostly through their books, Craig Childs and Amy Irvine. Finally, thank you Allison Stegner and Elliott West for the valuable interviews.

The Bears Ears celebration was the climax of the summer and I would not have attended were it not for Julie Mack of Salt Lake City. Huge thanks to Mark Maryboy and Kenneth Maryboy for taking time to sit down with me during that busiest of weekends. Thanks to Dine elder Jonah Yellowman for his wise words and to Willie Grayeyes for leading the fight. Thanks to Gavin Noyes for taking us on a tour of sites in Bears Ears; to my camping neighbor, Irene Hamilton, of Grand Canyon Trust; to Rob Vessels, who told me about his hike with Zinke; and to Tommy Rock for sharing his story. Thanks to Alastair Lee Bitsóí and Angelo Baca for their thoughtful guidance, and to Kevin Madalena, Tai Kooster, David Garrett, Seth Archer, and Robert McPhearson. And thanks to Ethel Branch, for leading the legal charge.

Good parts of the first draft of the book were written while my family had evacuated for Hurricane Florence, and thanks to my sister, Heidi Gessner, and her husband, Tim Auman, for making us feel at home during that stretch. At the University of North Carolina, thanks to Dave Monahan for suggesting we stop at Badlands National Park in his home state and to John Scherer for the Teddy bobblehead, as well as thanks to my colleagues in the creative writing department. Thanks to Michael Soulé of Paonia and Bruce Gordon of EcoFlight for one of the most exciting trips of my life, a huge lap from Colorado to Wyoming to Montana and back, and for Rick Bass and his daughter Lowry for generously letting me stay with them. (Thanks, Lowry, for the antelope sandwich.) Also thanks to the two organizations that sponsored the flights, the Yaak

Valley Forest Council and the American Prairie Reserve, for letting me tag along.

A huge thanks to Duane Jundt, for his conscientious and sharp-eyed last-minute reading, during which he caught some important mistakes on my part.

As I said of an earlier book, I see this more as a work of biographical adventure than as a biography, and I have leaned heavily on those who spent years researching Roosevelt's life, particularly Kathleen Dalton, Edmund Morris, David McCullough, and Douglas Brinkley. I also need to once again thank Walter Jackson Bate, who drew me into the world of biography in the first place.

At Simon & Schuster thanks to Jon Cox for his initial faith in this project and for Stuart Roberts and Emily Simonson for seeing it through. What might have been a dire and anxiety-ridden situation has been an exciting and pleasurable one, thanks to your professionalism and care.

And of course, as always, thanks to Nina and Hadley, the twin centers of my world.

Proclamations

The Antiquities Act

Text of the Act for the Preservation of American Antiquities
Signed into Law, June 8, 1906
16 USC 431-433

Be it enacted by the Senate and House of Representatives of the United States of America in Congress assembled, That any person who shall appropriate, excavate, injure, or destroy any historic or prehistoric ruin or monument, or any object of antiquity, situated on lands owned or controlled by the Government of the United States, without the permission of the Secretary of the Department of the Government having jurisdiction over the lands on which said antiquities are situated, shall, upon conviction, be fined in a sum of not more than five hundred dollars or be imprisoned for a period of not more than ninety days, or shall suffer both fine and imprisonment, in the discretion of the court.

Sec. 2. That the President of the United States is hereby authorized, in his discretion, to declare by public proclamation historic landmarks, historic and prehistoric structures, and other objects of historic or scientific interest that are situated upon the lands owned or controlled by the Government of the United States to be national monuments, and may reserve as a part thereof parcels of land, the limits of which in all cases shall be confined to the smallest area compatible with proper care and management of the objects to be protected: Provided, That when such objects are situated upon a tract covered by a bona fide unperfected claim or held in private ownership, the tract, or so much thereof as may be necessary for the proper care and management of the object, may be relinquished to the Government, and the Secretary of the Interior is hereby authorized to accept the relinquishment of such tracts in [*sic*] behalf of the Government of the United States.

Sec. 3. That permits for the examination of ruins, the excavation of archaeological sites, and the gathering of objects of antiquity upon the lands under their respective jurisdictions may be granted by the Secretaries of the Interior, Agriculture, and War to institutions which they may deem properly qualified to conduct such examination, excavation, or gathering, subject to such rules and regulation as they may prescribe: Provided, That the examinations, excavations, and gatherings are undertaken for the benefit of reputable museums, universities, colleges, or other recognized scientific or educational institutions, with a view to increasing the knowledge of such objects, and that the gatherings shall be made for permanent preservation in public museums.

Sec. 4. That the Secretaries of the Departments aforesaid shall make and publish from time to time uniform rules and regulations for the purpose of carrying out the provisions of this Act.

Land Saved by Theodore Roosevelt
Under the Antiquities Act

The Act for the Preservation of American Antiquities gave Roosevelt the ability to declare "by public proclamation historic landmarks, historic and prehistoric structures, and other objects of historic or scientific interest" as national monuments.

He didn't waste any time. Three months after signing the act he declared Devils Tower a national monument. He continued to declare monuments right up to his last days in office, in March of 1909, when he designated Mount Olympus (now a national park) a national monument. Here is a list of all of them:

- Devils Tower (WY)—1906—originally 1,194 acres
- El Morro (NM)—1906—originally 160 acres
- Montezuma Castle (AZ)—1906—originally 161 acres

- Petrified Forest (AZ)—1906 (now a national park)—originally 60,776 acres
- Chaco Canyon (NM)—1907—originally 10,643 acres
- Cinder Cone (CA)—1907 (now part of Lassen Volcanic National Park)—originally 5,120 acres
- Lassen Peak (CA)—1907 (now Lassen Volcanic National Park)—originally 1,280 acres
- Gila Cliff Dwellings (NM)—1907—originally 160 acres
- Tonto (AZ)—1907—originally 640 acres
- Muir Woods (CA)—1908—originally 295 acres
- Grand Canyon (AZ)—1908 (now a national park)—originally 808,120 acres
- Pinnacles (CA)—1908 (now a national park)—originally 1,320 acres
- Jewel Cave (SD)—1908—originally 1,275 acres
- Natural Bridges (UT)—1908—originally 120 acres
- Lewis and Clark Caverns (MT)—1908 (now a Montana state park)—originally 160 acres
- Tumacacori (AZ)—1908—originally 10 acres
- Wheeler (CO)—1908 (now Wheeler Geologic Area, part of Rio Grande National Forest)—originally 300 acres
- Mount Olympus (WA)—1909 (now Olympic National Park)—originally 639,200 acres

Roosevelt also established Chalmette Monument and Grounds in 1907, a site of the Battle of New Orleans. It is now a part of Jean Lafitte National Historical Park.

The source is *The Antiquities Act* edited by David Harmon, Francis P. McManamon, and Dwight T. Pitcaithley.

National Forests, Federal Bird Preserves, National Game Preserves, and National Parks Established During Roosevelt's Presidency

Theodore Roosevelt helped save 230 million acres of American land during his presidency. Working with Gifford Pinchot, the chief of the United States Forest Service, he established or enlarged 150 national forests, totaling 150 million acres.

In addition Roosevelt established more than fifty federal bird reservations, from Florida's Pelican Island (first) to Alaska's Bogoslof (last), and four national game preserves.

Unlike national monuments, Congress declares national parks, but during his time as president Roosevelt and Pinchot worked with the legislature, advocated for, and helped establish the following national parks:

- Crater Lake National Park (OR)—1902
- Wind Cave National Park (SD)—1903
- Sullys Hill (ND)—1904 (now managed by USFWS)
- Platt National Park (OK)—1906 (now part of Chickasaw National Recreation Area)
- Mesa Verde National Park (CO)—1906
- Added land to Yosemite National Park (CA)

The Declaration of Bears Ears as a National Monument

The declaration of Bears Ears as a national monument under President Barak Obama is in keeping with a relatively new tradition of eloquent and artistic declarations. Drawing heavily on the original proposal written by the Bears Ears Inter-Tribal Coalition, and then tweaked and refined by Interior Secretary Sally Jewell, who had hiked, rafted, and explored the area, and the acting chair of Obama's Council on Environmental Quality, Christy Goldfuss, it describes the land thoroughly and at times poetically.

Presidential Proclamation—Establishment of the Bears Ears National Monument

ESTABLISHMENT OF THE BEARS EARS NATIONAL MONUMENT BY THE PRESIDENT OF THE UNITED STATES OF AMERICA

A PROCLAMATION

Rising from the center of the southeastern Utah landscape and visible from every direction are twin buttes so distinctive that in each of the native languages of the region their name is the same: Hoon'Naqvut, ShashJaá,

Kwiyagatu Nukavachi, Ansh An Lashokdiwe, or "Bears Ears." For hundreds of generations, native peoples lived in the surrounding deep sandstone canyons, desert mesas, and meadow mountaintops, which constitute one of the densest and most significant cultural landscapes in the United States. Abundant rock art, ancient cliff dwellings, ceremonial sites, and countless other artifacts provide an extraordinary archaeological and cultural record that is important to us all, but most notably the land is profoundly sacred to many Native American tribes, including the Ute Mountain Ute Tribe, Navajo Nation, Ute Indian Tribe of the Uintah Ouray, Hopi Nation, and Zuni Tribe.

The area's human history is as vibrant and diverse as the ruggedly beautiful landscape. From the earliest occupation, native peoples left traces of their presence. Clovis people hunted among the cliffs and canyons of Cedar Mesa as early as 13,000 years ago, leaving behind tools and projectile points in places like the Lime Ridge Clovis Site, one of the oldest known archaeological sites in Utah. Archaeologists believe that these early people hunted mammoths, ground sloths, and other now-extinct megafauna, a narrative echoed by native creation stories. Hunters and gatherers continued to live in this region in the Archaic Period, with sites dating as far back as 8,500 years ago.

Ancestral Puebloans followed, beginning to occupy the area at least 2,500 years ago, leaving behind items from their daily life such as baskets, pottery, and weapons. These early farmers of Basketmaker II and III and builders of Pueblo I, II, and III left their marks on the land. The remains of single family dwellings, granaries, kivas, towers, and large villages and roads linking them together reveal a complex cultural history. "Moki steps," hand and toe holds carved into steep canyon walls by the Ancestral Puebloans, illustrate the early people's ingenuity and perseverance and are still used today to access dwellings along cliff walls. Other, distinct cultures have thrived here as well—the Fremont People, Numic- and Athabaskan-speaking hunter-gatherers, and Utes and Navajos. Resources such as the Doll House Ruin in Dark Canyon Wilderness Area and the Moon House Ruin on Cedar Mesa allow visitors to marvel at artistry and architecture that have withstood thousands of seasons in this harsh climate.

The landscape is a milieu of the accessible and observable together with the inaccessible and hidden. The area's petroglyphs and pictographs capture the imagination with images dating back at least 5,000 years and spanning a range of styles and traditions. From life-size ghostlike figures that defy categorization, to the more literal depictions of bighorn sheep, birds, and

lizards, these drawings enable us to feel the humanity of these ancient artists. The Indian Creek area contains spectacular rock art, including hundreds of petroglyphs at Newspaper Rock. Visitors to Bears Ears can also
discover more recent rock art left by the Ute, Navajo, and Paiute peoples. It
is also the less visible sites, however—those that supported the food gathering, subsistence and ceremony of daily life—that tell the story of the people
who lived here. Historic remnants of Native American sheep-herding and
farming are scattered throughout the area, and pottery and Navajo hogans
record the lifeways of native peoples in the 19th and 20th centuries.

For thousands of years, humans have occupied and stewarded this land.
With respect to most of these people, their contribution to the historical record
is unknown, but some have played a more public role. Famed Navajo headman
K'aayélii was born around 1800 near the twin Bears Ears buttes. His band used
the area's remote canyons to elude capture by the U.S. Army and avoid the fate
that befell many other Navajo bands: surrender, the Long Walk, and forced
relocation to Bosque Redondo. Another renowned 19th century Navajo
leader, "Hastiin Ch'ihaajin" Manuelito, was also born near the Bears Ears.

The area's cultural importance to Native American tribes continues to
this day. As they have for generations, these tribes and their members come
here for ceremonies and to visit sacred sites. Throughout the region, many
landscape features, such as Comb Ridge, the San Juan River, and Cedar
Mesa, are closely tied to native stories of creation, danger, protection, and
healing. The towering spires in the Valley of the Gods are sacred to the
Navajo, representing ancient Navajo warriors frozen in stone. Traditions of
hunting, fishing, gathering, and wood cutting are still practiced by tribal
members, as is collection of medicinal and ceremonial plants, edible herbs,
and materials for crafting items like baskets and footwear. The traditional
ecological knowledge amassed by the Native Americans whose ancestors
inhabited this region, passed down from generation to generation, offers
critical insight into the historic and scientific significance of the area. Such
knowledge is, itself, a resource to be protected and used in understanding
and managing this landscape sustainably for generations to come.

Euro-Americans first explored the Bears Ears area during the 18th century, and Mormon settlers followed in the late 19th century. The San Juan
Mission expedition traversed this rugged country in 1880 on their journey
to establish a new settlement in what is now Bluff, Utah. To ease the passage of wagons over the slick rock slopes and through the canyon lands,

the settlers smoothed sections of the rock surface and constructed dugways and other features still visible along their route, known as the Hole-in-the-Rock Trail. Cabins, corrals, trails, and carved inscriptions in the rock reveal the lives of ranchers, prospectors, and early archaeologists. Cattle rustlers and other outlaws created a convoluted trail network known as the Outlaw Trail, said to be used by Butch Cassidy and the Sundance Kid. These outlaws took advantage of the area's network of canyons, including the aptly-named Hideout Canyon, to avoid detection.

The area's stunning geology, from sharp pinnacles to broad mesas, labyrinthine canyons to solitary hoodoos, and verdant hanging gardens to bare stone arches and natural bridges, provides vital insights to geologists. In the east, the Abajo Mountains tower, reaching elevations of more than 11,000 feet. A long geologic history is documented in the colorful rock layers visible in the area's canyons.

For long periods over 300 million years ago, these lands were inundated by tropical seas and hosted thriving coral reefs. These seas infused the area's black rock shale with salts as they receded. Later, the lands were bucked upwards multiple times by the Monument Upwarp, and near-volcanoes punched up through the rock, leaving their marks on the landscape without reaching the surface. In the sandstone of Cedar Mesa, fossil evidence has revealed large, mammal-like reptiles that burrowed into the sand to survive the blistering heat of the end of the Permian Period, when the region was dominated by a seaside desert. Later, in the Late Triassic Period more than 200 million years ago, seasonal monsoons flooded an ancient river system that fed a vast desert here.

The paleontological resources in the Bears Ears area are among the richest and most significant in the United States, and protection of this area will provide important opportunities for further archaeological and paleontological study. Many sites, such as Arch Canyon, are teeming with fossils, and research conducted in the Bears Ears area is revealing new insights into the transition of vertebrate life from reptiles to mammals and from sea to land. Numerous ray-finned fish fossils from the Permian Period have been discovered, along with other late Paleozoic Era fossils, including giant amphibians, synapsid reptiles, and important plant fossils. Fossilized traces of marine and aquatic creatures such as clams, crayfish, fish, and aquatic reptiles have been found in Indian Creek's Chinle Formation, dating to the Triassic Period, and phytosaur and dinosaur fossils from the same period have been found along Comb Ridge. Paleontologists have identified new species of plant-eating crocodile-like reptiles and mass graves of lumbering sauropods, along with metoposaurus, crocodiles, and other dinosaur fossils. Fossilized trackways of early tetrapods can be seen in the Valley of the Gods and in Indian Creek, where paleontologists have also discovered exceptional examples of fossilized ferns, horsetails, and cycads. The Chinle Formation and the Wingate, Kayenta, and Navajo Formations above it provide one of the best continuous rock records of the Triassic-Jurassic transition in the world, crucial to understanding how dinosaurs dominated terrestrial ecosystems and how our mammalian ancestors evolved. In Pleistocene Epoch sediments, scientists have found traces of mammoths, short-faced bears, ground sloths, primates, and camels.

From earth to sky, the region is unsurpassed in wonders. The star-filled nights and natural quiet of the Bears Ears area transport visitors to an earlier eon. Against an absolutely black night sky, our galaxy and others more distant leap into view. As one of the most intact and least roaded areas in the contiguous United States, Bears Ears has that rare and arresting quality of deafening silence.

Communities have depended on the resources of the region for hundreds of generations. Understanding the important role of the green highlands in providing habitat for subsistence plants and animals, as well as capturing and filtering water from passing storms, the Navajo refer to such places as "Nahodishgish," or places to be left alone. Local communities seeking to protect the mountains for their watershed values have long recognized the importance of the Bears Ears' headwaters. Wildfires, both natural and human-set, have shaped and maintained forests and grasslands of this area for millennia. Ranchers have relied on the forests and grasslands of the region for ages, and hunters come from across the globe for a chance at a bull elk or other big game. Today, ecological restoration through the careful use of wildfire and management of grazing and timber is working to restore and maintain the health of these vital watersheds and grasslands.

The diversity of the soils and microenvironments in the Bears Ears area provide habitat for a wide variety of vegetation. The highest elevations, in the Elk Ridge area of the Manti-La Sal National Forest, contain pockets of ancient Engelmann spruce, ponderosa pine, aspen, and subalpine fir. Mesa tops include pinyon-juniper woodlands along with big sagebrush, low sage, blackbrush, rabbitbrush, bitterbrush, four-wing saltbush, shadscale, winterfat, Utah serviceberry, western chokecherry, hackberry, barberry, cliff rose, and greasewood. Canyons contain diverse vegetation ranging from yucca and cacti such as prickly pear, claret cup, and Whipple's fishhook to mountain mahogany, ponderosa pine, alder, sagebrush, birch, dogwood, and Gambel's oak, along with occasional stands of aspen. Grasses and herbaceous species such as bluegrass, bluestem, giant ryegrass, ricegrass, needle and thread, yarrow, common mallow, balsamroot, low larkspur, horsetail, and peppergrass also grow here, as well as pinnate spring parsley, Navajo penstemon, Canyonlands lomatium, and the Abajo daisy.

Tucked into winding canyons are vibrant riparian communities characterized by Fremont cottonwood, western sandbar willow, yellow willow, and box elder. Numerous seeps provide year-round water and support delicate hanging gardens, moisture-loving plants, and relict species such as Douglas fir. A few populations of the rare Kachina daisy, endemic to the Colorado Plateau, hide in shaded seeps and alcoves of the area's canyons. A genetically distinct population of Kachina daisy was also found on Elk Ridge. The alcove columbine and cave primrose, also regionally endemic, grow in seeps and hanging gardens in the Bears Ears landscape. Wildflowers such as beardtongue, evening primrose, aster, Indian paintbrush, yellow and purple beeflower, straight bladderpod, Durango tumble mustard, scarlet gilia, globe mallow, sand verbena, sego lily, cliffrose, sacred datura, monkey flower, sunflower, prince's plume, hedgehog cactus, and columbine, bring bursts of color to the landscape.

The diverse vegetation and topography of the Bears Ears area, in turn, support a variety of wildlife species. Mule deer and elk range on the mesas and near canyon heads, which provide crucial habitat for both species. The Cedar Mesa landscape is home to bighorn sheep which were once abundant but still live in Indian Creek, and in the canyons north of the San Juan River. Small mammals such as desert cottontail, black-tailed jackrabbit, prairie dog, Botta's pocket gopher, white-tailed antelope squirrel, Colorado chipmunk, canyon mouse, deer mouse, pinyon mouse, and desert woodrat, as well as Utah's only population of Abert's tassel-eared squirrels, find shelter and sustenance in the landscape's canyons and uplands. Rare shrews, including a variant of Merriam's shrew and the dwarf shrew can be found in this area.

Carnivores, including badger, coyote, striped skunk, ringtail, gray fox, bobcat, and the occasional mountain lion, all hunt here, while porcupines use their sharp quills and climbing abilities to escape these predators. Oral histories from the Ute describe the historic presence of bison, antelope, and abundant bighorn sheep, which are also depicted in ancient rock art. Black bear pass through the area but are rarely seen, though they are common in the oral histories and legends of this region, including those of the Navajo.

Consistent sources of water in a dry landscape draw diverse wildlife species to the area's riparian habitats, including an array of amphibian species such as tiger salamander, red-spotted toad, Woodhouse's toad, canyon tree frog, Great Basin spadefoot, and northern leopard frog. Even the most sharp-eyed visitors probably will not catch a glimpse of the secretive Utah night lizard. Other reptiles in the area include the sagebrush lizard, eastern fence lizard, tree lizard, side-blotched lizard, plateau striped whiptail, western rattlesnake, night snake, striped whipsnake, and gopher snake.

Raptors such as the golden eagle, peregrine falcon, bald eagle, northern harrier, northern goshawk, red-tailed hawk, ferruginous hawk, American kestrel, flammulated owl, and great horned owl hunt their prey on the mesa tops with deadly speed and accuracy. The largest contiguous critical habitat for the threatened Mexican spotted owl is on the Manti-La Sal National Forest. Other bird species found in the area include Merriam's turkey, Williamson's sapsucker, common nighthawk, white-throated swift, ash-throated flycatcher, violet-green swallow, cliff swallow, mourning dove, pinyon jay, sagebrush sparrow, canyon towhee, rock wren, sage thrasher, and the endangered southwestern willow flycatcher.

As the skies darken in the evenings, visitors may catch a glimpse of some of the area's at least 15 species of bats, including the big free-tailed bat, pallid bat, Townsend's big-eared bat, spotted bat, and silver-haired bat. Tinajas, rock depressions filled with rainwater, provide habitat for many specialized aquatic species, including pothole beetles and freshwater shrimp. Eucosmanavajoensis, an endemic moth that has only been described near Valley of the Gods, is unique to this area.

Protection of the Bears Ears area will preserve its cultural, prehistoric, and historic legacy and maintain its diverse array of natural and scientific resources, ensuring that the prehistoric, historic, and scientific values of this area remain for the benefit of all Americans. The Bears Ears area has been proposed for protection by members of Congress, Secretaries of the Interior, State and tribal leaders, and local conservationists for at least 80 years. The area contains numerous objects of historic and of scientific interest, and it provides world class outdoor recreation opportunities, including rock climbing, hunting, hiking, backpacking, canyoneering, whitewater rafting, mountain biking, and horseback riding. Because visitors travel from near and far, these lands support a growing travel and tourism sector that is a source of economic opportunity for the region.

WHEREAS, section 320301 of title 54, United States Code (known as the "Antiquities Act"), authorizes the President, in his discretion, to declare by public proclamation historic landmarks, historic and prehistoric structures, and other objects of historic or scientific interest that are situated upon the lands owned or controlled by the Federal Government to be national monuments, and to reserve as a part thereof parcels of land, the limits of which shall be confined to the smallest area compatible with the proper care and management of the objects to be protected;

WHEREAS, it is in the public interest to preserve the objects of scientific and historic interest on the Bears Ears lands;

NOW, THEREFORE, I, BARACK OBAMA, President of the United States of America, by the authority vested in me by section 320301 of title 54, United States Code, hereby proclaim the objects identified above that are situated upon lands and interests in lands owned or controlled by the Federal Government to be the Bears Ears National Monument (monument) and, for the purpose of protecting those objects, reserve as part thereof all lands and interests in lands owned or controlled by the Federal Government within the boundaries described on the accompanying map, which is attached to and forms a part of this proclamation. These reserved Federal lands and interests in lands encompass approximately 1.35 million acres. The boundaries described on the accompanying map are confined to the smallest area compatible with the proper care and management of the objects to be protected.

All Federal lands and interests in lands within the boundaries of the monument are hereby appropriated and withdrawn from all forms of entry, location, selection, sale, or other disposition under the public land laws or laws applicable to the U.S. Forest Service, from location, entry, and patent under the mining laws, and from disposition under all laws relating to mineral and geothermal leasing, other than by exchange that furthers the protective purposes of the monument.

The establishment of the monument is subject to valid existing rights, including valid existing water rights. If the Federal Government acquires ownership or control of any lands or interests in lands that it did not previously own or control within the boundaries described on the accompanying map, such lands and interests in lands shall be reserved as a part of the monument, and objects identified above that are situated upon those lands and interests in lands shall be part of the monument, upon acquisition of ownership or control by the Federal Government.

The Secretary of Agriculture and the Secretary of the Interior (Secretaries) shall manage the monument through the U.S. Forest Service (USFS) and the Bureau of Land Management (BLM), pursuant to their respective applicable legal authorities, to implement the purposes of this proclamation. The USFS shall manage that portion of the monument within the boundaries of the National Forest System (NFS), and the BLM shall manage the remainder of the monument. The lands administered by the USFS shall be managed as part of the Manti-La Sal National Forest. The lands administered by the BLM shall be managed as a unit of the National Landscape Conservation System, pursuant to applicable legal authorities.

For purposes of protecting and restoring the objects identified above, the Secretaries shall jointly prepare a management plan for the monument and shall promulgate such regulations for its management as they deem appropriate. The Secretaries, through the USFS and the BLM, shall consult with other Federal land management agencies in the local area, including the National Park Service, in developing the management plan. In promulgating any management rules and regulations governing the NFS lands within the monument and developing the management plan, the Secretary of Agriculture, through the USFS, shall consult with the Secretary of the Interior through the BLM. The Secretaries shall provide for maximum public involvement in the development of that plan including, but not limited to, consultation with federally recognized tribes and State and local governments. In the development and implementation of the management plan, the Secretaries shall maximize opportunities, pursuant to applicable legal authorities, for shared resources, operational efficiency, and cooperation.

The Secretaries, through the BLM and USFS, shall establish an advisory committee under the Federal Advisory Committee Act (5 U.S.C. App.) to provide information and advice regarding the development of the management plan and, as appropriate, management of the monument. This advisory committee shall consist of a fair and balanced representation of interested stakeholders, including State and local governments, tribes, recreational users, local business owners, and private landowners.

In recognition of the importance of tribal participation to the care and management of the objects identified above, and to ensure that management decisions affecting the monument reflect tribal expertise and traditional and historical knowledge, a Bears Ears Commission (Commission) is hereby established to provide guidance and recommendations on the development and implementation of management plans and on management of the monument. The Commission shall consist of one elected officer each from the Hopi Nation, Navajo Nation, Ute Mountain Ute Tribe, Ute Indian Tribe of the Uintah Ouray, and Zuni Tribe, designated by the officers' respective tribes. The Commission may adopt such procedures as it deems necessary to govern its activities, so that it may effectively partner with the Federal agencies by making continuing contributions to inform decisions regarding the management of the monument.

The Secretaries shall meaningfully engage the Commission or, should the Commission no longer exist, the tribal governments through some other entity composed of elected tribal government officers (comparable entity), in the development of the management plan and to inform subsequent management of the monument. To that end, in developing or revising the management plan, the Secretaries shall carefully and fully consider integrating the traditional and historical knowledge and special expertise of the Commission or comparable entity. If the Secretaries decide not to incorporate specific recommendations submitted to them in writing by the Commission or comparable entity, they will provide the Commission or comparable entity with a written explanation of their reasoning. The management plan shall also set forth parameters for continued meaningful engagement with the Commission or comparable entity in implementation of the management plan.

To further the protective purposes of the monument, the Secretary of the Interior shall explore entering into a memorandum of understanding with the State that would set forth terms, pursuant to applicable laws and regulations, for an exchange of land currently owned by the State of Utah and administered by the Utah School and Institutional Trust Lands Administration within the boundary of the monument for land of approximately equal value managed by the BLM outside the boundary of the monument.

The Secretary of the Interior shall report to the President by January 19, 2017, regarding the potential for such an exchange.

Nothing in this proclamation shall be construed to interfere with the operation or maintenance, or the replacement or modification within the current authorization boundary, of existing utility, pipeline, or telecommunications facilities located within the monument in a manner consistent with the care and management of the objects identified above.

Nothing in this proclamation shall be deemed to enlarge or diminish the rights or jurisdiction of any Indian tribe. The Secretaries shall, to the maximum extent permitted by law and in consultation with Indian tribes, ensure the protection of Indian sacred sites and traditional cultural properties in the monument and provide access by members of Indian tribes for traditional cultural and customary uses, consistent with the American Indian Religious Freedom Act (42 U.S.C. 1996) and Executive Order 13007 of May 24, 1996 (Indian Sacred Sites), including collection of medicines, berries and other vegetation, forest products, and firewood for personal noncommercial use in a manner consistent with the care and management of the objects identified above.

For purposes of protecting and restoring the objects identified above, the Secretaries shall prepare a transportation plan that designates the roads and trails where motorized and non-motorized mechanized vehicle use will be allowed. Except for emergency or authorized administrative purposes, motorized and non-motorized mechanized vehicle use shall be allowed only on roads and trails designated for such use, consistent with the care and management of such objects. Any additional roads or trails designated for motorized vehicle use must be for the purposes of public safety or protection of such objects.

Laws, regulations, and policies followed by USFS or BLM in issuing and administering grazing permits or leases on lands under their jurisdiction shall continue to apply with regard to the lands in the monument to ensure the ongoing consistency with the care and management of the objects identified above.

Nothing in this proclamation shall be deemed to enlarge or diminish the jurisdiction of the State of Utah, including its jurisdiction and authority with respect to fish and wildlife management.

Nothing in this proclamation shall preclude low-level overflights of military aircraft, the designation of new units of special use airspace, or the use or establishment of military flight training routes over the lands reserved by this proclamation consistent with the care and management of the objects identified above.

Nothing in this proclamation shall be construed to alter the authority or responsibility of any party with respect to emergency response activities within the monument, including wildland fire response.

Nothing in this proclamation shall be deemed to revoke any existing withdrawal, reservation, or appropriation; however, the monument shall be the dominant reservation.

Warning is hereby given to all unauthorized persons not to appropriate, injure, destroy, or remove any feature of the monument and not to locate or settle upon any of the lands thereof.

IN WITNESS WHEREOF, I have hereunto set my hand this twenty-eighth day of December, in the year of our Lord two thousand sixteen, and of the Independence of the United States of America the two hundred and forty-first.

Donald Trump's Reduction of Bears Ears

On December 4, 2017, President Donald Trump signed a "Presidential Proclamation Modifying Bears Ears National Monument," dramatically reducing the land saved. The proclamation states:

"WHEREAS, it is in the public interest to modify the boundaries of the monument to exclude from its designation and reservation approximately 1,150,860 acres of land that I find are unnecessary for the care and management of the objects to be protected within the monument . . ."

Though there are precedents for presidents slightly modifying national monuments, the massive reduction is unprecedented. Lawsuits, led by Native American tribes and environmental groups, are challenging the reduction, as well as that of Grand Staircase-Escalante National Monument, in court.

As of this writing, March 1, 2020, there has been no ruling in the courts on the legality of the Trump reductions to Bears Ears and Grand Staircase-Escalante National Monuments. A lawyer deeply involved in the case writes: "The Court has set a briefing schedule that will have briefing concluded by middle of May 2020 and we expect that the Court will set oral argument and issue a decision before the end of the year."

Meanwhile, on Thursday February 6, 2020, the Trump administration announced that they would permit drilling, mining, and grazing in areas of southern Utah that had once been protected in the two national monuments.

In a news release, the administration touted the local support for this and for the reduction of Bears Ears, despite the fact that the San Juan County Commission is now made up of a majority of Native Commissioners who support the original Bears Ears boundaries.

In language that would be familiar to readers of Bernard DeVoto, the administration and its allies defended the opening of these public lands to the extractive industries.

"The approved plans keep the commitment of this Administration to the families and communities of Utah that know and love this land the best and will care for these resources for many generations to come," said Acting Assistant Secretary, Land and Minerals Management Casey Hammond. "These cooperatively developed and locally driven plans restore a prosperous future to communities too often dismissed and punished by unilateral decisions of those that would not listen to the voices of Utahns."

"These management plans are the result of meaningful collaboration that was clearly lacking in the politically motivated monument designations by past administrations," said Utah Congressman Robert Bishop. "Well-funded special interest groups that aren't from our state will spread outrageous misinformation, but the fact remains that this administration has continued to take actions that reflect the will of Utahns who call these places home. Unfortunately, this work can all be undone by bureaucrats and the political whims of future presidents, unless Congress tweaks the Antiquities Act. Despite this reality, thanks and praise is warranted for this new and better approach at the Department under President Trump."

"When President Trump reduced the size of both Bears Ears and Grand Staircase-Escalante National Monuments, he did it with the full support of Utah's federal delegation and the elected officials who represent those areas," said Utah Congressman Chris Stewart. "By contrast, the Obama and Clinton Administrations snubbed and ignored Utah's local, state, and federal elected officials who objected to the creation of both monuments. Thanks to this administration's attitude towards local input, these new plans will benefit Utahns. I proudly stand with my friends, the county commissioners in Kane and Garfield Counties, in thanking President Trump, Department of the Interior, and BLM staff for listening and responding."

Voices

During my time out West I collected stories, from the people I talked to and the books I read. Since they could not all fit inside this book, I want to share some of those voices here. I found, as I have found during earlier trips like my journey to the Gulf of Mexico during the BP oil spill, that the reality on the ground was more interesting than what we see on TV, not the simple dichotomy of FOX vs. CNN, but something messier: more varied, more complex, more contradictory.

> Our history is written on the land. It is written on the rock walls. You let them destroy that and you're ripping out my textbook, my history, and my history is my grandchildren's history.
>
> Regina Lopez-Whiteskunk,
> interview with the author,
> January 2018

> Frankly, I'm tired of Bears Ears issues. I am very tired of the manipulation on both sides of talking points. And you talk to one side and you're told one story, you talk to the other side, you're told an entirely different story. And in my mind, on too many of these, these stories are concocted for political gain and not necessarily to reflect the on the ground reality in San Juan County.
>
> Bill Boyle,
> editor, publisher, and janitor of the *San Juan Record,*
> interview with the author,
> July 2018

I would say that this is a continuing struggle between Native Americans and non–Native Americans, specifically in this area since 1879, when the Mormons arrived.

Mark Maryboy,
interview with the author,
July 2018

My worst fear, truly, is that those lands will become private. We can deal with oil and gas exploration. An oil well will come in, if we're careful with it, it's going to do some damage, but it will be gone in twenty years. And we can smooth that well pad over and pick up the pipelines. But if we lose it from public ownership, and it becomes someone's private property, we'll never see that again. . . . We're seeing a greater division between those who have and those who have not. And public lands, the public places, are shared places for all of us to share and enjoy. If we lose those things, we've really lost much of the value of these wild places.

Kevin Jones,
former Utah State archaeologist

Some people think that the natural resources of Utah should be controlled by a small handful of very distant bureaucrats located in Washington. And guess what? They're wrong.

Donald Trump

If you like Teddy Roosevelt, you'll love me.

Interior Secretary Ryan Zinke

Our aim is not to do away with corporations; on the contrary, these big aggregations are an inevitable development of modern industrialism. . . . We are not hostile to them; we are merely determined that they shall be so handled as to subserve the public good. We draw the line against misconduct, not against wealth.

Theodore Roosevelt,
State of the Union,
1902

Natural history and national history proceeded in sync, a cultural fugue to Manifest Destiny. The national epic found its monuments, as often or not, in the American landscape. Nature, which America had in abundance, replaced the built environments that it lacked. . . . The natural, the big, the distinctive—all challenged the artifice of ancient and aristocratic societies, while arguing strenuously for a republic of native, once-and-future virtue.

Stephen J. Pyne,
How the Canyon Became Grand

Our whole national history has been one of expansion.

Theodore Roosevelt

To protect wilderness was in a very real sense to protect the nation's most sacred myth of origin.

William Cronon,
"The Trouble with Wilderness"

Preservationist efforts did not succeed until the latter half of the nineteenth century, however, when outdoor enthusiasts viewed wilderness as an uninhabited Eden that should be set aside for the benefit and pleasure of vacationing Americans. The fact that Indians continued to hunt and light purposeful fires in such places seemed only to demonstrate a marked inability to appreciate natural beauty. To guard against these "violations," the establishment of the first national parks necessarily entailed the exclusion or removal of native peoples. . . . Americans regarded reservations, rather than the "wilderness," as the appropriate place for all Indians to live.

Mark David Spence,
Dispossessing the Wilderness

We have had more trouble with the Indian tribes we have pampered and petted than with those we did wrong.

Theodore Roosevelt

These are sacred ancestral hills. For thousands of years our ancestors drew strength from them. The minerals, the vegetation, the woods, the birds, all the traditional uses. In Navajo it is a way of life. We want to teach that way to future generations. That's what Bears Ears is all about.

> James Adakai,
> president of the Oljato Chapter of the Navajo Nation

Although he earned a reputation as a conservationist—placing more than 230 million acres of land under public protection—Roosevelt systematically marginalized Indians, uprooting them from their homelands to create national parks and monuments, speaking publicly about his plans to assimilate them and using them as spectacles to build his political empire.

> Alysa Landry,
> *Indian Country Today*

The Indians, they don't fully understand that a lot of the things that they currently take for granted on those lands, they won't be able to do if it's made clearly into a monument or a wilderness. . . . Once you put a monument there, you do restrict a lot of things that could be done, and that includes use of the land. . . . Just take my word for it.

> Orrin Hatch,
> Utah senator, 2017

The question has been asked but we get no response: what part of sacred don't you understand? Essentially we are saying why isn't it enough for us to say a site is sacred and should be set aside and protected and respected because it is integral for our spiritual practices to be continued?

> Klee Benally Navajo,
> dancer, anarchist, musician, filmmaker

I feel like there should be some sort of fence.

> Tourist in Yellowstone watching a grizzly
> and her cubs in a meadow

By the close of 1883, the last buffalo herd was destroyed. The beaver were trapped out of all the streams, or their numbers so thinned that it no longer paid to follow them. The last formidable Indian war had been brought to a successful close. The flood of the incoming whites had risen over the land; tongues of settlement reached from the Mississippi to the Rocky Mountains, and from the Rocky Mountains to the Pacific. The frontier had come to an end; it had vanished.

Theodore Roosevelt,
The Wilderness Hunter

I don't care what a think tank in Washington says, and I don't care what a think tank in Boulder says. I'm interested in the dirt on the ground in San Juan County. And I think all too often, the reality on the ground has been left far behind in these battles that are spinning out of control. But that's where we are in our society today.

Bill Boyle,
San Juan Record

The Antiquities Act, in fact, is the most important piece of preservation legislation ever enacted by the United States government.

Hal Rothman,
America's National Monuments

The vision for the Bears Ears is something very beautiful. Native people have different ways of knowing about the world, and I think now western science is beginning to catch up. Where we realize that tree roots communicate with each other and trees will actually send nutrients to other trees that are in trouble. We are learning how every bit of the world is sentient and connected. That is something that native peoples have known and had in their knowledge system for a long time. And the vision for Bears Ears was for people who have lived in this difficult, arid land of the southwest for thousands of years to say "Let's take our traditional way of knowing and blend it with western science and see what the two knowledge systems can do to illuminate one another. And see if we can't learn to live in this place."

> Bill Hedden,
> former president,
> Grand Canyon Trust

Hasn't the government taken enough of our land already? Yes, they have. But they keep taking more.

> Guy sitting at the bar at Eddie McStiff's,
> Moab, Utah

The history of Hopi people is recorded upon the landscapes of their ancestors. Thus, maintaining Hopi culture is more than merely an act of writing down those events and places; it must encompass the actual preservation of those places where ancestors dwell.

> Lyle Balenquah,
> Hopi archaeologist

What we are seeking to do with Bears Ears National Monument is to stabilize our community and to bring youth back to the reality of the natural world. We want to teach them how to utilize these resources in a way that not only benefits them in their pocket, but spiritually. To teach them that water from this spring is pure—it's good to drink. It's a healing substance that will not give you headaches but will clean you from the inside out and give you better health.

> Jonah Yellowman,
> Navajo Elder

There is no way our traditional culture and worldview can persist without being permitted actual space in the physical world to live out those ideas. . . . These cultural values my great-great-aunt records cannot be intellectual concepts: they must be lived. And yet our homelands and cultural and sacred space are constantly being taken and reallocated for money-making ventures with no regard for toxic outcomes and necessary cleanup or of our lived histories on the land.

Jacqueline Keeler,
Navajo/Yankton Sioux writer,
Edge of Morning

The traditional ecological knowledge amassed by the Native Americans whose ancestors inhabited this region, passed down from generation to generation, offers critical insight into the historic and scientific significance of the area. Such knowledge is, itself, a resource to be protected and used in understanding and managing the landscape sustainably for generations to come....

Barack Obama,
Establishment of the Bears Ears National Monument
December 28, 2018

They are too big.

Interior Secretary Zinke,
speaking about national monuments

I wrote this book with the hope that as conservationists and native people converge uneasily they can come to agreement that they both own the interdependent causes of biodiversity conservation and cultural survival, that they need each other badly, and that together they can create a new conservation paradigm that honors and respects the life ways of people who have been living sustainably for generations on what can only be fairly regarded as their native land. And it is my hope that native people will blend their ancient traditional knowledge systems with the comparatively new sciences of ecology and conservation biology, in search of new and better ways to preserve the diversity of species that is not only vital to their own security but also to all life on earth. At this point, as the entire planet seems poised to tip into ecological chaos, with almost forty thousand plant and animal species facing extinction and 60 percent of the ecosystem services that support life on earth failing, there may be no other way.

Mark Dowie,
Conservation Refugees

If cooperation on cultural issues does further tribal efforts to exercise some control over national parklands, this could revolutionize the way all Americans experience the wilderness.

Mark David Spence,
Dispossessing the Wilderness

This is the one example that is going to lead us into the bigger conversation about public lands throughout the country. This is setting the tone. This is going to set those precedents that others will follow and use.

Regina Lopez-Whiteskunk,
interview with author,
July 2018

These sacred lands have held our songs, our stories, and our prayers since time beyond memory, and these lands continue to hold the promise of our future. They are places of peace. Bears Ears National Monument is the source of our healing and shared humanity, not just for Native peoples but for all people, for generations to come.

Willie Grayeyes, chairman of the Utah Dine Bikeyah,
"An Open Letter to President Donald Trump"

RECOMMENDED READING

Biographies of Theodore Roosevelt

Roosevelt loved books, claiming he was addicted to them, and he'd be happy to know there are so many about him. Here are a few of my favorites:

You still can't go wrong with Edmund Morris's great three-volume life. I agree with the general consensus that the rousing Pulitzer Prize–winning first volume is the best, but the others are almost as good. The titles are *The Rise of Theodore Roosevelt* (1979), *Theodore Rex* (2001), and *Colonel Roosevelt* (2010).

As I mention in the text, David McCullough's story of the young TR, *Mornings on Horseback: The Story of an Extraordinary Family, a Vanished Way of Life and the Unique Child Who Became Theodore Roosevelt* (1981) rivals Morris's first volume.

Kathleen Dalton has written my favorite one-volume life of TR, 2002's *Theodore Roosevelt: A Strenuous Life*. In it she reimagines Roosevelt, acknowledging his flaws while arguing that his great transformation was not the remaking of his scrawny body, but his movement toward greater empathy and a truly liberal political vision.

Another popular, rollicking, and relatively recent book is Candice Miller's *The River of Doubt: Theodore Roosevelt's Darkest Journey*, which covers Roosevelt's trip to the Amazon in 1913–14.

For a brisk overview of Roosevelt's life, including some prescient thoughts on the Republican Party's migration away from TR, I recommend *Theodore Roosevelt* by Louis Auchincloss.

On the other extreme is Douglas Brinkley's exhaustive *The Wilderness Warrior: Theodore Roosevelt and the Crusade for America*. Though it lacks the narrative power of Morris's books, it is monumental, providing the full picture of TR's love of nature, environmental advocacy, and achievement in the saving of millions of acres of American land. Its predecessor in this regard was P. R. Cutright's *Theodore Roosevelt: The Making of a Modern Conservationist,* published in 1985.

Two recent books that I happily devoured focused on Roosevelt's love and study of the natural world: Michael Canfield's *Theodore Roosevelt in the Field* (2015), replete with gorgeous re-creations of his field notes, and Darren Lunde's *The Naturalist: Theodore Roosevelt, a Lifetime of Exploration, and the Triumph of American Natural History* (2016).

And while it approaches hagiography, 1905's *Camping and Tramping with Roosevelt* by John Burroughs is still a fun read. First cousin Nicholas Roosevelt's accounts of Theodore, including the Grand Canyon hike, enliven *Theodore Roosevelt: The Man as I Knew Him* (1967).

Clay S. Jenkinson helped me get to know the TR of the Badlands through two books, *A Free and Hardy Life: Theodore Roosevelt's Sojourn in the American West* (2011) and *Theodore Roosevelt in the Dakota Badlands: An Historical Guide* (2006). While in Medura, I also read *Theodore Roosevelt and Tales Told as Truth of His Time in the West* by Douglas W. Ellison (2017).

My favorite early biography of Roosevelt is Edward Wagenknecht's *The Seven Worlds of Theodore Roosevelt,* written in 1958. Other one-volume accounts that I enjoyed include *Theodore Roosevelt: A Life* by Nathan Miller (1992), *T.R.: The Last Romantic* by H. W. Brands (1997), Patricia O'Toole's *When Trumpets Call: Theodore Roosevelt After the White House* (2005), and *A Bully Father: Theodore Roosevelt's Letters to His Children* by Joan Patterson Kerr (1995).

The Folly of Empire: What George W. Bush Could Learn from Theodore Roosevelt and Woodrow Wilson by John B. Judis (2004) helped me imagine TR into the present, and *Leadership in Turbulent Times* by Doris Kearns Goodwin (2018) gave me insight into TR's leadership style.

One of the fascinating things about reading these lives is to see how each of the biographies is, to some extent, a product of its time. It will be interesting to watch how TR is portrayed in years to come as his environmental vision becomes more and more urgent and the chauvinistic aspects of his personality grow ever more dated.

On Bears Ears and the Antiquities Act

To learn about the history of the Antiquities Act, I highly recommend *America's National Monuments: The Politics of Preservation* by Hal Rothman, published in 1989. Another good resource is *The Antiquities Act: A Century of American Archaeology,*

Historic Preservation, and Nature Conservation, edited by David Harmon, Frank P. McManamon, and Dwight T. Pitcaithley (2006).

Red Rock Testimony, which collects the work of three generations of writers writing about Bears Ears, was edited by Stephen Trimble and Kirsten Allen of Torrey House Press. It was published as a chapbook and delivered to Obama Administration officials and every member of Congress in June 2016, as decision-makers deliberated between a destructive public lands bill and a national monument proposed by the Bears Ears Inter-Tribal Coalition. In 2017 the essays were collected in book form as *Red Rock Stories,* edited by Stephen Trimble.

That same year Jaqueline Keeler edited a collection of Indigenous writers in *Edge of Morning: Native Voices Speak for the Bears Ears.* A wide variety of voices can also be found in Rebecca M. Robinson's *Voices from Bears Ears,* published in 2018.

As Long as Grass Grows: The Indigenous Fight for Environmental Justice, from Colonization to Standing Rock by Dina Gilo-Whitaker (2019) provides an overview of Native environmental battles written by a Native writer.

A tension I discovered in my reading, and that I hope is reflected in the book, is between the American ideal of saving land and the fact that that land already belonged to someone. Two books, *Dispossessing the Wilderness: Indian Removal and the Making of the National* Parks by Mark David Spence (1999) and *Conservation Refugees: The Hundred Year Conflict Between Global Conservation and Native Peoples* by Mark Dowie (2009), work to debunk the myths of pristine parks. I found it helpful to read these in conjunction—and lively argument—with another pair of books. The collections *Keeping the Wild: Against the Domestication of Earth* (2015) and *Protecting the Wild: Parks and Wilderness, the Foundation for Conservation* (2014), both edited by George Wuerthner, Eileen Crist, and Tom Butler, argue for the inspiration and vital necessity of parks, both past and future.

Connecting Migratory Pathways/Yellowstone to Yukon/ Grand Canyon

Rewilding North America: A Vision for Conservation in the Twenty-First Century. Dave Foreman. 2004.

Walking the Big Wild: From Yellowstone to the Yukon on the Grizzly Bear's Trail. Karsten Heuer. 2004.

Half-Earth: Our Planet's Fight for the Future. Edward O. Wilson. 2016.

Yellowstone to Yukon. Douglas H. Chadwick. 2000.

Yellowstone to Yukon: Freedom to Roam. Florian Schultz. 2007.

Empire of Shadows: The Epic Story of Yellowstone. George Black. 2013. A comprehensive history.

National Geographic 229, no. 5 (May 2016), "Yellowstone: The Battle for the American West." David Quammen's articles in this issue are a subtle and powerful overview of the battles and what is at stake.

Grizzly Years. Doug Peacock. 1990. Classic story of a man living with grizzlies after his time serving in Viet Nam.

In the Presence of Buffalo: Working to Stop the Yellowstone Slaughter. Daniel Brister. 2013.

Engineering Eden. Jordan Fisher Smith. 2016.

Grand Canyon for Sale. Stephen Nash. 2017.

How the Canyon Became Grand: A Short History. Stephen J. Pyne. 1998.

On American Lands

These are some of the books about the land that migrated on and off of my desk during the writing of *Leave It As It Is*:

House Made of Dawn. N. Scott Momaday. 1968.

The Western Paradox. Bernard DeVoto. 2001.

Ceremony. Leslie Marmon Silko. 1977.

Hour of Land: A Personal Topography of America's National Parks. Terry Tempest Williams. 2016.

Rough Beauty: Forty Seasons of Mountain Living. Karen Auvinen. 2018.

American Holocaust: Columbus and the Conquest of the New World. David E. Stannard. 1992.

The Haida Gwaii Lesson: A Strategic Playbook for Indigenous Sovereignty. Mark Dowie. 2017.

In Defense of Public Lands: The Case Against Privatization and Transfer. Steven Davis. 2018.

Debunking Creation Myths About America's Public Lands. John D. Leshy. Delivered as the 2018 Wallace Stegner lecture at the University of Utah.

Seeing Things Whole: The Essential John Wesley Powell. Edited by William deBuys. 2001.

Beyond the Hundredth Meridian: John Wesley Powell and the Second Opening of the West. Wallace Stegner. 1953.

The Sound of Mountain Water. Wallace Stegner. 1958. 1963.

Where the Bluebird Sings to the Lemonade Springs. Wallace Stegner. 1992.

Cadillac Desert: The American West and Its Disappearing Water. Mark Resiner. 1993.

Eating Stone: Imagination and the Loss of the Wild. Ellen Melloy. 2005.

Desert Solitaire: A Season in the Wilderness. Edward Abbey. 1968.

Desert Cabal: A New Season in the Wilderness. Amy Irvine. 2019.

Lasso the Wind. Timothy Egan. 1998.

When the Rivers Run Dry: Water—the Defining Crisis of the Twenty-First Century.
    Fred Pierce. 2006.

I was thrilled to also read advance proofs of the following books, both of which give me hope that the tradition of thoughtful Western environmental writing is alive and well:

Confluence: Navigating the Personal & Political on Rivers of the New West. Zak
    Podmore. 2019.

This Land: How Cowboys, Capitalism, and Corruption Are Ruining the American West.
    Christopher Ketcham. 2019.

The Ancestral Puebloans/Anasazi and Archaeological History

The Professor's House. Willa Cather. 1925.

Richard Wetherill: Anasazi Pioneer Explorer of Southwestern Ruins. Frank McNitt.
    1957.

Reaching Keet Seel: Ruin's Echo and the Anasazi. Reg Saner. 1998.

Finders Keepers: A Tale of Archaeological Plunder and Obsession. Craig Childs. 2010.

Sandstone Spine: Seeking the Anasazi on the First Traverse of the Comb Ridge. David
    Roberts. 2006.

In Search of the Old Ones: Exploring the Anasazi World of the Southwest. David
    Roberts. 1996.

A Guide to Southern Utah's Hole-in-the-Rock Trail. Stewart Aitchison. 2005.

Canyon Lands Country: Geology of Canyonlands and Arches National Park. Don
    Barrs. 1989.

Books by Theodore Roosevelt

I'll list them all here, but my focus for this project was on his more personal books. *Theodore Roosevelt: An Autobiography*, written in 1913, is eminently readable, and the early books about the West are great if you can handle TR's taste for blood. These include:

Hunting Trips of a Ranchman. New York: G. P. Putnam's Sons. 1885.

Ranch Life and the Hunting Trail. New York: The Century Company. 1888.

The Wilderness Hunter. New York: G. P. Putnam's Sons. 1893.

On the other hand, his more overtly political essays, like 1899's "The Strenuous Life," require more strenuous reading. 1916's *A Book Lover's Holidays in the Open*, a collection of his essays that includes his Grand Canyon trip and his birding trip to the Gulf, is a return to the earlier form and one of my favorites. *The Selected Letters of Theodore Roosevelt* gives you a sense of the wide range of interests and passions of this gregarious polymath.

The four-volume *The Winning of the West* (with individual volumes listed below) is generally considered his most durable scholarly achievement.

He also wrote:

The Naval War of 1812, Part I. New York: G. P. Putnam's Sons. 1882.

The Naval War of 1812, Part II. New York: G. P. Putnam's Sons. 1882.

Thomas H. Benton. American Statesmen. Boston: Houghton, Mifflin and Company. 1886.

Essays on Practical Politics. New York: G. P. Putnam's Sons. 1888.

Gouverneur Morris: The Study of His Life and Work. Boston: Houghton, Mifflin and Company. 1888.

The Winning of the West, Volume I: *From the Alleghanies to the Mississippi*. New York: G. P. Putnam's Sons. 1889.

The Winning of the West, Volume II: *In the Current of the Revolution*. New York: G. P. Putnam's Sons. 1889.

New York. Historic Towns. London: Longman's, Green, and Co. 1891.

American Big Game Hunting. New York: Forest and Stream Publishing Co. 1893. (with George Bird Grinnell)

The Winning of the West, Volume III: *The War in the Northwest*. New York: G. P. Putnam's Sons. 1894.

Hero Tales from American History. New York: The Century Company. 1895. (with Henry Cabot Lodge)

Hunting in Many Lands. New York: Forest and Stream Publishing Co. 1895. (with George Bird Grinnell)

The Winning of the West, Volume IV. New York: G. P. Putnam's Sons. 1896.

American Ideals. New York: G. P. Putnam's Sons. 1897.

Trail and Campfire. New York: Forest and Stream Publishing Co. 1897. (with George Bird Grinnell)

Some American Game. New York: G. P. Putnam's Sons. 1897.

American Naval Policy: As Outlined in the Messages of the Presidents of the United States. Washington, D.C.: Government Printing Office. 1897.

The Rough Riders. New York: Charles Scribner's Sons. 1899.

The Naval Operations of the War Between Great Britain and the United States, 1812–1815. Boston: Little, Brown, and Company. 1901.

The Deer Family. New York: The MacMillan Company. 1902. (with T. S. Van Dyke, D. G. Elliot, and A. J. Stone)

Outdoor Pastimes of an American Hunter. New York: Charles Scribner's Sons. 1905.

Good Hunting: In Pursuit of Big Game in the West. New York: Harper & Brothers Publishers. 1907.

Outlook Editorials. New York: The Outlook Company. 1909.

African and European Addresses. New York: Charles Scribner's Sons. 1910.

African Game Trails. London: John Murray, Albemar Street. 1910.

American Problems. New York: The Outlook Company. 1910.

The New Nationalism. New York: The Outlook Company. 1910.

The Conservation of Womanhood and Childhood. New York: Funk & Wagnalls Company. 1912.

Realizable Ideals: Earl Lectures of Pacific Theological Seminary. San Francisco: Whitaker & Ray-Wiggin Co. 1912.

History as Literature and Other Essays. New York: Charles Scribner's Sons. 1913.

Progressive Principles. New York: Progressive National Service. 1913.

Through the Brazilian Wilderness. New York: Charles Scribner's Sons. 1914.

Life-Histories of African Game Animals, Volume I. New York: Charles Scribner's Sons. 1914. (with Edmund Heller)

Life-Histories of African Game Animals, Volume II. New York: Charles Scribner's Sons. 1914. (with Edmund Heller)

America and the World War. New York: Charles Scribner's Sons. 1915.

Fear God and Take Your Own Part. New York: George H. Dornan Company. 1916.

The Foes of Our Own Household. New York: George H. Dornan Company. 1917.

National Strength and International Duty. Princeton: Princeton University Press. 1917.

The Great Adventure: Present-Day Studies in American Nationalism. New York: Charles Scribner's Sons. 1918.

Theodore Roosevelt's Letters to His Children. New York: Charles Scribner's Sons. 1919.

ILLUSTRATION CREDITS

Index

ABOUT THE AUTHOR

David Gessner is the author of eleven books that blend a love of nature, humor, memoir, and environmentalism, including the *New York Times* bestselling *All the Wild That Remains: Edward Abbey, Wallace Stegner and the American West* and *The Tarball Chronicles*. In 2003 Gessner taught environmental writing as a Briggs-Copeland Lecturer at Harvard, and he now serves as chair of the Creative Writing Department at the University of North Carolina Wilmington, where he is also the founder and editor in chief of the literary magazine *Ecotone*. His prizes include a Pushcart Prize, the John Burroughs Award for Best Nature Essay, the Association for Study of Literature and the Environment's award for Best Book of Creative Writing, and the Reed Award for Best Book on the Southern Environment. In 2017 he hosted the National Geographic *Explorer* episode "The Call of the Wild."

Gessner lives in Wilmington, North Carolina, with his wife, the novelist Nina de Gramont, and their daughter, Hadley.